The Wrong Camp

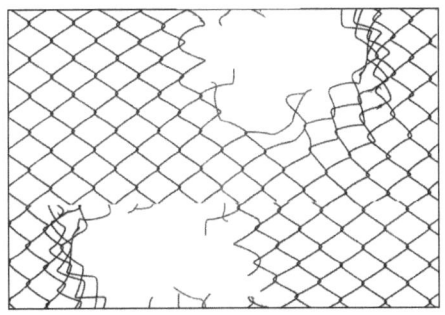

Bol Majok Adiang

ISBN 978-0-6482591-6-9
© Bol Majok Adiang

Published by Africa World Books Pty. Ltd.

All rights reserved. No part of this publication may be reproduced, stored in a retrieval system, or transmitted, in any form, or by any means, electronic, mechanical, photocopying, recording or otherwise, without the prior permission of the publishers.

This book is sold subject to the conditions that it shall not, by way of trade or otherwise, be lent, re-sold, hired out or otherwise circulated without the publisher's prior consent in any form of binding or cover other than in which it is published and without a similar condition including the condition being imposed on the subsequent purchaser.

DEDICATION

This book is dedicated to Commander (Lt. General) Bona Bang Dhel, who saved my life in 1995, when Commander (Lt. General) Anthony Bol Madut sentenced me to death. If Commander Bona Bang Dhel had not been present on that fateful day, I would have been hacked to death with a machete. I would not have lived to witness the independence of South Sudan and to write this book.

Contents

	Introduction	7
	In the Wrong Camp	9
Chapter 1	My Birth and Childhood	12
Chapter 2	The Legacy of a Remarkable Leader	20
Chapter 3	School Days	23
Chapter 4	Rumbek	40
Chapter 5	Anya-Nya	45
Chapter 6	Back Home	62
Chapter	University	70
Chapter 8	Local Government and Time in Shilluk Kingdom	75
Chapter 9	Transfer to Renk	101
Chapter 10	Cueibet	110
Chapter 11	Malakal	116
Chapter 12	Gogrial	120
Chapter 13	Family	137
Chapter 14	An Attempt on my Life in Aweil	143
Chapter 15	Growing Unrest	152
Chapter 16	Trouble with the Arab Cattle Raiders (Marahliin)	160
Chapter 17	Joining the SPLA	166
Chapter 18	A Life of Hardship	178
Chapter 19	Itang, the End of our Journey	191
Chapter 20	A Cold Reception by Dr John Garang	198

Chapter 21	The Death of an Innocent Man	209
Chapter 22	Military Training	215
Chapter 23	Mistreatment and Victory of the Malou Ci Guak Recruits	221
Chapter 24	Distressing News	227
Chapter 25	Tharpam to Kapoeta	230
Chapter 26	More Frustration	236
Chapter 27	Mutiny	241
Chapter 28	Some Order Established	244
Chapter 29	Trouble	249
Chapter 30	Prisoners	258
Chapter 31	More Bad Blood	265
Chapter 32	Surviving	271
Chapter 33	From Pillar to Post	280
Chapter 34	After the Comprehensive Peace Agreement (CPA)	288
Chapter 35	The States	290
Chapter 36	Excluded	294
Chapter 37	Dr Riek Machar Teny	296
Chapter 38	The Future	299
	Appreciation	307

Introduction

This book mainly tells my own story, but I could not write it without mentioning the ethnic groups I worked with during my career as an administrator, and the ones I came to know in the course of the Sudanese civil war. I also recall the names of some individuals I encountered before and during the war and those whose actions affected me directly or indirectly, physically or psychologically. It contains some anthropological, political and administrative elements. I mention, for example, the Sholo Shilluk Kingdom in the hope that my narrative may lead to a better understanding of their culture.

My defection from the Sudanese government to join the SPLM/SPLA Movement was a political decision. And the treatment I received – during the war and even now, in the post-war period - has often been politically motivated.

I talk a great deal about the administration, and at some points the reader may feel that I am repeating myself, but I simply wish to emphasize certain important ideas.

I avoid using the word 'late' in my book, although some of the persons mentioned have passed away. Any reader who may not be happy with what I say about them, is welcome to dispute my judgment. It is not easy to record unfavourable impressions of persons who are still alive. But history cannot be altered. When what happened is truthfully recorded, it does not cheat nor favour anyone. I invite anyone who may disagree with what I have written to challenge my observations, preferably in writing.

The many comrades who have shared my experiences will be the best judges of my book. Hopefully they will write their own stories, perhaps when the main players have left the stage. As for me, I have opted to write now, because my days are not in my hands.

In the Wrong Camp

This is a short history of my life. I have survived many difficulties and experiences, some of which have been extremely dangerous. The fact that I survived when others, personal acquaintances of mine, did not, convinces me that my life is unique.

I may mention Agok Bol Mayom, my sister's son, as an example. We were together at the SPLA base at Wunrok at the time when the forces of Kerubino Kuayin Bol, known as 'Nyigat', were compelled to withdraw from Twic and fled to Abyei, where they aligned themselves with the Sudanese government forces. From Abyei, the force returned, fighting their way through the Twic area up to Gogrial. There they settled, side by side with the government forces. From Gogrial they used to come out from time to time to attack the SPLA positions or loot the villages.

My nephew, Agok, used to go to Panliet airstrip alone from time to time to attend the distribution of relief items. I warned him that he would one day fall into Nyigat's trap and that since he, like me, was a wanted man, they would kill him. But Agok was convinced that, even if he found himself in the jaws of Nyigat soldiers, he would be able to escape. It did not help that I explained to him what it was like when I was captured in the battle of Wunrok on 15 July, 1995.

He did not heed my advice. One day he heard that there would be another relief food distribution at Panliet. He left alone, and spent the night on the southern side of the airstrip in the direction of Gogrial. Meanwhile Nyigat soldiers had also got word of the same relief food distribution, and they came out the same evening to loot the food items. When the Nyigat soldiers arrived just before dawn, they found Agok fast asleep behind the wall of a half-built hut, his head resting on his gun. The entrance was very small, like a hole in the wall, but they pointed their loaded guns at Agok over the open wall. "Get up!" they ordered. "Don't touch your gun!"

Agok got up and surrendered to them. He now found himself in the "jaws of Nyigat soldiers", with no way to escape, as he had vowed he would. His hands were tied and he was taken with them. More SPLA soldiers were caught at different locations and young men were rounded up from the villages and cattle camps; also some women who had come to the airstrip for the distribution. They were all made to carry the looted goods to Gogrial. From here the women were allowed to return to their homes. The young men were sent to an orientation training centre. The captured SPLA soldiers were asked whether they wanted to remain with Nyigat or return to their SPLA units. They opted to remain. They had no choice. They knew what it would mean if they refused. "You are no longer prisoners," they were told. "You have become soldiers of Gogrial, Aweil, Tonj, Rumbek and Yirol (GATRY)."

Agok had left his mother and his wife with a very young infant behind at home. He wanted to escape, but it was impossible, as the base was heavily guarded and no-one was allowed to leave. He knew that his only chance would be when the soldiers left the base to fight or loot. His family hoped that he would be back soon, but I had no hope, and what I expected happened. After four days, a senior Nyigat officer from our area recognized Agok among the soldiers. He went straight to Kerubino Kuanyin and told him that the son of Bol Majok's sister was among the latest soldiers brought to the base, and that, like his maternal uncle had done, he was sure to attempt to escape. Kerubino immediately ordered his arrest and execution. That same evening Agok was arrested, together with his relatives Deng Majok Anguei, Malong Cyer Mabok and Mayar Majak Adiang, who were already members of the Gogrial, Aweil, Tonj, Rumbek and Yirol (GATRY) forces. They spent the night in custody. Early in the morning Agok was led out and executed. Two days later Deng, Malong and Mayar were taken to Kerubino, who told them that Agok had died for his crimes. The three of them were allowed to return to their units, under supervision.

When we received the news at home, I did not blame Agok. I accepted it as his destiny. When your day arrives and you do something you shouldn't, or fail to do what you should, it is the end.

My own survival I do not attribute to being cleverer than others. I simply consider it to be my destiny, the design of my creator. It was his will that I should be born and live to see the day South Sudan gained its independence from the Republic of Sudan, and continue to witness further post-independence events. It is my belief in the uniqueness of my life that has prompted me to write my life story for my children and their children and generations to come to read. Some of them have been witnesses to a number of the difficulties I faced. And I hope that these notes will assist whoever undertakes to write my biography when I am no longer there. May God help me!

CHAPTER 1

My Birth and Childhood

I was born in 1946 in a village called Wunrok. At that time (like it still is today) there was no registration of births and deaths in Dinka villages. But when I grew up and went to school, and learned to count the days of the week, the months and the years, I started wondering about my own birth date. One day I approached my mother:

"In which year was I born?" I asked her.

"It was the year of Hou," she said.

"When was that, Mother?"

"It was when a man called Hou was killed by the people of Adiang in the Battle of Alal. He was believed to be from Ajuong section of Dinka Malual in Aweil. You were born in the dry season, five days before his death."

"But which year was it? How many years ago?"

"Many years ago, my son."

My mother, like her contemporaries, had difficulty counting years. They would sometimes count one year twice. When I asked an elderly person about his age, he would often say "A hundred years or more", and when I told him that it was too much for his age, he would simply reply that he had existed for a very long time.

I knew that our neighbour's son had attended school at the time when Hou was killed, and I asked him for a date. "It happened on 8 March 1946," he told me. So, using simple mathematics, I subtracted five days from eight, and I had determined the date of my birth: 3 March 1946!

My Birth and Childhood

My mother did tell me a story I would remember all my life. With gratitude.

"I have given birth to four daughters and four sons, as you know," she told me. "Your four sisters were born first – Ajok, Alek, and then Aluel and Nyibol, my twins. After them came my four sons – Ngor, Piol, Deng, and then you, Bol. After Deng, I conceived another child, but I became sick in the first month and had a miscarriage in the second month." It took her two months to regain her health. There were no health services in the area, and people had to rely on the herbs they could gather.

"Three or four months later I fell pregnant again. The sickness returned and I actually lost some blood. But fortunately my child survived. It was you!" She said.

After nine long months I was born - a healthy baby. Although my mother was weak, she continued to breastfeed me for two and a half years. At that time children were nursed for up to three years. After me, she tried for another baby, but failed. So I was her last-born child, known in Dinka as 'kun'.

Whilst of course I was sorry for my mother who had lost a child before I was born, it suddenly occurred to me one day that I was actually very lucky. Suppose she had had that child, and nursed it for two or three years – my chances of being born afterwards would have been very slim!

The village of Wunrok is divided into two by the Lol River, with three-quarters to the north, and about a quarter to the south of it. The river has its source in the west and runs through the Aweil area and Twic, then flows down east, through Bentiu. There it joins the Kiir River and enters a lake, and emerges on the other side to meet Bahr el Jebel River, which comes from the far south through

Juba, flowing north. The two rivers meet to form the White Nile, which flows through many towns, such as Bor, Tonga, Malakal, Kodok, Renk and Kosti and then continues to Khartoum. Here the White Nile joins the Blue Nile coming from Ethiopia to form the Nile, which flows further north to Egypt and empties itself into the Mediterranean Sea.

The main road from the far south passes through Wau, Kuajok and Gogrial. It crosses the Lol River at Wunrok, and the Kiir River at Akech-nhail and continues to Abyei, sixty-four miles north of Wunrok, and then proceeds to Muglad and the far north.

When I was a child, all the inhabitants of Wunrok were farmers. They cultivated the land and kept some cattle, sheep and goats. But Wunrok was (and still is) also famous for its fish. The Lol River passes through many villages, but the one-and-a half mile stretch through Wunrok is particularly rich in fish. It is known as Kolbith; 'kol' meaning the deepest part of a river, and 'bith' denoting a fishing spear. Someone once lost his spear there and could not find it again – hence the name. During the dry season, which is the fishing period, people used to come from the villages south and north of the river to Wunrok to fish.

In the fifties fishing implements were still traditional. There were no hooks or nets, but a great quantity of fish was caught and dried, which, at the start of the rainy season and the cultivation period, would be carried home to the villages. Villagers were free to fish in all parts of the Lol River around Wunrok, but Kolbith alone was reserved for the time of the first rains. This would provide enough fish to feed families while the fields were being cultivated.

Kolbith's fish has inspired many songs. One of them says, *Aci kolbith weng dhieth*, Kolbith gave birth to a cow – a truth that the people of Wunrok cannot deny. When our great-grandfathers settled at Wunrok, only a few of them had cattle, but as they continued to live there, they began to catch a lot of fish, some of which they dried and took to far places to barter for sorghum (locally known as dura). Money was not commonly used in those days. Then, when food was scarce, people could be persuaded to part with their cattle in exchange for sorghum. In the sixties, money was introduced to the area, and both fresh and dried fish was sold for money, which could then be spent on more cattle. This enabled Wunrok's residents, who had originally arrived with hardly any cattle, to acquire impressive herds. It was indeed the river that had given them their cows.

In the late fifties there was only one small shop at Wunrok, owned by Jalaba, an Arab trader. Limited supplies were brought in by porters from Wau or Gogrial. They included clothes (mainly domuria), salt and beads. Items like sugar, tea, soap and onions came in very small quantities, and were intended for use only by the trader himself. Clothes were a novelty, and those who could afford to buy an item, would wear it until it was torn and had to be discarded. Soap was unknown, and clothes were not regularly washed, or washed in water only.

Ninety percent of the male population went naked. Only a few acquired tight knee-length jalabiyas of domuria, and wore them without any underwear – and only on journeys. A jalabiya might be shared with a brother or neighbour. The women wore the skins of small wild animals, sheep or goats. The animal skins were treated with oil, which made them very soft; and decorated with beads, which made them look beautiful, and lent them some weight, so that the wind could not blow them off too easily. About twenty percent of the ladies owned lengths of cloth, about the size of a single bed sheet or smaller, with which to cover themselves, or to wear over their skin dresses. Grown-up girls also wore the decorated skin of animals on special occasions or for dances, but at home they used a piece of black cloth tied around their waists, reaching down to their knees and open on the left side. Small girls went naked, but like almost everyone else, they wore beads round their necks and waists. Adults sold goats to buy beads. Young girls and even some women cut bundles of firewood or poles to barter for beads and salt.

Twic Bol Nyuol or Twic Bol Chol as it was known by many (Twic Mayardit), located in the northern part of Bahr el Gazal, was divided into four main sections. The Amiol section had its headquarters at Turalei, the Adiang section had its headquarters at Wunrok, the Akuar section, to the east, and Aweng respectively; and Thon, to the west, had Akoc as its headquarters.

The head-chief of a section was the sole authority over his people. He was highly respected and his orders were promptly carried out. He was the arm of the law in his area. He had runners or retainers who were strong men selected from among his people, who carried out the present functions of the police and prison warders. They did not wear uniforms, but wore on their left arms a flat yellow metal badge which was stamped with the image of a shoebill, the emblem of the former Bahr el Ghazal Province, which served to distinguish them from other men, even when they were naked. They separated fights, and arrested and imprisoned criminals. They also assisted in collecting pole taxes, performed administrative functions and carried out any other orders of the head-chief and his sub-chiefs.

My section, Adiang, had thirteen sub-sections: Kak, Majok, Audeng, Gumtor, Jokabar, Hol, Aruet, Liang-arol, Goi, Luit, You, Akak and Alueth. Each was administered by a sub-chief, who did not have his own retainers, but could call on those of the head-chief from time to time to assist him in maintaining the law in his area. The retainers could also assist the clan or Gol leaders in the collection of taxes. Once collected, the money was taken by the head-chief and the Gol leaders to the district headquarters. The head-chiefs, sub-chiefs and the retainers received a small monthly amount each, while the Gol leaders received a percentage of the amount they collected.

Life in general was simple. The numerous demands we are subject to today did not exist in the fifties. The chiefs benefited from free services rendered to them by their subjects, their houses were built and their fields cultivated. They were given rams as gifts; the hunters offered meat and the fishermen fish. Cooked food and locally brewed beer were delivered to their homes. These gifts were not considered bribes, because gifts were brought by everyone, whether they had cases before the chief or not, and the food was shared with others, including visitors who had come to the court centre from distant villages.

In those days Dinka chiefs were generally selected from rich families, and they became richer in office. The position could become hereditary. They served as both administrators and judges in their sections. Minor cases were settled by sub-chiefs, and only major ones were referred to the head-chief.

Villagers were unsophisticated and their problems were simple. Telling a lie, whether in court or outside, was thought bad form. Crimes which have now become quite common, were then considered dangerous and damaging, and were consequently rare. Young men treated women with respect, because if they eloped, or conceived a child with a girl, it would result in fighting between families or clans, and many would die. Girls were just as careful not to get involved in activities that could cause the loss of lives. If a single girl had a sexual relationship with a man or men before her marriage, she had to confess to it at the time she delivered her first child. If a woman died in childbirth or lost her first child, she would be suspected of not revealing the truth.

In Dinka tradition, adultery ranged with murder, and was heavily punished. A man who had committed adultery, would be made to pay ten cows to the husband of the woman as well as pay additional fines, and might be imprisoned. There was no specific punishment for the woman, but the treatment she received from the community was worse than a fine of cattle. If anyone in her house was ill, she would be evicted. When she paid a visit to neighbours or relatives, and there was a sick person in the house or compound, people would come running to prevent her from entering. And when the sick person left the house, he or she had to put on shoes made of the skin of a cow or giraffe, for fear of stepping on the footprints of an adulterous woman. This was hardly better than being stoned for adultery, and the humiliation she suffered caused many an unfortunate woman to commit suicide.

Theft was also rare. Cattle, goats and *dura* were considered to be special gifts from God to human beings, and stealing any of these would ruin the reputation of the thief's family. Items such as hoes, spears and axes were likewise inviolable. A hoe is used for burial, and to steal one could cause death. Someone who stole a knife or spear would suffer pain, it was believed. Thus the crimes which have today become all too common, once were prevented by the norms, customs, traditions and taboos of the communities and tribes.

I was barely six when I had my first brush with death. My sister Alek. my babysitter, took me to her house. As her husband was away, she gave me the job of taking the cattle down to the river. I left the cattle at the riverside to graze, and went down to the water to have a drink. I had squatted at the edge of the water, and was washing my hands, when I sensed a movement behind me. I jumped up. It was Malual Ring Lual, a notorious boy in the village for making mischief! He was close behind me, and there was no escape. He pushed me, hard, into the water about two metres from the edge, then quickly climbed the bank and ran away.

I was fortunate that a man called Jong Nhom Majak saw him running. Because he knew Malual's reputation, Jong rushed to the river bank to see what had made him run away. And there he saw me in the water, going down, then coming up again. I was trying to reach the bank by pushing very hard on the ground under the water, and every time I did manage to come up to the surface for air, but I was making no progress towards the edge. I was inhaling water, and was about to disappear finally, when Jong caught my hand and pulled me out of the water. He left me on the river bank to recover, while he ran after Malual, who had, however, drowned. I was vomiting when Jong joined me again, but after an hour I was able to get up and walk. Jong took me to my sister's house and explained what had happened. She immediately set off to tell the story to Malual's parents. It was very late in the evening when Malual went home, to be met by his angry parents. He was badly beaten by his father and denied food for the night. In those days parents never sided with their children when they did something wrong.

When my mother got the news, she rushed to my sister's house and took me back home, never to return. My father told my brother Deng to take me down to the river and teach me to swim, which I managed to do in less than a week, putting their minds at rest. I spent another two years at home, herding goats, before I was taken to school.

CHAPTER 2

The Legacy of a Remarkable Leader

At this point I would like to pause to bring homage to a great man, Head-chief Paulino Cyer Rehan Nuer, whose influence shaped the Adiang section – to which I belong – into what it is today.

Paulino Cyer Rehan was one of the South Sudanese children who attended school at Stack Memorial College in Wau. He then worked as a clerk for some time, before he took over the position of head-chief from his stepbrother Mawiir Rehan in 1946, a few months before I was born. Both Rehan Nuer and his son Mawiir were very capable and powerful, but Cyer had the advantage of education over them. He established a strong connection with the government authorities, and was always the first head-chief to maintain roads and collect pole taxes. Any self-help projects initiated by the government were promptly carried out. He became renowned for the eloquence with which he addressed meetings and conferences. He represented Twic at the famous Juba Conference in 1947 and again in 1953 in the first Sudan Legislative Assembly. In 1958 he and his lifelong friend, Head-chief Benjamin Lang Juk of the Akuar Section, represented Twic in the Second Sudanese Parliament – Paulino Cyer in the Senate, and Lang in the House of Representatives.

Paulino Cyer Rehan became the most prominent head-chief in the former Gogrial District, and in 1952 he travelled to the United Kingdom to be awarded the Belt of Honour, First Class, by Her Majesty the Queen.

His impact was particularly apparent in two major fields, education and trade. He started by sending his own children and those of his close relatives to school. Then he got all his sub-chiefs, leaders and retainers to enroll their children in schools as an example to the ordinary citizens, who were quick to follow suit. My father was one of the first.

The result is that today, in Kuajok, the headquarters of Warrap State, the majority of the educated people come from Twic, particularly from the Adiang Section. Adiang has more educated persons than any other section of the Warrap State (which formerly included Apuk, the largest section in the state, now an independent county).

Traditionally trading was regarded as the work of Arabs only, but Cyer Rehan opened the door to Dinka traders when he built a shop in Wunrok for his brother Deng Rehan, the first of its kind in Dinka history. The youth of the Adiang section, followed by others in Twic, immediately picked up the trading profession. In the late sixties and early seventies our own traders moved to Gogrial market in great numbers and erected small kiosks alongside the big shops of the Arab traders. Up to then, apart from one Greek gentleman, every single shopkeeper in Gogrial had been Arab.

As the Aguok people from around Gogrial also joined in, the Arabs lost their customers. Within a few years all the Arab trader had disappeared from Gogrial market, many moving their shops to Wau. The Greek trader's business dwindled too, and after his death his son went broke and left. Soon the Dinka traders followed the Arabs to Wau, and in the late seventies, especially after the Addis Ababa agreement, they dominated Wau market as well. Many of our own people, mainly those from Adiang acquired lorries.

To my knowledge, the first South Sudanese man to become a millionaire in the early nineties, was Cypriano Cyer Ayuel Rehan, the son of our head-chief's stepbrother.

At the time of my writing, most of the leading traders in Juba, the capital city of the Republic of South Sudan, are from Twic, mainly from the Adiang section.

The head-chief, Cyer Rehan Nuer, died in August 1981. His death left a vacuum which could not be filled. At that time I was the assistant commissioner of Gogrial Area Council, the area now divided into the Twic, Gogrial West and Gogrial East counties.

CHAPTER 3

School Days

When I first went to school there were only one elementary and six bush schools in Twic, all run by the Catholic Church, which was based at Mayen Abun. One bush school was Akoc for Thon, others were Pan-Nyok and Abindau for Adiang, Turalei for Amiol and Pawil and Ajak for Akuar.

In 1951 my brother Piol was the first from our family to be sent to school – Mayen Elementary School, twelve miles north of Wunrok, on the main road to Abyei. After two months he was back home, complaining of beatings by the teachers, and poor food. My father took him back to school, but a month later he ran away again, and this time my father allowed him to go to the cattle camp instead.

Then, in 1953, my brother Ngor Majok, who was at that time a petty trader who knew something about town life, told my father that I should be taken to school. My mother was bitterly opposed to the idea, and suggested that my other brother, Deng, should go. But Deng was not at home. He was staying with our elder sister, Ajok, who had just lost her husband and had four children to look after. Deng was there to take care of her cattle and the cultivation of the land; and he brought them fish during the fishing season. I was too young to take over from Deng, and leaving our sister Ajok alone with the children was impossible. For my father it was very important to have at least one child in a school at a time when many other parents were sending theirs. Deng and I were both keen to go, but would not be allowed to without our parents' approval. The children left behind in our village envied those boys who came back from school, wearing clothes and talking foreign languages, like English and Arabic. And they could read and write! This was like witchcraft to those at home!

At last my mother allowed me to be taken to school. Ngor went to Gogrial and promised to send clothes, but when the schools reopened in April, he had not sent any yet. Still, my father took me to Abindau Bush School, on the Lol River two miles east of Wunrok, on the same side as my home. He handed me over to Korado Cyer Deng Aken-guet, a very good teacher from Wunrok.

For a month I went naked, like some of the other children, especially those in the first year. Even our beads had been left at home – they were not allowed at school. Then one day the priest who was in charge of schools arrived with some rolls of white cloth, which were cut into pieces and issued to us. We tied them around our waists. They reached our knees and were open on the left side, like the black cloth worn by the girls in the villages. The boys' ones were known as *abong'a*, a name used by the Luo tribe. We did not want to resemble the girls too closely, so we tied the lower ends of the cloth between our legs, and decided that wearing abonga was better than nothing, for at least they covered our private parts. When I eventually received a pair of shorts and a shirt, I wore them alternately with my *abong'a*.

Teaching started well and the teachers were very kind. Some big boys tried to bully the younger ones, but they were punished when found out. The only heavy work we were required to do was to take turns pounding the *dura* into flour. We gathered firewood too, and did the cooking ourselves. We also cleaned the school compound.

We were close to the river. The priest brought some fishing nets and hired local people to catch fish, part of which was dried and distributed to all the schools in Twic. As our school was on the river, we received fresh fish as well, a special privilege. Once a month we used to visit the houses of the chiefs and other notable persons of the surrounding villages, marching, and singing the school song, accompanied by a teacher or two. In most cases, we were given an ox to slaughter for meat. During the three years I spent at Abindau, we never went to the same person twice, and we never returned without a bull.

Our first and second years passed smoothly. But in August 1955, when we were in our third year, the school was abruptly closed. We did not know what was going on, neither did the teachers. The priest in charge of schools just appeared and issued orders to the teachers for the closure of the school. It was only much later, when we reached intermediate school, that we came to know the reason – destabilization caused by the Torit mutiny. In 1956 we were able to complete our third year, and I was one of five pupils to be promoted to Mayen Elementary School.

When we arrived at Mayen, we found that everything had changed. All the schools in the south, most of which had been run by various Christian churches, had been taken over by the Sudanese government.

A headmaster was brought from Wau to run the school and his administration came up with a new policy – they abolished third-year classes at Abindau (where pupils from Akoc used to go) and Pawil (for students from Turalei and Ajak). It was also decided that second-year pupils in the six bush schools were to compete with those at Mayen for admittance to third year. There were only forty spaces.

Those of us who had done our third year in a bush school, were denied entry to fourth year at Mayen elementary school. We had to repeat our third year – and only if the teachers deemed us good enough to do so. Standards at Mayen were higher and the teachers were better educated than at our previous school, but we had no problem with that, since we were repeating our third year.

We were not expected to do a lot of manual work. We only collected firewood for cooking and we cleaned the compound. I was exempted from those duties as I was appointed office boy. I cleaned the headmaster's office and issued chalk to the class monitors every morning, changed used exercise books and issued pens and pencils to the boys.

The food, however, was horrible – the very same poor quality that had earlier caused my brother Piol to run back home. The *dura* issued from the store was never clean, and was ground into flour by a certain Mading Bith using a hand-operated mill. Mading used to set the machine loose to make the work easy, and what he produced could not be called flour in the real sense of the word. When cooked, this '*asida*' looked very black in the locally forged iron dishes known as 'alela'. When it was put in broth, it disappeared from your hand, and you had to reach to the bottom of the dish to collect some. The broth was equally bad.

Big bulls were brought from Gogrial – one for each month we spent at school – that meant one bull per month for 160 pupils. Certainly that was not enough! When a bull was slaughtered, only the entrails were eaten on the first day, and the next day the head and legs – only the bones that did not have much meat on them. The meat was smoked, but it was not properly done, and flies bred on the meat, especially the bones. The bones were made to last for a week, and then, for the remaining days, a very small piece of meat was boiled in a lot of water each day, with a little groundnut paste added to it. We bravely ate on, regardless of the maggots we found in this broth.

Towards the middle of our fourth year, even fewer bulls were brought, and instead of meat, white beans were added to the broth. They might have been as good as grain, but looked like lizard's eggs, and some pupils decided that they had had enough and went home.

Then they started bringing dried meat from Wau, provided by the Tsetse Fly Eradication Team which was working in the areas between Tonj, Wau and Gogrial, combating the testse flies that were killing the cattle. This area teemed with a variety of wild life, and the team was authorized to reduce the number of animals by hunting them and drying the meat for use in the schools. The problem was that the team members were mainly from the Fertit and Luo (Jurcol) tribes, people said to eat monkey's meat. Dinkas do not eat monkey meat, and we assumed that the dried meat included the forbidden variety. More pupils left school.

I was one of those who ignored the food, and stuck it out. We sat for our intermediate entrance examinations and I was the only one of the boys from Abindau to pass. Seventeen boys from Mayen were accepted by Kuacjok Intermediate School. I was one!

As the time approached for the new school year to start, I was pondering the long journey to Kuacjok. From Wunrok to Gogriel is thirty-eight miles, and from Gogrial to Kuacjok nineteen, a long distance to cover on foot. In those days people were not used to travelling too far per day. (Our grandfathers and great-grandfathers even less so.) When I was a young boy, my father used to go to Maker, where his brother Piol Adiang lived, about a mile south of Mayen. He would sleep over at Acuanac, in the house of his stepbrother

Col Adiang, only to reach Maker the next day. He followed the same route on his way back. When I went to school in Mayen, I walked the distance in one day. No-one has been able to give me a convincing reason for our fathers' reluctance to walk far. Perhaps it was because of the wild animals that were so common then, they say.

People would start their journeys when the sun was high in the sky, and settle for the night before sunset. Let's say my father left at nine o'clock in the morning and walked until four in the afternoon, alone, in broad daylight, one would expect him to have been able to cover the distance of twelve miles between Wunrok and Mayen Abun in a day – if he walked two miles per hour, with a few minutes' rest at water points.

But our forebears do not seem to have been particularly energetic. This is shown by the size of the fields they cultivated. A family of six able bodies used to till a plot which nowadays requires only two persons. Some hard-walking persons now cover the distance between Wunrok and Gogrial in a day, and arrive before sunset.

Wunrok was the assembly point for all students from Twic going to schools outside the Twic area. From east to west, Twic is divided into four main sections: To the east is Akuar, which shares a border with a small Nuer area and the Dinka Ruweng (Alor) of Upper Nile Province. Amiol is situated next to Akuar, and then Adiang and Thon, which border an area occupied by the Dinka tribes of Aweil. To the north, all four areas border an area where the Dinka Ngok have settled in Abyei. Originally, the entire Twic area was on the northern side of the Lol River, and Dinka Rek on the southern side. Gradually Akuar, Amiol and Adiang pushed Rek southwards and away from the river, for a distance of six to fifteen miles. Rek, again, pushed Thon northwards for at least six miles.

Students from other parts of Twic found it impossible or very difficult to take a shortcut from where they lived to Gogrial, particularly if they were using a car. Everyone had to pass through Wunrok. When all the Twic boys, bound for Kuacjok and beyond, had arrived at Wunrok, we started our journey. We spent the night at Karaduet, about halfway between Wunrok and Gogrial, and reached Gogrial at about six o'clock the next evening.

In Gogrial we stopped in front of some shops which lined both sides of the main road to Wau. Each shop had a brick wall attached to it, behind which the trader and his family lived. There was no electricity, but the traders had small hurricane lamps to use in their homes.

Soon the boys who had been there before, disappeared into the direction of the houses of people they knew and where they could spend the night. That left seven of us to fend for ourselves. We knew that there were about six government officials and some traders from our section currently in town, but we did not bother to look for their houses. Instead, we asked the Greek merchant to allow us to sleep on the veranda of his shop. He agreed, and showed us where to sleep. His shop was the largest in town, sturdily built of baked bricks, and with a corrugated iron roof. It had a wide open veranda which, on the southern side, did not have a door into the shop. We had to climb two steps to get on to it. It was smooth and clean and we each found a spot to sleep. We were very tired, but also very hungry. One of the merchant's servants soon brought us some water in a pail, with a cup for drinking. The same merchant also had a bakery, north of the shop, and as we had some money, his servant took one of the boys there to buy bread. It was fresh and hot from the oven, and although we had no broth to eat with it, we all agreed that it made a great meal with water.

We lay down to rest, but before we could go to sleep, a police patrol arrived to check whether the shops were properly locked. They found us on the veranda and asked what we were doing there.

"We're students from Twic. We have nowhere else to sleep," we said.

"No problem! Just stay where you are until morning."

In the morning we tied up our belongings, and put the bundles against the wall of the shop. We went out to meet the other boys, and together we went to the office of the assistant district commissioner (ADC). The ADC and the executive officer were both Arabs. They told us that those going to Wau and beyond were to assemble with their belongings in front of the police station where they would be put on lorries and taken to Wau. Those who, like me, were bound for Kuajok were to continue on foot.

We promptly decided to remain in Gogrial for another three days. We could have our clothes mended there, and of course we wanted to see more of the town which we, village boys, found fascinating. We went through almost all the shops, just gazing at the merchandize, and at the merchants themselves. We visited the ADC's office several times, just to see it from the outside, built on high ground and looking quite imposing. Close to the office was a police station, and then, further south, a dispensary. There was no hospital. Some distance south-east of the office, were the quarters for junior staff – a house built of baked bricks, and thatched. The ADC's own house was about a mile away, to the east, situated on the Jur River. Of course we went to see it. The executive officer had a house south of the office.

The residential area or *'malakai'* was small, composed of huts, most of which were unfenced. This was where the labourers and local traders lived. There was also a small market where locally produced items and produce were spread out on the ground and on small tables. Women were selling cooked food in whatever shade was available, and it was here that we took our meals. We had no choice as there were no restaurants in town.

For the three days we spent in Gogrial, our belongings remained on the veranda. We knew that no one would steal anything, or tamper with our bags.

Very early on the third day, we set out for Kuacjok. About eight miles from Kuacjok, the road started getting very rough. The gravel was sharp, and there were no footpaths on either side – only trees and tall grass. About a mile from the school the surface of the road had become extremely jagged, with sharp stones sticking up. We hit them with sticks. They were very hard. Our bare feet were bleeding. Coming from Twic, a muddy area, we had never seen such stones before, only heard people talk about them. A few boys possessed canvas shoes but reserved them for going to church on Sundays. They could never wear them at Kuacjok! The stones would destroy them. Most of us did not have shoes anyway.

It was about five o'clock in the afternoon when at last we arrived – the first pupils to get there. We found a teacher who took us to a dormitory and told us that it was too late to issue rations and that the cook was out. Fortunately we still had some bread from Gogrial, which we soaked in cold water and ate, with a little sugar added to it. The following morning the cook appeared and issued rations according to our number.

There were two long dormitories with small verandas and a storeroom between them. They were built of baked bricks, and thatched. The walls were very high and there were proper windows, with mosquito screens. Inside, the walls were plastered with cement. It was very cold in these rooms!

To the north of these dormitories was the main school building, built of bricks and with a corrugated iron roof. It was designed in a T-shape. Each wing consisted of a classroom and an office, with a hall in the middle. There was a veranda supported by pillars, and above it was a board with "Kuacjok Intermediate School" written on it. To the north was another thatched building consisting of two more classrooms, also built of bricks, and a little distance away, the teachers' houses. The police station was situated south-west of the school, close to the main road. Two hundred meters south of the police station, on the other side of the road, was Deng Agany's shop. Apart from some salt, black cloth for girls, beads and *domuria*, it did not stock much.

The pride of the area was the famous Catholic Church, about half a kilometer east of the school. It looked like the church at Mayen, but much larger, built of special bricks and with a corrugated iron roof. The main door facing west was closed, but you could enter by a side door. Inside it was very beautiful, with wonderful pictures on the walls. The palm trees painted on the walls, inside and outside, looked like actual trees growing there. Above the altar was a painting of a lamb which looked so real, you would expect it to get up and walk away. The furniture was mahogany. We were truly impressed to see this great church, which we had read about in Dinka books.

The priests' compound south of the church was a modern building in a fenced lemon and mango orchard, with a workshop to the west of the garden, where logs of mahogany and teak were sawed and made into furniture for the school and church when they were under the church's administration.

North of the church was the sisters' compound with the girls' elementary school annexed to it. The boys' elementary school was about a hundred meters east of the church. Behind it, open grassland stretched east to the Jur River, two or three kilometers away, and north and southwards along the river to Wau and Gogrial.

To the north was a small forest, and behind it were river-flooded grassland (*toch*). Along the western side of the main road was a thick forest that extended for many miles. South of the intermediate school there were only two or three houses. The Dinka Kuac village was situated about a mile away on both sides of the main road.

Kuacjok in those days was not a town, nor was it a typical Dinka village. It was just a church, with three schools around it. Kuacjok Catholic church was the largest church in the area, and the first in Dinkaland. Kuacjok Intermediate School had started as a vernacular teachers' training centre (VTTC) under the Catholic Church but was turned into an intermediate school when the government took over. The first batch of student teachers had been drawn from Akon, Mayen Abun, Nyarkec and Kuacjok elementary schools. Five students originally came from Tonj elementary school, mostly sons of Gogrial. When we arrived, the final batch of VTTC students were in their fourth year - men, not children, some of whom were married. Most of them had come from Yirol and Rumbek, two from Wau, two from Awiel and one each from Gogrial and Twic. There was no-one from Tonj.

Their educational standard was rather low. They used to come to us, first year pupils, for help, especially in mathematics. When they sat the secondary entrance examination only two chaps from Wau made it to Rumbek Secondary School. The rest went home or had to look for jobs elsewhere.

For those of us who had come from Mayen, Akon and Kuacjok elementary schools, life was relatively good. We ate asida, a boiled dura flour pudding. This time the dura was clean, and ground using an electric grinding mill, not hand-operated like the one at Mayen. We had fresh meat daily, plus rice or lentils or beans, and vegetable oil and onions. Sugar was issued to us, and tea boiled for everyone. I'd never had a steady supply of tea before!

We slept on iron beds and each of us received two blankets. We were not used to this life, and the first few nights some of the boys would fall off their beds. In the classrooms we sat on proper chairs and we each had our own desk in which we could keep our books, under lock and key.

Teaching was very good. We did not have much manual work to do as firewood was brought by a contractor and we only had to clean our rooms and the school compound. I was put in charge of the pressure lamps which lit the classrooms and the kitchen in the evenings. For the first time we also received school uniforms – two pairs of shorts and two shirts each. Nevertheless, the students from Nyarkec and Tonj found cause for complaint. Why weren't they given bread to eat, they wanted to know, and why didn't the dormitories have corrugated iron roofs?

Our first, second and third years at Kuacjok passed smoothly. It was only in our fourth year that we encountered trouble – not only us, but all the people of southern Sudan. It happened when the government in Khartoum under General Ibrahim Aboud issued a decree abolishing Sunday, which was a day of rest in the south, and imposing Friday – a day of rest in northern Sudan – on the entire country. This was rejected by the people of the south. The first to receive the news, were the students in the bigger towns, and they went on strike. We watched as students from Wau passed through Kuacjok, perched on cars and singing songs. They were not allowed past the police station, but they managed to drop letters informing us why they were going home. Most of us had never heard of a strike before, let alone how to start one. But there were four boys from Tonj who said that they knew. It was not difficult to go on strike, they told us, and said that if all the students in the south joined in, and only Kuacjok Intermediate School remained functioning, it would give our young school a bad name.

The elementary schools at Kuacjok, likewise, were reluctant to strike if their elders did not take the lead. But then, one morning, it was agreed that the strike would begin the following day. It was decided that all the students would enter their classrooms as usual, but, as soon as the teachers appeared, the students would march out, the fourth-year students leading. So, the next morning, as the teacher entered our fourth-year classroom, we got up and walked out – only to discover that only twelve of us had done so while the rest, including the four ring-leaders, had remained in their seats. Eight third-year boys joined us outside, and four or five from the second and first-year classes.

We marched to our dormitories as the teachers went to the headmaster's office. The school authorities were fully aware of the pending strike, so the headmaster told the teachers to take down the names of us culprits and allow the rest of the boys to follow us to the dormitories.

We were angry. "Why didn't you follow us outside?" we asked the four ring-leaders. "What made you stay in the classroom?" "We stayed to see who the back-legs were who would give our names to the teacher," they said. Of course it was a lie! The teachers knew our names and could write them down without being told by anyone! But these four town boys, we realized, knew what the consequences would be for ring-leaders in a strike. They had deceived us, put the blame on the twelve of us and the boys who followed from the other classrooms.

After breakfast, a parade was called, and the headmaster declared the school closed. The following day two lorries arrived, one to take those going to Wau away, the other to take the boys bound for Gogrial and beyond.

After our first long walk from Wunrok to Kuacjok we never travelled on foot again, at least not all the way. Every year we were taken in cars to and from school. The only problem facing the students from Twic was floods. When schools closed in December Twic was always flooded and the road would become impassable. Every year the driver would drop us north of Panliet, and we would proceed on foot for seven to twelve miles, depending on the severity of the floods. The pupils from Turalei and Aweng took the road to the east of Wunrok and those from Mayen Abun and beyond, took the road to the north. Pupils from Pan-nyok and Akoc had an additional problem. The streams they had to cross were narrow, but deep, and short boys would need the support of their friends to cross with their belongings. At the time of the strike, though, the road was still good up to Wunrok, and the *toch* was not yet flooded.

The students were called back to school after about a month, and another month later the school authorities met to decide our fate. A teacher later told us that their first decision had been to dismiss the twelve of us who had walked out of the fourth year classroom. But when they checked our records, they found that our behaviour had always been exemplary and that, as for academic achievement, we were the best in the class. Our dismissal would result in our new school that was to sit for national examinations for the first time that year, performing poorly. So the authorities changed their minds and decided to punish us with lashes instead. Twelve of us were given ten lashes each, and those of the third year five lashes each. This was the second time I was punished in my school career. The first time I was lashed was at Abindau Bush School when I remained swimming in the river with some other boys when we were supposed to be on parade. Then we were given five lashes each, but with a thin branch. At Kuacjok they used a real hippo skin whip. A very strong young teacher was instructed to whip us – five lashes on the first day, and five on the next. We asked for the lashing to be finished on one day, but they would not allow that. The teacher first checked what we were wearing, and if we were found with underwear inside our shorts, the shorts were removed and we were lashed wearing underwear only.

On the second day, our bottoms were swollen, some of them bleeding. We did not understand why we were treated so severely as the issue of Sunday as a day of rest concerned everyone in southern Sudan. All of our teachers were southerners and Christians, except for one man from Egypt, who taught Arabic but was a Christian. As a matter of fact, the Egyptian was the only teacher to show us any sympathy. He called what was done to us a wild act. One third-year boy from Wunrok refused to be lashed and left school.

Things returned to normal and our studies continued. But then something very strange happened. Two days after the lashing, the teacher responsible for it came into the classroom and began his lesson as usual, but halfway through the period he threw down his chalk and walked out, back to his house. On the second day he was back in the classroom, but only sat on his table until the bell rang, and went home. This time the class monitor reported the matter to the headmaster. On the third day, Friday, the teacher did not appear at all, but stayed at home. He had no wife, and lived alone in his brick house with a corrugated iron roof. In his yard he had a thatched mud hut where he used to cook his meals. That Sunday evening he carried all his belongings, including his bed and his box, to the hut and set it on fire. Helpers arrived too late to save anything. The fire consumed everything. He was asked why he had done it, but refused to talk, and when at last he uttered a word it was in his mother tongue which nobody could understand. The school store supplied him with another bed and mattress and a labourer was sent to sleep on his veranda to monitor his behaviour that night. The next morning the labourer reported that the teacher had spent the whole night walking in the school compound, visiting the church several times. The labourer followed him, and asked him about it, but the teacher was unable to tell him what he was looking for or what his problem was. This was dangerous as the area teemed with wild animals. Moreover, the teacher had stopped eating and drinking, and the headmaster feared that he might starve to death. The headmaster therefore arranged for a car to take him to Wau, accompanied by a teacher and a labourer. At Wau he was put on a plane and flown to Juba, as he was a Latuho from Eastern Equatoria. Nothing was heard of him since.

Some people said the teacher must have been bewitched by the students he had lashed. Others said it was just coincidence. It is left to the reader to form his own opinion, depending on how superstitious he is.

When the time arrived for us to sit for the secondary school entrance examinations, we were fully prepared. We finished the papers and went home. When the results came out, we were happy to learn that seventeen students from Kuacjok Intermediate School had been accepted by Rumbek

Secondary School. The twelve of us whom the authorities had threatened to dismiss were among them. None of the ringleaders who had instigated the strike had made it. The results were deemed very good for a young intermediate school sitting for the exams for the first time, as the competition for spaces at Rumbek was fierce.

CHAPTER 4

Rumbek

Rumbek was the only academic secondary school in the south, catering for the three provinces of Bahr el Ghazal, Equatoria and Upper Nile. In our year the intake was raised to one hundred and sixty students in four streams, but still some intermediate schools had fewer than ten students accepted.

When I received the news that I had been accepted as a student at Rumbek Secondary School, I was elated! In those days secondary school graduates were very scarce. Most of the officials in the South were intermediate school leavers. If I continued to work hard, I knew, this might be a step to university! I couldn't wait for July to come, and the school to open. Meanwhile I stayed at home and helped my parents cultivating our fields.

In the second week of June a car was sent from Wau to collect all the students bound for Rumbek Secondary School from the whole Gogrial district – from Wunrok and Abyei. (In those days most Ngok students received their education in Bhar el Ghazal, particularly at Mayen Elementary School in Twic.) At Gogrial we were joined by some more students and we left for Wau. I was among the students who had not been to Wau before, but some of the boys knew exactly what to expect and they made it clear that it was well worth seeing. When I was at Kuacjok Intermediate School, there were boys who walked forty miles, just to go and see Wau. I remember how exhausted and how hungry they were when they came trudging back after a week – they knew nobody in Wau who could house or feed them. Now, on the route to Rumbek, it would be my chance to see the city! When we arrived, we dispersed and went to different houses to find accommodation. Those of us who came from the Adiang section and some others who had nowhere else to go, went to the house of our head-chief, Cyer Rehan.

Wau was beyond imagination, much more impressive than I had ever expected, much bigger than Gogrial. The large shops were sturdily built, and they stocked a great variety of goods. The offices and government houses were very beautiful, all built of permanent materials. The provincial headquarters were the best building in town. Even today it has not been surpassed – the modern building that has now been erected looks inferior compared to it. There were affordable restaurants at which we took our meals. And there was a cinema! For the first time in our lives we could see movies! There were so many residential areas (*malakai*) that it was impossible to visit all of them. We could only explore the town from the point where we entered it, to the point from which we would depart again.

We also went to pray in the huge Catholic church of Wau, and gaped at the Muslim mosque in the Muslim shopping district. We had heard of mosques, but had never seen one. In Gogrial there was no mosque. We visited the railway station and stared in amazement at the trains. The bridge across the Jur River had not been built yet, but there was a ferry, much larger than the ferries at Wunrok and Gogrial, to take people and cars across this river and the Lol.

We stayed for five days; then had to leave for Rumbek. The roads were quite good in those days because traffic was not heavy – you could sometimes drive all the way from Wau to Rumbek without meeting a single car – so we covered the sixty-three miles to Tonj in two hours. Tonj was a small town, almost like Gogrial, except that it had a good number of schools in it and a mosque near the police station. We got out of the car for a thirty-minute rest, then continued to Rumbek, seventy-five miles away. It was afternoon when we were dropped at the school.

Rumbek Secondary School is situated about a mile east of the town, south of the main road from Rumbek to Yirol, which is seventy five miles away. It is on flat ground – fine sand mixed with black soil – among thornless trees. When we arrived it was already an established school – it had been opened in the late forties. There was a large u-shaped north-facing building consisting of classrooms and, in the middle, two offices, one for the headmaster and one for the teachers. In the western wing there was a library, and in the eastern wing a laboratory. As the school was expanding, and additional classrooms were needed, another building had been erected north of the main building.

Close to the main road there was a football field, used for all kinds of games and also for athletics. The dormitories were south of the classrooms, each with its own kitchen and dining hall. A main dining hall was still under construction. There were two chapels, one for Catholics (to the west) and one for Protestants (to the east). Between the classrooms and the dormitories there was a large flat area where, at weekends, the students used to dance or present concerts. Some good distance away to the west, towards the town, were houses for the teachers and also some small villages.

We were well fed. Twice a day we had meat cooked with vegetables and served with rice or lentils. The Egyptian beans (*ful masr*) which we ate either for breakfast or for supper were particularly good. We were issued with sugar and took tea with milk twice a day.

In the dormitory each of us had a bedside cupboard where we could keep our belongings and the roasted groundnuts we received, under lock and key. Whenever we felt hungry, we could have a snack.

The teaching was equally good. We had a number of teachers, different ones for each subject. There were southerners and northerners, plus three foreigners – two from Britain and one from Egypt – all of them university graduates (unlike the teachers in our schools today). The headmaster came from the north.

After a year of good teaching and good food, time to go home for the holidays came just too soon. "You have grown so tall!" My mother exclaimed when she saw me. "You are a big boy now! I am so happy that they are taking such a good care of you."

But the good times were not to last. We were still on holiday when we became aware that a rebel army was on the rise in the south, and when we reached school there was a lot of talk about the Anya-Nya having reached the Aweil and Gogrial areas. The people of the south were shaken. A number of arrests were made in the town. Then the unrest reached the school.

The security personnel in the town secretly recruited several students to spy on the others. This led to a number of students actually being arrested, and caused a quarrel between the headmaster (a very strong man married to an Englishwoman) and the District Commissioner (DC). Every time a student was arrested, the headmaster would go to the DC's office in person, and he would not leave until that student had been released. It was lucky that he was a northerner. If he had been from the south, he could have been arrested together with the students, and killed. The nickname the students had given him, was Brutus, which to them meant brute. But actually they liked and admired his strong personality and administration. He was able to control the tough southern Sudanese students who would look at every problem from a political angle. When eventually he was transferred to a school in the north, he would tell his new students that in the south he had dealt with men, not children like them.

I do not know who was responsible for the decision, but two months later the school was closed and we were sent home.

CHAPTER 5

Anya-Nya

When we got home, we found that the situation had changed a great deal in the short period of two months. All the Arab traders in the villages in the Gogrial district had disappeared. Those who had not been killed by the Anya-Nya had fled to Gogrial town. There were not many Arab traders left in Twic, only a few single men without families. They also left the area before the arrival of the Anya-Nya freedom fighters.

The traders in the Rek area, however, did not leave in time, and when they did flee, or were killed, they left the women and children behind. The strong Anya-Nya presence in the area made it impossible for the families to escape to Gogrial, so a number of them went to Wunrok, hoping to make their way from there to Abyei town. But Abyei was sixty-four miles from Wunrok, and the terrain was difficult and hostile. Wild animals or even ordinary citizens could pose a threat. Our head-chief Cyer Rehan Nuer in whose house they had assembled took it upon himself to hastily transport them to Abyei before the arrival of the Anya-Nya rebels. It was not Dinka custom to kill women and children. When the Anya-Nya reached Wunrok they were furious with the head-chief for saving the lives of the families of the enemy. When Nuer received word of this, he did not return to Wunrok after handing over the families to the authorities in Abyei, but proceeded to Muglad from where he took the train to Wau. It was only after a month in the north that he returned to Gogrial. Here he found that all the head-chiefs of the Gogrial District had been called to the town, and told to stay there to prevent them from collaborating with the Anya-Nya, although the sub-chiefs had stayed in their areas. All the outside police stations were closed. Some of the policemen joined the Anya-Nya, whilst others came to the town.

There was no other form of government presence in the countryside, and connection between the town and the rural areas had been severed. Anyone arriving in town from the villages was considered to be a member or agent of the Anya-Nya. Likewise, anyone leaving the town for a rural destination was accused of being a spy for the Arab government.

During the time I remained at home, the government in the town made no effort to restore their presence in the rural areas. The Anya-Nya, however, launched sporadic hit-and-run attacks on the towns, as well as on vehicles travelling between towns. This necessitated the use of convoys guarded by the army and the police. The Anya-Nya tactics were purely guerilla, and they avoided direct combat with the government forces. They continued recruiting soldiers, although they did not have enough arms, only a few guns, mostly of very inferior quality compared to what the government had.

The situation changed when the soldiers who defected from the government forces came properly armed. The rebels were mobile and in our area they used to come and go. They tried to persuade us to join the movement too, and some of my friends did, but many of us were not ready to join the Anya-Nya yet. As for me, I told them that I wanted to continue my education and was just waiting for the road to the town to reopen to go back to school. As soon as I had completed my studies, I would join, I promised. Fortunately there were some officers who agreed with me. They said that I was still too young to fight, and since they expected the war to continue for a long time, those who were willing to go back to school should do so. The movement would eventually need educated members. Those of us remaining at home, made the best of the simple village life, like any other young man would. We went fishing, attended dances in the evenings, and sometimes went to distant villages to converse with the girls.

One day there was a fight between our section, Adiang, and the Amiol section. I went with my uncle's son, Kuel Abekjok Adiang. We assembled at a place called "Muon", on the border between the two sections, three miles east of Wunrok. We from Adiang stood facing east, with our backs to our homes. Our opponents from Amiol faced us, with their backs towards their homes in the north.

More and more people joined the two sides as the day drew on. Women traditionally accompanied the men to a fight, but did not take part, and neither did young boys. That day, however, the Amiol section tricked us. They knew that our southern wing was always the strongest, so they grouped their women and boys together, holding *dura* (sorghum) stalks. Young boys were not supposed to take part in a fight, and they were not killed when found among the warriors. To us they appeared to be fighters and we concentrated on them while Amiol moved their real fighting force south to the river.

The fighting men went down to the river, one by one, as if they were going to drink water, and remained there. My friend and I were in the southern wing, near the river. At about three o'clock that afternoon, the two sides started approaching each other. The two of us were in the second wave. We were directly behind a man from Wunrok, Mathiang Akok, whose mother was from Amiol. We found ourselves facing his two maternal uncles, and when they saw the two boys behind Mathiang, they thought that we were his twin sons, Malual and Makuac, so they repeatedly called him by his mother's name, urging him to send us away. I do not think Mathiang Akok was even aware of our presence behind him. He continued to insult them and sing war songs. Then the two sides clashed. We pushed Amiol back three times; then their concealed force emerged from the long grass on the river bank and joined the fight. I saw one of our men, Majok Bol, being speared. A man called Atem Mawien Dau pulled him back, and advanced ahead. Atem was also speared but continued fighting. When Majok, who had been retreating, saw this, he turned around and came back fighting. He was again speared, this time fatally, and he fell down flat. Then the Amiol fighters overwhelmed us, and we pulled back and ran.

Atem Mawien Dau could not run. There were many spears in him, I could not tell how many, but he did not fall down. He put down one knee, and held his buffalo skin shield close to his chest, and kept singing the Adiang war songs. He had killed two of the Amiol men, so now the Amiol fighters gathered round him, caught the handles of the spears, pushed him down and killed him. This delayed them, and enabled us to flee. We were already more than a hundred meters away, out of reach of their spears, when Deng Bol, Majok's brother who was ahead of us, heard about his brother's death. He turned around and walked back, calmly. We could not stop him. He hurled spears, but they were caught. He then continued walking, undaunted, unarmed. And he was speared, hit several times. His foolish act gave us the opportunity to get away from those who were still following us.

The Amiol warriors returned to their place just outside Wunrok. The sun was setting, and the women were sent to collect the bodies of all who had been killed, and bring them home. The men crossed the Lol River to the southern side, leaving only the women and children in the houses. The dead would be buried the next morning.

We spent the night in the house of my maternal uncle, Nyuol Aguan Nyuol. I lay on the bare floor, unable to sleep. Late that night my aunt came and offered me some food. I took a mouthful, but just could not swallow it, so I threw the food away, took a sip of water, and lay down again. Not all of us were trying to sleep. Some young men were patrolling the riverside in case the Amiol fighters decided to strike again. In the morning we got up and went to the river to wash away the dust that covered us. Then we went to the houses of those killed, to bury them.

In all, thirty of our men had been killed, and only three from Amiol, including the two killed by Atem Mawien Dau. Atem was buried in his house. The two other Wunrok men who were killed, Majok Bol and his brother Deng Bol, were buried in the house of their brother Bek Bol because their houses were far south of the river.

For a few days the situation remained tense, but then the Anya-Nya came to our area and things calmed down. After suffering such a defeat, I thought nobody would mention fighting again. After a month, however, the young men were regrouping and discussing ways to take revenge. Some ambushes would be organized by both sides, and a person or two killed.

Kuel Abekjok and I never took part in fighting again. I blamed myself for having participated in such a senseless sectional fight. If we were to ask the men, "But *why* did you fight?" They would not know what to say. The fact that we ourselves had not been killed, could only be put down to luck. If those Amiol fighters had not mistaken the two of us for their nephew Mathiang Akok's twins, they would have killed us. They did hurl a number of spears at another boy, Deng Nyuol Aguan, but he was very good at dodging them and was not hit. If they had done that to me, I would probably have been killed.

In 1966, when I was in Khartoum, another battle took place between Amiol and Adiang. In that single fight, Amiol lost between one hundred and two hundred men, while Adiang lost only one young man, a relative of mine by the name of Mayou Anyang Mayou. To this day there has not been another fight between them.

I spent the last months of 1964 and the whole of 1965 at home, until circumstances allowed me to return to school.

It then happened that a certain First Lt. Deng "Manoon" Mawiir Rehan of the Anya-Nya ordered his soldiers to beat and imprison another of their commanders, Lt. Dut Deng Atak. First Lt. Deng "Manoon" lived in a village called Kurum, about twelve miles north of Wunrok, with his stepbrother Captain Athuai "Mahmoud" Mawiir Rehan. They used to camp at Wunrieng, about twelve miles west of Wunrok, from where they would go home from time to time.

A few days later, Lt. Dut Deng managed to escape from the Anya-Nya camp at Wunrieng where he had been held captive and found his way to Gogrial town, where he surrendered to the government forces. After two days he asked to be given some soldiers to accompany him to capture First Lt. Deng "Manoon" Mawiir and his stepbrother. This arrangement between him and the soldiers, who were mostly Arabs, was leaked to Head-chief Cyer Rehan Nuer, whose stepbrother Mawiir Rehan Nuer was the father of the two officers. So very secretly, Cyer Rehan sent a messenger, someone he could trust implicitly, to warn the two officers. It was kept top secret, for if the Arabs were to learn of it, it would mean death for both messenger and chief. So the messenger bypassed us in Wunrok and went to Kurum, where he delivered the message and then returned secretly to Gogrial.

We in Wunrok were unaware of the beating of Lt. Dut Deng Atak by the Anya-Nya and his escape to town. Our contact with the Anya-Nya was a fellow student, Victor Kuol Malek, who had joined the movement, but would come back to spend some time in Wunrok from time to time and stay with us. He might have known about these events, but he never told us.

Late one afternoon Lt. Dut Deng Atak and his Arab soldiers left Gogrial for Twic. They had planned their journey carefully so that there would not be time for the news of their approach to reach Twic. In those days people did not have telephones, like now.

It was dark when the cars arrived at Kuelbuut, about a mile from the Lol River and Wunrok. So as not to alarm the people of Wunrok on the northern side of the river, they had not used headlights. They now left the cars and continued to the river on foot. They knew that the people of Wunrok would keep to the road as both sides were flooded. The soldiers allowed travellers coming from Wunrok to pass, but they prevented those who were coming from behind them from going to Wunrok, telling them to wait a while before they proceeded.

Just then, a friend of mine, Deng Kuot Malou, who had spent the day with us in Wunrok, was on his way home south of the river on his bicycle. He was lucky that his bicycle didn't have lights. When he was about two hundred meters from the soldiers, he noticed something black in the middle of the road. He stopped. What could it be? He was alarmed. At that spot there wasn't any bush, and even if there were, it would not be in the middle of the road. Then he saw a flicker of light. Someone smoking! And the black objects could only be cars! He turned his bicycle and rushed back to the river. He threw his bicycle into the long grass, jumped into the flooded river fully clothed, and swam across. The river was deep – the water would reach the shoulders of a six-foot man. He came directly to the market where he found us.

We were about to have supper, when he approached and called us aside. He told us what he had seen on the road. Then Majok Abekjok Adiang, my uncle's son, came running and told us that the Arab soldiers had crossed the river. He did not see his brother Kuel Abekjok among us, and he immediately ran to their house to warn him to hide from the Arab soldiers. We were students and the Arab soldiers were always arresting students in villages on the accusation of their being Anya-Nya sympathisers. We all dispersed into different directions.

Bol Bek Bol and I crossed the *toch* and the river Katuak to Gol village. We later found out that Deng Kuot and others had run to Panyang, two miles west of Wunrok on the river Lol. Victor Kuol Arop, an Anya-Nya soldier who had some information, and who believed that it was Lt. Dut Deng Atak that had come back with the Arab soldiers, ran to the Anya-Nya camp at Wunrieng.

When Majok Abekjok did not find his brother Kuel at their house, he wanted to cross the road to my house but he was caught by the Arab soldiers. What actually happened was that a certain Magor Malim saw the cars on the road and went to the house of Majok Abekjok and told him about the coming of the Arab soldiers and that they were spending the night at Kuelbuut and they were going to cross to Wunrok that night to kill all the students.

Majok therefore, took the footpath that went through a swamp to bypass the soldiers and reached the crossing point of Lol River. But when he arrived there, he found that the soldiers were already on the river and were taking off their clothes to cross. Majok jumped into the river fully clothed. The soldiers called to stop him but he did not listen. After he had found his brother missing among us, and did not find him in their home, he wanted to cross the road to my house, to see whether he was there.

Lt. Dut Deng Atak, knew the area very well and when Majok went ahead of them, he told the soldiers to move very quickly to get to the road leading out of Wunrok to the north before anybody else did. Dut knew that even if the people of Wunrok were aware that they had come and had taken the road to the north, there would be no way to pass them to spread the news. The soldiers followed Majok very quickly and when they caught him, they recognized him as the man who had refused to listen to them and had run ahead. Majok's clothes were still wet.

Majok however, told the soldiers that he had not recognized them in the darkness and that he was following a cow that had crossed the river and run towards Wunrok. He told them that the cow was missing from their byre (*luak*). He was crossing the road to the house of his uncle, to see if it had gone there. While the soldiers were talking to Majok, Kuel approached them from the north, following the road. Kuel did not recognize the soldiers and he too was caught. Another man, Mawut Madut, followed behind him and was caught also.

Fortunately Lt. Dut knew the three captives very well. He told the soldiers that none of them had any connection with the Anya-Nya. But the soldiers did not release them. They did not want the people of Wunrok to know that they had passed during the night. They took the three with them.

In the morning, the soldiers who had stayed at Kuelbuut with the cars, came to the river. The citizens of Wunrok had slept peacefully all night unaware that the Arab soldiers had come to their village and proceeded to Mayen Abun.

About a mile from Wunrok, the road had been washed away in many places, and the soldiers had to wade through water. They took off their boots, tied them into three bundles and handed them to the three captives, Majok Abekjok with his brother Kuel Abekjok and Mawut Madut, to carry. When the soldiers reached a place called Agar, ten miles from Wunrok, they turned and took the road to the west.

The soldiers entered Apioth village about a mile from the junction. They went to the house of our subchief, Atem Barac Atem, where they found his son, Ambrose Barac Atem, who was a senior clerk on leave. There was a big byre (*luak*) in the compound of the house of the subchief where many intellectuals, who were on leave and some students around Mayen Abun used to sleep. Lt. Dut Deng Atak, knew very well that they were inside the *luak*, asleep.

On their arrival, Lt. Dut knocked at the door of the byre, and called the name of Ambrose Barac. Ambrose recognized Dut's voice. He was aware of of what had happened to Lt. Dut and his escape to town. Ambrose answered Dut by saying "Yes Dut". Dut requested Ambrose to come out. He opened the byre and came out alone.

Lt. Dut then told Ambrose that he knew who was inside the *luak* but he had nothing against any of them. He said he had come for specific persons, the sons of Mawiir Rehan. Dut then introduced Ambrose to the Arab soldiers, and told him that he and others who wanted to go back to the town, were welcome to join him when he returned from Kurum after arresting Mawiir Rehan's sons. Then he left with the soldiers.

Soon they were on the road leading to Kurum, and Ambrose realized that there was no way any messenger would be able to pass them to go and warn the two officers, Mawiir Rehan's sons, that Lt. Dut was on his way to arrest them. The terrain between Apioth and Kurum was extremely difficult. The *toch* between the two villages was water-logged and halfway to Kurum there was a deep river. All along the river Ador tall thick grass grew, intermingled with trees called *peth*, with thorns like fishing hooks.

It was that difficult terrain that had deceived the two soldiers, captain Athuai and 1st Lt. Deng (sons of Mawiir Rehan), when they were told by their uncle, headchief Cyer Rehan to leave Kurum and also to move the Anya-Nya camp from Wunrieng to a new site. Instead of carrying out their uncle's instructions, they decided to post guards on the road coming into the village, day and night. But the guards did not go down far enough. If they had gone down right to the river bank, and guarded the passage leading from the river, no-one would have reached the village without their noticing it. Instead they stayed at the edge of the *toch* near the village.

Lt. Dut knew exactly where the guards could be found. When they were near the place, he told the soldiers to leave the road and wade through the water. That part of the *toch* was shallow with shorter grass and no thorn trees. They bypassed the guards and reached the village where they surrounded the two houses, built close together, of the two officers.

Lt. Dut knocked at the door of 1st Lt. Deng "Manoons" Mawiir Rehan's hut. He knew that he Deng "Manoon" was inside with his wife and a baby.

"I have come for you, Deng," he called.

"How did you come?" 1st Lt Deng asked.

"With the Arabs. Come out, unless you want your wife and baby to die with you! If you resist, if you want to fight, you'll die with your family."

"Will you please allow my wife to leave the house with the baby?"

"All right, but if you offer any resistance once they are out, even if you inflict no harm on any soldier, your family will not be spared."

The negotiations were in Arabic for the soldiers to understand, and they added their voices to that of Lt. Dut Deng Atak. Deng's wife and the baby would be safe and free if he caused no problems or harm to the soldiers.

Meanwhile Captain Athuai Mawiir was still sleeping – or staying quiet - in his own hut.

1st Lt. Deng said that he had only a pistol with him in the room and passed it out to the soldiers, through the window, in exchange for the lives of his wife and the only baby that they had. 1st Lt. Deng was asked to open the hut from the inside to allow the woman and the baby to come out. His wife, Wieu Mangokdit, at first declined. She expressed the desire to die inside the hut with her husband, but her husband persuaded her to leave the room for the sake of their only child. She came out and 1st Lt. Deng locked the door again. He said that he did not want to be tortured and asked questions about the Anya-Nya, but preferred to die in his room and his dead body to be buried at home. He sat down in the middle of the hut. "Here I am," he said. "Shoot me!" And they did, through the window.

It was the sound of the guns that told the guards what had happened. They ran away. Captain Athuai came out of his room and was apprehended. His hands were tied.

"I won't go with you," he protested. "Let me die here, at home, like my stepbrother!"

But the soldiers merely set fire to his hut and left, taking Captain Athuai "Mahmud" Mawiir Rehan with them.

The three prisoners brought from Wunrok, threw down the boots they had been carrying and ran back to the road and found their way to Wunrok. The villagers had run away, and only came back in the morning to discover what had happened.

The soldiers kept their word, and allowed 1st Lt. Deng "Manoon"'s wife and baby to go free. When the soldiers reached Apioth, they did not find Ambrose Barac there and the force proceeded to Wunrok.

As for us at Gol, we thought the army was going to surround Wunrok and search it in the morning. Later that day we received news from some people coming from Wunrok of what Arab soldiers had done at Kurum.

As we were not sure whether the Arabs had left Wunrok, we spent a second night in Gol, in the house of Ayuel Rehan who was to become my father-in-law in 1982. Ayueldit was not at home, but his wife Angok Piyom Bol, who today is my mother-in-law, took proper care of us. The Arabs left Wunrok on the same day they returned from Kurum.

But that very night, the second we spent at Gol, two other sons of Mawiir Rehan, Muon and his stepbrother Deng, did something we found atrocious. Inspite of the fact that the head-chief Cyer Rehan had informed the two officers of the truth, and the fact that everybody in the area knew that it was Lt. Dut Deng Atak that had killed 1st Lt. Deng "Manoon" and captured, Captain Athuai "Mahmud", those two men went to Panyang during that night. They asked for Cyer Cyer Rehan, the son of the head-chief Cyer Rehan who was a secondary school student in El-obeid. Cyer Cyer knew

Muon and Deng – they were his uncle's sons – and went out to them. Other people who were present also thought they were to meet as a family, to discuss how they were going to handle what Lt. Dut Deng Atak had done to them.

But as soon as the three of them were some distance away from the house, Mawiir's sons speared Cyer Cyer and killed him, saying that it was his father who had sent the Arabs to kill their brothers.

We intended to spend the day at Gol because a he-goat had been slaughtered for us, but when we received the bad news, we left for Wunrok immediately to bury Cyer Cyer. Cyer was a very good boy and his death was condemned by the whole Adiang section and other sections of Twic who knew him, especially the students' body.

It called for revenge. Rehan Nuer, their grandfather, had many wives, but when Cyer Cyer was murdered by the sons of Mawiir, the feud was limited to the children of two wives, Acol Kon, mother of Mawiir and Ajak Mayom, the mother of Cyer, the headchief. All the sons of Mawiir went into hiding, while the children of Ajak Mayom were hunting for them. The feud was between Mawiir and his brothers with their sons.

Mawiirdit did not go into hiding. He openly condemned the act perpetrated by his sons. He said that he could be killed in revenge for the death of Cyer Cyer, except that he was not equal to the young boy, who had a bright future ahead of him.

The Anya-Nya blamed the head-chief, Cyer Rehan, for what had happened. They should have known better – they were perfectly aware of what had transpired between Lt. Dut Deng Atak and the two officers – but they remembered how Cyer Rehan had saved the lives of the families of the Arab traders when he took them to Abyei, and decided that he was their enemy. So they looted his cattle and those of his brothers. They burned their houses and destroyed their property. In Wunrok, they went to the house of his wife Anok Kuanyin Agoth, and destroyed all his documents. They opened the box of utensils which Cyer had bought in Rome and London - beautiful, original items, not like the fakes people use today – and destroyed them. These utensils could have fetched a huge amount of money if taken to Aweil or Tonj or other parts of Gogrial to sell, and the Anya-Nya needed money badly, but they used heavy blocks of wood to crush them, rendering them useless. The head-chief was well known for his hospitality - no one in Gogriel treated official and private guests better - and he had used those precious items for this purpose.

When Head-chief Cyer Rehan got word of what was going on in his area, he came to Wunrok with his army. He remained on the southern side of the river with the soldiers who were guarding the cars they had come in, while the army went to Kurum. They spent the night there and returned the following day. The soldiers did not do anything in Kurum.

The head-chief then sent people to bring all his children to safety. I did not think twice when I was invited to accompany them. He called a meeting with his brothers in Wunrok, and told them that there should be no revenge, and that no-one was to touch Mawiir Rehan, his stepbrother, for the murder of his son. Both Cyer Rehan and his brother had sons in the Anya-Nya Movement, but they were still away in Congo at the main Anya-Anya base. Before he left with us, he gave instructions that if his son Madut and Jel Maror came home, they should not take revenge on the Anya-Nya soldiers who looted their cattle and destroyed their homes and property. He did not want the movement in Twic to be paralysed because of the death of his son and the destruction they had wreaked. The sons, however, did not heed their father's wish, and some months later, they killed Mawiir Rehan's favourite son, Lueth Mawiir. Lueth was not an educated man like Cyer Cyer, but his death was a great loss.

In Gogrial we received word that a number of students from Rumbek Secondary School had made their way to Khartoum and had been sent to Kassala, in Eastern Sudan, where they completed the academic year in 1964-1965. Two months later the head-chief took us to Wau and went to see the Commissioner of Bahr el Ghazal province to arrange for our transport to Khartoum. The commissioner was not very helpful. "I'm not responsible for the transport of secondary school students to the north," he said. "But as you are a chief, I will help your children – and your own children only. Give me a list of their names."

When the head-chief presented the list to the commissioner, all the names ended in "Rehan", except my name, which was totally different. "I can't pay for this boy," the commissioner said. He is obviously not your son." "I regard him as my son," the head-chief said. "He is the son of my maternal uncle and he grew up with my children." He explained that in Dinka society the uncle is a very important person in the life of his sister's son. If he treats the son badly, the son would not take revenge. If a son did something very bad, such as committing many murders, and he is disowned by his own clan and his paternal uncles, he will be welcomed by his mother's brother and become a member of his clan. "If my children leave without this boy, their journey to Khartoum will not be peaceful," he said.

The commissioner relented and issued all of us with second-class train tickets. When we arrived in Khartoum, the city was new to us, but we had no difficulty in finding people from our own section to put us up. Our arrival coincided with the return of those other students from Rumbek Secondary School who had travelled from Kassala to Khartoum.

Third and fourth year students attended classes at the Khartoum Government Secondary School, near the main campus of the University of Khartoum. The first and second years were accommodated at Omdurman. My former classmates from Kassala were now in their third year. Those of us who had been delayed at home, were supposed to start our second year, but I made up my mind to join my friends in the third year. We were accommodated at Shambat, on the river Nile, and had a bus for transport. I completed my third year without any difficulty, spent the holidays in Khartoum, and continued to fourth year. When we sat for the school certificate exams, I was confident. I knew that my work was good, and that I was going to pass. So I decided to return home to see my parents in the south before I went to university.

CHAPTER 6

Back Home

I left Khartoum for Wau by air, and waited for a week for the convoy going to Gogrial. Upon our arrival at Gogrial, we saw a large number of people gathered at the graveyard. Someone came close to our car, and told us quietly that the Anya-Nya had captured Tiaraliet station and killed all the government policemen. Fear had caused the entire population of Gogrial to come out to the graveyard to attend the funeral of the policemen, many of them from the north. I stayed in Gogrial at the house of an acquaintance for about a fortnight before I left for Wunrok.

This time, the situation was quite different in Wunrok. The government had deployed new army soldiers as well as policemen, mostly from the North. All the headchiefs of Twic had been brought to Wunrok and ordered to run the administration of their sections from there. Actually, the soldiers and police officers treated me well, but sometimes I was not happy with how they treated other people. Without proper investigation, they would torture to death people who were suspected of having links with the Anya-Anya. The soldiers and policemen had no wives with them and at times went after the wives and daughters of the local people, and when asked about it, it became a crime for which somebody could be tortured or killed.

When it was time for me to go back to school, I decided to go to Abyei and take a car from there. The route through Gogrial would delay me as a convoy from Gogrial to

Wunrok came only once a month, and then I would have to wait in Gogrial for another day for a convoy to Wau.

Moreover, my father had given me a bull and a cow to sell so that I would be able to support myself in Khartoum. There was no cattle auction in Wunrok and the Anya-Nya did not allow cattle to be driven to Gogrial. The only way open for both people and cattle was to Abyei, as the Anya-Nya also received supplies from Abyei and sent their own cattle there for sale. I gave my two head of cattle to Adhar Majic Agurwel, the husband of my niece Nyadeng to take to Abyei. I followed with some other people. Upon arrival in Abyei, Adhar went directly to the cattle auction where my bull and one of his were bought, but a man from Abyei, Can Dau, alleged that the cow was his and had been stolen by the Anya-Nya, along with twenty others. The money Adhar had received for the bull was confiscated, and the cow was taken to the police dairy. Adhar Majic was accused of being an Anya-Nya collaborator, and detained in police custody. During the investigation, Adhar told the police that the cow was not his, but belonged to a student called Bol Majok Adiang (me), who was on his way to Abyei. So they decided to wait for me to arrive, with Adhar remaining in custody.

While I was spending the night at a house on the Kiir River en route to Abyei, it happened by coincidence that the man at whose house I was sleeping over, had knowledge of what had happened at the cattle auction earlier in the day. He told me that my cow was identified as one of the cows that had been stolen by the Anya-Anya rebels and therefore Adhar was detained together with the cow awaiting my arrival to be questioned by the police. "Don't go to Abyei," he warned me. "You will be killed. Rather bypass the town, and wait for a car on the other side. When a car comes, jump in, and go to Khartoum."

But I did go to Abyei, and when I got there, a man took me straight to Head-chief Deng (Majok) Kuol Arop, who was also the judge. When he heard my name, he told a retainer to take me to the police station. A police officer took me straight to the investigation room. What I told them confirmed what Adhar had said - that the cow was mine, given to my family by my stepsister's husband, Ring Aguek Ajang. The police told me to find someone to pay Adhar's bail so that he could go to Wunrok to fetch Ring Aguek Ajang. Just then an old friend from my elementary school days, Deng Majok Deng from Twic, a trader at Abyei market, came to the station for a different purpose. He was surprised to find me there, and agreed to help. The police knew him well and allowed him to bail Adhar.

The next day, while I remained in police custody, Adhar left for Wunrok, carrying a letter from the police to their colleagues in Wunrok, requesting them to arrest Ring Aguek Ajang and send him to Abyei. As I was a student, the police allowed me to do light jobs such as sweeping around the offices, and to sleep on the veranda. Then suddenly I was moved inside again to join the other prisoners. I had no idea why.

The condition in the cells was horrible. There was a bucket for the use of detainees with stomach problems, or who wished to urinate. I was pushed to right next to the bucket, and prisoners visiting the bucket during the night stepped on me and sprayed urine on me. I begged them to stop using the bucket, but to no avail.

Before daybreak three more men were pushed into the room. They were all from Twic, and I knew them by name. They told me that they had come to Abyei to sell their cattle, but had been accused of being members of the Anya-Nya by a man from Thon, in Twic. The man was Atem Madut Atem

– a person whose reputation we knew. Atem used to be an Anya-Nya soldier himself, but after some disagreement with his officers he had defected to Abyei. He was now being used by the government army as an informer, and to identify Anya-Nya soldiers when they visited the town. Atem would often accuse innocent persons just to have them killed so that he could confiscate their cattle to sell at the market. Atem was from Akoc, while the three men he had accused this time were all from Wunrok. They told me that their cattle had been taken away and that they had been tortured all night to force them to admit that they were Anya-Nya soldiers, but they had refused. They were locked up to be tortured again the following night.

In the morning, I with some others were allowed out of the cell, and I resumed my sweeping duties.

The Abyei representative of the people from Adiang was a man called Bol Bol. When he was informed of the arrest of the three men, he came to the police station and testified that they were his people, and that he knew them very well, and that they had no connection with Anya-Nya. "Atem Madut Atem also knows them and he assures us that they are members of Anya-Nya," a police officer said. "Well, send for Atem, and ask him what their names are. If he knows them so well, he should know their names."

So Atem was called. He knew the names (he had obviously sought information), but he could not tell who was who, and which villages they came from. It was obvious that Atem lied, so the three men were released and their cattle returned to them. That night I was allowed to sleep on the veranda again. I don't think the police wanted me to witness people being tortured.

When Adhar Majic reached Wunrok, he discovered that Ring Aguek had heard of the problems in Abyei, and had gone into hiding. The Wunrok police arrested his father Aguek Ajang instead and handed him to Adhar Majic to take to Abyei. "We authorize you to kill him if he tries to escape," they told Adhar. Adhar was very careful. Wherever they slept over, he would put Aguek in a hut, while he himself would guard the door. It was a long journey – from Abyei to Wunrok and back took eleven days.

On the morning of the eleventh day after Adhar had set out, they arrived in Abyei. The police took Aguek Ajang's statement and we were all taken to the courthouse. Ajang admitted that he was the one who had given the cow, Nyiel, to my father. He had exchanged a bull for the cow, he said, with a man from Aweil called Hou. "Can you go back and bring Hou to this court?" he was asked. "No, I'm afraid not," Aguek replied. "There has been a fight between Adiang, our section and Abiem section of Aweil and since then, for several months, there has been no movement between the two sections. Not even the Wunrok police can move between the two, because of the fear of Anya-Nya rebels."

The members of the court now spoke in turn, not all of them in our favour. One called us the three Anya-Nya boys. Another said the Anya-Nya couldn't be blamed, rather the Twic people. The Twic people had stolen the cattle, and as we had been caught, we had to compensate for the loss of Nyiel and the twenty-two other cows.

When everyone had spoken, the head-chief Deng "Majok" separated us, the accused. He would decide the case of each of us individually. First, he picked Adhar. Adhar had testified that the cow did not belong to him, but to me, Bol Majok, and I had confirmed it, so he said Adhar had no connection to the cow, and would be acquitted. Adhar was told to take a back seat.

I, Bol Majok, was next. "Bol Majok testified that he had acquired the cow from Aguek Ajang, and Aguek confirmed it," the chief said. He added that what counted in my favour was that, even when I heard that Adhar had been arrested, I still came to Abyei. "If he was a member of Anya-Nya, he would not have come," he said. "The Anya-Nya do not help one another when caught. Furthermore, Bol has a school identity card. He could not possibly have been at school and in the bush at the same time." I was a free man!

Head-chief Deng "Majok" then turned to Aguek Ajang. "Have a good look at Aguek Ajang," he told the members of the court. "What do you think a man like him could do for the Anya-Nya? Cook? Carry loads? You cannot accuse a man his age of working for the Anya-Nya! He is innocent."

He ordered that the cow Nyiel be returned to Can Dau. Aguek Ajang would not be compensated for the bull he had lost in exchange for the cow. We were all released.

I paid one last visit to the police station, to collect my watch and my shoes which the police removed and kept when I was arrested. But what I really wanted to do was to say goodbye to a friend of mine, Bol Bulabek, also known as Bol Wunbiong. He had had some dispute with the head-chief (to whom he was related) and had been placed in custody, where he remained indefinitely. He refused to eat the food provided by the prison and went for several days without eating or drinking anything. The authorities feared that he would starve to death, and allowed him to have his meals brought from his house. I could understand his aversion of prison food - on my first day there I could not eat it either. "You will just have to eat it eventually, whether you like it or not," an unsympathetic policeman said. Bol heard about it and called me. "You are welcome to share my meal with me," he said, "every day, until they release you."

Since taking leave of Bol Bulabek on that day, I have never been back again to see him and to thank him for his support when I was desperate. He died before we could meet again. It haunts me to this day.

When I arrived in Abyei eleven days earlier, there were a good number of cars in town, preparing to leave. But by the time I was released from prison there was only one lorry left, one with mechanical problems. It was raining heavily, and no more cars came from Muglad. The next day it was announced that the lorry had been repaired and was ready to go, and I boarded it. We did not get far. Only ten miles from Abyei we got stuck in heavy mud, and however hard we tried, we could not push it out. At midday the driver told us that he was going to abandon the lorry just there, and return for it in the dry season. There was no other way. This was a problem! It would take three or four days for us to reach Muglad on foot, and we had no food to eat on the way. Neither would we be able to buy anything as there were no villages or cattle stations anywhere between Abyei and Muglad. Adhar Majic and some other passengers announced that they were going to walk back to Abyei to buy food for the journey, and left.

At about three o'clock in the afternoon – Adhar and the others were not back yet - a military vehicle on its way from Abyei to Muglad appeared and we noticed that they were going to try to cross the muddy belt about a hundred meters from where we were stuck. It also got stuck. The army vehicle was a reliable one, and the soldiers worked very hard, trying to pull it out of the mud. At first I was reluctant to go and talk to them about a lift, but when I considered the difficulties ahead of us, I realized that I had no choice. So I picked up my belongings and those of Adhar Majic and approached the soldiers. The other passengers followed me. "Sorry," a soldier said, "we are not allowed to take civilians. But we will take the two students." Mayen Majok Jong and me! I offered to help them pull the car out (I was old enough, I thought), but they refused. They succeeded in another half hour, and we got onto the vehicle. I realized that I could not leave Adhar Majic's belongings behind as they would get stolen, so I took them with me.

    The soldiers did not want to run the risk of again running into mud in the dark, so we stopped for the night at a place called Dhunydhuol, or Tebeldi, as it is known in Arabic. The soldiers had enough food and clean water, and they invited us to join them for supper. We were only too happy to do so. I had not had a proper meal since I shared Bol Bukabek's food in prison. At about twelve o' clock the next day we reached Muglad where we were told to get down, as the soldiers were proceeding to El Nahud. This time, fortunately, there was public transport, and we took a car to Babanusa, and from there, the next day, to Kosti, where we decided to wait for Adhar Majic. When he eventually arrived about a week later he was exhausted, so we stayed for another two days to allow him to rest before we left for Khartoum.

CHAPTER 7

University

It was at Kosti, on the day we left for Khartoum, that I received the good news: I had passed my exams. My name was in the Arabic newspaper! Late that evening as we arrived in Khartoum I went to the house of Bol Bek Bol, where I was to wait for the university to open. Within a week it was announced: I had been accepted as a student at the Faculty of Economic and Social Studies at the University of Khartoum!

This was exceptional! It was July 1968, and it was quite unusual for a Southerner to study at a university. In those days many uninformed northern Sudanese (and even some educated ones) did not believe that Southerners were capable of doing so. There were only a handful of us. The only other student from Twic when I arrived was Philip Akot Akok from Akoc Thon. I know of only two other persons from Twic who had graduated from the University of Khartoum – Dr. Justin Yac Arop and Chan Malual Chan – but that was years before our time. Of the four students from Twic who had sat for the school certificate, I was the only one to have been accepted.

From the whole of the Adiang section, I was the second person, after Chan Malual Chan, to enter university. He graduated in 1965, three years before I joined. After me, however, the number of Twic students at the University of Khartoum increased considerably.

Lectures started smoothly. The university was very good. Teaching was excellent, and so were both the accommodation and the food. We would never be able to afford such first-class food again, not after graduation, nor when we were employed and received our first salaries. I completed my first year, and spent the holidays in Khartoum, as government policy did not allow southern students, especially those studying at university or secondary school, to go home. The government authorities in the south, mostly Arabs, did not want students to come back and witness the atrocities being committed by the security organs. They feared that the students, once they were aware of what was being done to their people, would join the Anya-Nya movement. It was true that the government administration in the south was paralyzed by the military activities of the Anya-Nya, and that the whole region was engulfed in rebellion.

We university students were given temporary employment for two months to keep us in Khartoum. We were paid very little, only nine Sudanese pounds per month, but the standard of living in Khartoum at that time was low, and food was cheap, so we were able to buy everything we needed without asking for more money from home.

When the university reopened, I started my second year. We were divided into various groups. Some students went to the Faculty of Law, which one could only enter after completing a year of arts and economics. The rest of us had a choice: economics, business administration, accounting, anthropology, statistics or political science. My tutor advised me to do accounting, although, coming from an academic, not a commercial secondary school, I had no knowledge of the field. He told me that my good marks entitled me to specialize in accounting, which would guarantee employment after graduation. I accepted his advice and went ahead. We were to be the first batch of accounting graduates from the University of Khartoum – thirteen northerners, and only Ananias Modi Lolik and me from the south.

At the end of that year, I decided to go home again, and I flew to Wau. The journey from Wau to Wunrok took me about a month, because of the convoy system. I found Wunrok a changed town. The security situation had worsened. The soldiers and policemen I used to know had all been transferred, and new ones had been brought in.

A number of young men had been recruited from the local population and trained as home guards (*huras el waton*). They were not paid a salary, but were supplied with rations. They were mainly responsible for identifying Anya-Nya members, and leading the soldiers when they went out to hunt for them. The soldiers and policemen trusted them more than anyone else, including the head-chiefs. But at times they did give false reports to serve their personal interests, or they accused a person of being Anya-Nya, simply because he had differed with them. They looted the properties of villagers, and when these people complained to the head-chiefs, they called them Anya-Nya, and when the head-chiefs ordered them to return the looted items, the *huras el waton* would accuse the chiefs of collaborating with the Anya-Nya.

I was not allowed to travel more than a mile from the station. My home was just a kilometer away, but I was told to sleep at the station. If I disobeyed, the soldiers could not be held responsible for my life. One day a member of the home guard laid a charge against me. He said I was slandering them, blaming them for what they were doing, turning the people against them, so that once things were back to normal, they would have nowhere to go. The station commander was furious. I denied the charge, but he would have lashed me if the police radio reporter had not reminded him of the lies that members of the home guards had told in the past. He warned him of the implications if he lashed a university student, particularly in front of his own people. If the student himself did not join the Aya-Nya as a result, some angry youths from among his relatives would probably do so. So I was left alone. But a few days later the radio operator told me that it would be better for me to return to Khartoum.

Before I went back to Khartoum in 1968 to start my first year at university, I had got married, and the next year my wife Acai Ayuel Dual had given birth to a girl Aker, named by my father after his mother Aker Tueny Deng. As I did not intend to return home until peace came to the South, I decided to take my wife and daughter with me to Khartoum. My parents agreed. I was not to visit again while war raged in the country, they said.

The radio reporter knew of a convoy coming our way, and when it arrived, we took the golden opportunity to escape. The convoy took us all the way from Wunrok to Gogrial and then to Wau. There my family and I boarded a plane for Khartoum. My quickest trip ever! In Khartoum I took my wife and child to the house of Bol Bek and his brother Deng. They were both married, and the two of them rented a house together. As soon as the university opened, I moved into the hostel, and visited my family at weekends.

After a year, however, I thought it better to send my wife and child home, so that I would be able to complete my final year without having to worry about them, or spending time trying to solve family problems. During my third year I sometimes had to skip lectures to take the child and her mother to hospital. Moreover, I had run out of money, and in order to support them I had to depend on others for assistance. I was confident that a woman would be safe at home, as only educated persons were targeted by the army and the police. I therefore arranged with a friend of mine in Wau to meet them and help them to get into the convoy going to Gogrial and Wunrok. They arrived safely.

When the university reopened I returned to the hostel. The year passed smoothly, and in March 1972 we sat for our final examinations. At that very time, the Anya-Nya and the Government of Sudan were conducting peace talks in Addis Ababa in Ethiopia. I was fortunate to have been able to complete my four years without interruption. The 25th May Revolution, and the 72 hour aborted coup of Hashim el Atta in July 1971, had not caused the university to be closed; neither had the three or four student demonstrations against the regime.

CHAPTER 8

Local Government and Time in Shilluk Kingdom

The Addis Ababa Peace Agreement granted Southern Sudan local autonomy. Anya-Nya soldiers poured into the towns from the countryside, especially in Southern Sudan. A new government was formed in Juba. But, unlike what happened later in the case of the SPLM/SPLA, the government in Juba was headed by Said Abel Alier Kwai, who had been the chief negotiator of the Sudan Government during the peace talks. The ministers he appointed included some Anya-Nya politicians as well as members of his own former party, the Southern Front, and others.

Some of the Anya-Nya soldiers, including General Joseph Lagu, the head of the movement, were absorbed into the new Sudan army. Others were given jobs in the police, prison or wildlife services. Those members of the Anya-Nya Movement who had never been soldiers, as well as the soldiers who did not want to continue in the organized forces, were employed in the civil service.

This happened quickly. The arrangements were concluded even before we received our final university results. When the results did come out, what my tutor had told me about employment, proved true. During Nimeiri's regime, all the industries and factories had been nationalized and grouped under the National Industrial Corporation. Now representatives from this corporation came to the university, and before we could even apply for jobs, they looked at the list of graduates and invited all fifteen of us for interviews at their headquarters. All of us were employed! We accepted our assignments and set to work. After two months, however, our northern colleagues started leaving one by one, until soon only the two of us, the southerners, remained in the corporation. It transpired that most of these northerners were the children of prominent business people in Khartoum and for them using their family connections to find profitable positions in the banks, proved easy.

They invited us to follow suit. "Why don't you apply for jobs in the banks? There is still a great need for people with our qualifications," they said. But before we could put in our applications for the banks, we came across an interesting advertisement. The regional Ministry of Local Government in Juba was looking for qualified Southerners to fill the posts of officers in local government.

My main interest was local government, so I applied at once. My friend Ananias Modi Lolik followed suit. We sat for the examination and attended an interview in Khartoum - and waited for the results. I was employed, but my friend was rejected. So I resigned from the National Industrial Corporation and joined local government. My friend remained with the corporation for a while, but soon he too found employment in Juba, with the Regional Ministry of Finance.

The local government officers from Khartoum as well as Juba were now sent for training at the Khartoum Academy for Local Government Officers. While I was there, my mother came to visit with my wife and two children. (My wife gave birth to a second child, a boy, in 1972.) The course lasted for only three months after which we were posted to the three southern provinces of Bahr el Ghazal, Equatoria and Upper Nile. I was to go to Upper Nile.

I left Khartoum with my mother (who had just recovered from an illness), my wife and children. We travelled by train to Kosti, and from there took a steamer to Malakal. When I arrived in Malakal I found that I was to work in the Kodok district, which meant a journey back from Malakal to Kodok. If only they had informed me earlier! My mother did not wish to accompany me there, so I had to arrange for her to travel to Wunrok. That left me with my wife and two small children, Aker and the baby boy Ajal, plus my stepsister, Alek Majok, who had joined us to help take care of the children.

In Kodok I found two officials already employed in the office – the local government inspector (LGI) and a general service officer, both Northerners. I was supposed to take over as the executive officer (EO), but the LGI regarded himself as my superior. As I expected the two of them to be leaving soon, because the local government was southernized, I did not complain. Exactly two months later Ajang Bior Ajang was transferred to Kodok as acting local government inspector, taking over from the inspector I had found there on my arrival. The general service officer was retained by Ajang, for reasons known only to himself. I complained, but to no avail. I was expected to work under the general service officer. My job was to collect revenue, but the general service officer spent the money so carelessly, that I relaxed the collection, and the council ran into financial difficulties. The northern administrators who knew very well that they would be leaving the south, had cleared the bank of any cash that might have been in it. The small amount of cash brought in by the rate collector from the market was not enough to meet the salaries of the council employees. The main source of income was the social service taxes which needed to be collected from the chiefs in their areas, but I was not ready to visit them yet. Two and a half months later a letter came from Malakal instructing Ajang Bior to leave on the first steamer from Malakal. He had been appointed as acting assistant commissioner in Renk, a big *dura*-producing district whose status had recently been raised and had to be administered by a grade five officer. Ajang was a DS (Distinguished Scale) officer.

The same letter authorized me to take over as acting local government inspector of Kodok. Ajang and his Arab friend had no choice but to leave on the next steamer – which they did without bothering to formally hand over to me. And I had no choice but to pick up the pieces. Three junior officers, all citizens of Kodok, soon joined me.

The former district of Kodok, which has today been divided into a number of counties, was a vast area. It stretched all the way from Bir Kodok in the far north near Kosti and opposite Jebellen, all the way along the western bank of the White Nile to Tonga, south of Malakal and bordering the Nuba Mountains. It shared a border with Bentiu and the present White Nile State to the north. Certain areas on the eastern bank of the White Nile were also included: Wau-Shilluk, Malakal, Doleib Hill, Atar and Nakdiar.

I sat down with the three new officers to determine our strategy. We all agreed that the area was too large and the distances too long to be administered from a single office in Kodok town, so we decided that they would run the outstations, leaving me alone in Kodok. Denis Aywok Yor, a very bright officer, would go to Tonga, Yithaya Amum to Malakal, and David Lam Atong to Wedakona and Kaka.

These officers were well acquainted with the area and

I valued their advice. They talked to me about the Shilluk people and said that if we were to succeed in our work, we would need the full co-operation of the Reth, their king.

The Shilluk people are not spread across Sudan, but live only in a limited area in the Kodok district. They are members of the Luo Nilotic groups, said to be related to the Anyuak of Pochalla, and the Balanda Bor, Acoli, Lango and Jur Col of Western Bahr el Ghazal.

The fact that the Shilluk nation has a king, the Reth, makes Kodok a unique place. The Reth has administrative, judicial, and above all spiritual powers, and the Shilluk pay full allegiance to him. They regard him as the spiritual representative on earth of Nyikang, their first ancestor and god. One may sometimes hear a Shilluk man complaining about the Reth or something he has done, but when you suggest that it would be better to abolish the system, he will never agree with you. For them the Reth is a symbol of their unity and wellbeing.

All the sons born into the royal family are called Kuanyreth, and the daughters are known as Nyakuanyreth. The direct children of the Reth are known as Wareth (boys) and Nyareth (girls), meaning prince and princess. The Reth's deputy must always be a Kuanyreth.

When a daughter of the Reth gets married, no bride price is paid. She would choose a man and they would live as husband and wife, but they will be supported by the Reth, and their children would belong to the royal family. A daughter of a Kuanyreth is married in the normal way, and the bride price goes to her parents. However, if the daughter of a Kuanyreth is made pregnant by a man who is not her husband, the compensation in cattle (usually six cows) belongs to the throne, which means the cows are handed over to the Reth. The Shilluk community is highly organized. At that time the bride price was fixed at ten cows. If a man made a girl pregnant, he was made to pay six cows to the girl's parent as compensation for making the girl pregnant outside marriage and he was given the child born of that particular pregnancy. This was an indirect way of inducing people to pay the remaining four cows to make the total of ten cows, which was the official bride price. If the remaining four cows were paid the man would be given the girl as his wife.

If someone committed a serious crime, a murder perhaps, the family of the culprit had to go to the Reth with a cow to inform him about it. The relatives of the deceased had to do the same. The Reth had the power to expel someone from the Shilllukland – something no government authorities could do.

Dual authority in the same community could make it very difficult for a government representative to function independently of the Reth. The people would take the Reth much more seriously than they would do to government representative. I was fortunate that the Reth I worked with was one of the best Shilluk kings ever. Reth Kur Papiti, who was in his seventies, was a very wonderful man. In spite of the great power he wielded over his people, he was a simple person who treated everyone, including his own subjects, with great respect and humility. His deputy, Kuanyreth Thabo, was of the same age and also a very nice man.

I invited Kuanyreth Thabo to my office and asked him to tell me everything about the Reth, and the best way to approach him. The two of us agreed to meet the Reth in his house at Ywodo, a private village belonging to Reth Kur Papiti, about two miles from Kodok town, some distance away from the Nile River.

Every Reth is entitled to a private home, away from the other villages. Even after his death, that home and everything in it, continues to belong to him. The most important such palace is Fashoda, where the shrine of Nyikang is preserved. Only one king, Reth Nyikwac, was buried there. Other kings are buried in their private homes or villages. Kings are the only ones to be buried in their homes. Other members of the family, including his wives and children, are removed and buried by the clan responsible for the royal family in their villages. Everything in Fashoda, including the women, is always inherited by the next Reth.

One morning Kuanyreth Thabo duly accompanied me to Ywodo to visit the Reth. It was not the first time I had met him. During Ajang Bior's time he had come to our office about four times, but I just greeted him and excused myself. In Ywodo the Reth lived in a fine concrete house, larger than the house of the local government inspector, with a neat fence around it. Outside, but very close to the entrance, there were twin tukuls or huts facing each other, with a fence built in the same style around them. I was told that one tukul was the future tomb of the Reth, and the other one was for the use of the guard. More huts were scattered around the place.

When we arrived, we remained standing near the car while one of the Reth's bodyguards went in to inform the king of our arrival. He returned with another guard, and two chairs, which he carried into one of the huts. I was taken there. After some time, the Reth himself came and we talked, alone, although his Arabic was poor, for an hour. He was very happy that I had come to see him. No other administrator had ever tried to involve him the way I was doing it, he told me, and promised me his full support.

He listened to my name, then called me "Bol Nyajwok", meaning "Bol, the son of God". In Dinka, Bol is a name given to a son born after twins and it is the same with Shilluk people. Both Dinka and Shilluk people and even Nuer people – consider twins to be a special gift from God, and the twins as well as the child born after them are called Children of God.

We agreed that the two of us would tour the district together, as soon as we had informed the head-chiefs of our intention. So after our conversation, the Reth sent out runners to the northern sector of the district, with a message requesting the head-chiefs to be at home when we arrived, though he could not give exact dates.

One morning we duly set out for the northern sector. I was using a small type of Commer, called half Commer, a vehicle I had only come across in Kodok. The Reth travelled in a much larger Commer, which befitted his status as he had a number of guards and elders travelling with him. He told me to lead the way since I was the local government inspector, flying the district flag. At first I would wait for him to catch up when I could not see his car behind me, until one of my passengers told me that the Reth wanted to allow for some time between my arrival and his at every stop. My role was to herald his arrival.

Every time we reached the border of a section, the head-chief would be there to receive us. Someone in my car then announced the coming of "Nyajwok" - the son of God – and everyone present began to sing special songs, songs that sent a clear message to the whole village that the Reth was near. Men and women rushed out in large numbers, the men singing songs and playing and jumping about, carrying spears and shields, while the women sat down, lined up at the entrance to the compound, singing and clapping their hands.

When the Reth arrived, the villagers moved to the edge of the village to receive him and perform rituals, leaving me behind. They took him to a special seat, one which I believe was reserved for him in every village. It was only when he asked for me that someone would come to escort me to him. Everyone then sat down on the ground in front of the Reth. Only the Reth and I had chairs. The two of us were also the only persons to wear shoes – no-one else was allowed to in his presence. We talked to the villagers, concentrating on security and the collection of social service taxes.

In some of the villages we merely addressed the people and resumed our journey. In others we slept over. We went up to Wedakona in the far north and then returned to Kodok.

We were about to start our next trip, to the southern sector, when the Reth fell ill. So, instead of visiting them, we called all the head-chiefs of the southern Shillluk – including Jago Ajobwong of Tonga, Jago Okiech, Jago Deng Parac, Kuanyreth Laa Adwok and many others - to Kodok. While I was in a meeting with them, a number of head-chiefs from the northern sector of the district arrived with the taxes they had collected, such good amounts that we were able to pay not only them but also the head-chiefs who had come from the south their salaries as well as all arrears. This gave a clear message to the southern chiefs, and they left, happy and ready to complete the collection of social service taxes in their own districts in the shortest possible time.

In Shilluk tradition the Reth's people are not informed when he falls ill, and he is not left to die like a normal person. His great-grand aunts gather around him, and when his condition is judged to be grave, they strangle him. I therefore arranged for him to be brought to Malakal as for a normal visit. He visited some sections, where he was honoured by his subjects, but while he was there he also received medical treatment before he returned to Kodok.

After that the Reth came to visit Malakal more frequently. He lived about two miles from the town, and I urged him to send for a car whenever he wanted to come. He preferred to walk, though, owing to the large number of people who would always follow him and who could not all fit into the vehicle. In Shilluk tradition, when people accompanied the Reth, they would allow him to go ahead, and they would follow at a distance. If he stopped on the way, everyone present had to sit down and listen to what he wanted to say. Only when he continued his journey, would they get up and follow as before.

On his way to my office, Reth Kur would sometimes stop at my house to talk to my children, Aker and Ajal, whom he loved. He would touch them, and give them some money, and wait for them to go back into the house before he proceeded. His followers would just sit down and wait for him to finish talking to the children. He once gave them two cows as a gift.

When I first met the Reth of the Shilluk in the office of the local government inspector I was not sure how to greet him. I just assumed that, like with Dinka spiritual leaders, one cannot shake hands with him. So I kept my distance and just raised my hand to him, and he responded by raising his hand also. My assumptions were correct because during the time I spent in Kodok, I never saw the Reth shaking hands with anybody, Shilluk or non-Shilluk. I only saw him touching the heads of my kids.

During my visits to Ywodo, I never saw children, big or small at Reth's palace. I was told that the children of the Reth are born and brought up in the homes of maternal uncles.

When he came to Kodok town, Reth Kur would not accept an invitation to sit down in my house even if he found me in the house. He used to sit only in two places, his private house in the town or in the office of the local government inspector. Whenever he was coming to me and found me still in the house, I would at once go with him to the office.

Although the Shilluks, like the Dinkas and Nuer, do not possess poison themselves, Reth Kur would not drink water or tea brought to him in my office, unless he was sure it was brought from the house. I used to send the messenger together with his bodyguard to my house when I wanted to offer him some water and tea. His bodyguard would be the one to carry the water and tea from my house and to serve the Reth.

I visited Reth Kur at Ywodo regularly, so I was no longer seated in the outside *Tukuls*. Whenever the Reth was informed about my arrival, he would tell the guard to lead me into the saloon where he used to sit with a handful of wives, most of them teenage girls. I would sometimes hear them giggling, murmuring or singing. Some of them used to stand with their arms aroundthe Reth's shoulders behind the great armchair on which he used to sit in the middle of the saloon. The women would then leave the Reth's side in a single line as soon as I entered the saloon. Some of them would greet me and walk out of the saloon into their rooms. The guards remained outside, including the one who brought me in. I would then remain alone with the Reth for up to an hour before I left. As I held discussions with the Reth, there would be no sound in the house but as soon as I had left, I would hear the movement of the Reth's wives returning to the saloon.

When I first arrived at Kodok, I tried to establish a social relationship with some officials and citizens but I found nobody. Most of the officials were juniors, mostly on the council's supporting staff. I visited the headmaster of an elementary school in the area twice in his house to establish a friendship with him but he failed to return the visit in spite of the fact that he appreciated my courtesy call, so I gave up on him. The only person who used to visit me in my house was the area's medical assistant but most of his time was spent at the hospital.

One day I came back from the house of the Reth at about six o'clock in the evening. I had my dinner and went to a small social club about a hundred yards from the police station to play cards with some young men. That was the only place I used to go in the evenings. I got back to my house from the social club at about 10:30PM and went to the room that I shared with my wife and three children. My wife had just given birth to my son Wal Bol. My stepsister, Alek Majok used to sleep in another room alone. We had the habit of locking the doors leading to the veranda and only leave the rooms open at night. As I was about to lie down to sleep, the wind blew the door and it was becoming a nuisance so I got up and bolted the door.

That night an incident occurred, something I considered to be an attempt on my life. I was asleep when my stepsister (she was only eleven years old) knocked at my bedroom door and asked, "Brother, have you just been in my room?" No, I hadn't! An intruder had clearly entered the house! My wife and I both got up and rushed to the door leading to the kitchen. We found it open. We ran out and discovered that the door of the veranda outside the kitchen was also wide open. The moon was bright, right above our heads, enabling us to see clearly, but there was no-one in sight, no-one behind the house, where my wife checked, and no-one hiding among the trees, where I went to investigate.

There was no sound, except the voices of a veterinary assistant whose house was about fifty meters from ours, and his wife, quarrelling. We went back to the house to see if anything had been stolen, but nothing in the kitchen had been touched. The clothes were still on the line. Nothing was missing from the storeroom where we kept boxes on shelves and which we usually left unlocked.

"Tell me exactly what happened," I asked my stepsister.

"I woke up when someone came into my room," she said. "He knelt down and removed the sheet that covered my head, very carefully. I asked who he was, but he just told me to keep quiet, and tiptoed out onto the veranda. I followed, but he was gone. That's why I came to your room. It was bolted, so I knocked."

I was unable to go back to sleep. I sat up, trying to connect what had happened in my house to the quarrel in my neighbour's. I did not like my neighbour. Some time back heand a friend had come to my office with an official from the department of agriculture. They were drunk, and talked a lot of rubbish – until I got angry and chased them out of the office, warning them that I would take measures against them if they came back. Actually I had no quarrel with them, but they were great friends with that northerner who had been the general service officer when I first arrived. They used to drink together, and he was the main source of their cash. When he left, they could not obtain the favours they were used to, and blamed me for his transfer, although they were aware of the government policy to send northerners back to the north, and allow southerners to take over.

"He was smelling of liquor," my stepsister had said of the intruder.

In the morning my wife and I went to see the neighbours. It was nine o'clock, and the husband was still asleep. "Why were you talking so loudly late last night?" my wife asked his wife. "He came back late," she replied, "and he had been drinking again. The door was locked, so he was angry."

We did not talk to him or arrest him. I decided not to open a case against him, although I was convinced that he was the one who had come to my house – but I did report the incident to the police and I told the Reth about it.

"I do not believe that the person came to your house to steal," the Reth said. "He wanted to kill you. He was probably watching you through an open window, and got in. When he found your door bolted, he went to the girl's bedroom, and found someone in bed. It was a small person, though, and he lifted the sheet to make sure. She was obviously not the person he was looking for, so he left."

I saw my neighbour the next day, and the guilty look on his face confirmed my suspicions.

Time passed. Reth Kur Papiti became ill again, and I arranged for him to go to Malakal. From there the commissioner had him flown to Khartoum, where, some months later, he passed away. His death was treated as top secret. The commissioner in Malakal was the only person to be informed, and he passed the information to no-one but me. There were no mobile phones yet, and the post office was very efficient at handling government secrets, so no-one else received the news.

There was a very important reason for this secrecy. In Shilluk tradition, the period between the death of a Reth and the election of a new Reth is considered to be a time when there is no law - "*wangyom*" in Shilluk. Crimes committed during this period need not to be accounted for.

I called the deputy Reth, Kuanyreth Thabo and broke the news to him. I told him to take courage. Together we would handle the situation. Shilluk society, as I have mentioned before, is well organized and tradition dictated the procedure they would follow. My only problem was to put security in place. Kuanyreth Thabo told me which areas needed protection. These included Kodok town, where the crown princes would soon assemble. Unlike in other kingdoms, in Shilluk culture the crown princes are not known in advance, but are elected by the electoral board from a number of princes. Other important places to be protected were Ywodo (the house of the late Reth Papiti), Fashoda (the palace), Debalo and Athodhuai. Thabo told me that as soon as the security forces reached those places, the Shilluk people would, without having to be told, know that the Reth had passed away. He explained that the Reth would not be mourned like people usually are. The people would not cry, but they would come out in great numbers to dance and perform rituals. They knew in advance who would beat the drums and who would dig the grave, as those duties were traditionally entrusted to certain clans, who would now automatically perform them. I called a meeting of the security committee and made arrangements. All the organized forces – the army, police and prison warders - were involved. We completed their deployment during the night, and in the morning the forces were in their positions. By nine o'clock, as Kuanyreth Thabo had predicted, the roar of about six huge drums could be heard loudly and clearly from Ywodo. The sound of the drums was heard and repeated from village to village, the rhythm conveying the message. Within less than twelve hours the news had reached all corners of the Shilluk kingdom.

The late Reth Kur Papiti's body was flown from Khartoum to Malakal and immediately put on a speedboat and taken to Kodok, accompanied by the local government inspector, Charles Mabil Riak. It was midnight, and raining, when it arrived. I arranged for a car to take the body to Ywodo. "It is not necessary for you to accompany it," Kuanyreth Thabo told me. "The Shilluk people will know how to handle the body when it arrives." So I remained at the port to properly receive Inspector Charles Mabil Riak, but he and the crew of the boat wanted to return that same night. I went home and left it to the Shilluk to carry their dead king to Ywodo. There were so many people around the port by then, singing songs, that I had to leave without even seeing the coffin.

The following morning I did go to Ywodo and sat with Kuanyreth Thabo under a tree. The place was crowded with dancing people, including the late Reth's wives. The group entrusted with the burial were inside the fence of the twin tukuls, digging the grave and preparing objects connected with the burial of the Reth. One of the most important items was an elephant tusk, which, according to custom, had to be cut and prepared to be put on the arms of the late Reth before he was buried in the tomb. Three pieces of ivory were to be placed on each arm – one on the upper arm above the elbow, one lower down, and one on the wrist. From time to time Kuanyreth Thabo would get up and walk over to the twin tukuls to see how work was progressing. He told me that they were digging a hollow into the wall of the big hole and shaping a seat like an armchair in it. On this the body would be seated and sealed off. This took a whole day.

Meanwhile people were busy in the house where the body lay. It was about five o'clock in the evening when everything was ready. I was hoping that they would take me to the house to pay my last respects to the Reth, who had been like a father to me, and to see his body being placed in the tomb. "I'm afraid we cannot take you inside," Kuanyreth Thabo told me. "There is no way we can ensure your safety. The people will step on you, and your guards cannot push them away." It was true that people were pushing to get into the house and lining up to enter the twin tukuls. But I knew that was not the true reason why the deputy Reth did not want me to enter the house. I was a foreigner in Shillukland. I realized that it was probably not permissible for me to be present on such an occasion.

So I remained under the tree while Kuanyreth Thabo went into the house and the body was brought to its final resting place, amidst the singing and dancing of the huge crowd. Many bulls were slaughtered, but I never found out what was done with the meat, whether it was cooked, or distributed and carried away. I sat there until the burial was over, and went home.

Whenever a head of state dies, a successor has to be elected as soon as possible to fill the vacuum created by his death. The Shilluk were no exception. The morning after the burial I sent for Kuanyreth Thabo and asked for his advice. What should we do next?

He told me that the Electoral College was already in town, waiting for a directive from me, the local government inspector. The Electoral College, he said was not appointed by anybody. The seven members, all head-chiefs, came from certain predetermined sections of the Shilluk nation. The Padhiang section always provided the chairman. Also present in town, he told me, were the three sons of Reth Anei. They were waiting in different locations, each with his own supporters, under heavy guard.

As mentioned earlier, the children of a Reth are always brought up by their maternal uncles. In the past the princes used to fight among themselves for the position of Reth, aided by their own supporters which always included their maternal uncles. The victorious prince would take up the throne. That custom, however, was frowned upon by the colonial government, and, later by the government of Sudan, and the idea of an election was introduced. The Sudanese government had ruled that the three royal families – the house of Anei, the house of Dak and the house of Papiti - would occupy the throne in turn, without the use of violence. But that has not stopped the persistent infighting among the different houses and within each house. As soon as the throne has gone to one house, the remaining two will do all they can to make their own turn come sooner. That is the reason why a reigning Reth is given such good protection. Likewise, within each group, there is fierce competition for the position. The sons of a reigning Reth are not brought up in the same place, as their maternal uncles take responsibility for them. Each of them grows up wishing the others dead, so that when the turn of their house comes, he will be the only eligible contender.

Of the three princes in town, two were the sons of Shilluk mothers – Prince Othow Anei and Prince Tipo Anei. The third prince, also called Tipo Anei, had a Dinka Dong-jol mother. (It was an acceptable practice for a reth to marry a woman from a different tribe. Reth Kur Papiti himself was a child of a Nuba mother, I was told.) These three princes were the only legitimate contenders because they were the sons of Reth Anei.

One other person tried his luck. John Papiti, the younger brother of Reth Kur Papiti, came with a forged document that stated that Reth Kur had wanted him to rule the Shilluk, but he found no support as his claim was contrary to Shilluk tradition and he had not been included in the arrangements.

Another prince, Wareth, also known as Othwon Dak, arrived from Khartoum, but made no claim to the throne as he was well aware of the fact that it was the turn of the house of Anei to rule. He only came, he said, to make sure that John Papiti's claim would not succeed.

I called the members of the Electoral College to my office. The chairman was Kuanyreth Laa Adwok, the head-chief of the Padhiang section. (Dhiang is the Shilluk word for 'cow', so Padhiang must have had something to do with a cow in the past.) I told them that I would not interfere, but would leave them alone to deliberate over the three princes and elect the one they believed would govern the Shilluk nation the best. They assured me that they had done their homework and that they had examined the personalities of the contenders and knew enough about their characters. I left them for further deliberations, then, five hours later, they sent for me.

"Which of the three does the government prefer?" they asked. "It is not for the government to choose," I replied. "The Reth is going to rule only the Shilluk people, not anybody else. As for me, I have never met any of the princes, they are all the same to me." I assumed that certain prominent Shilluks were watching the proceedings to ensure that the Electoral College was not influenced by any government representatives, or anybody else who was not a member of the college, so I had to count my words.

I left them to their deliberations, knowing that they would eventually give me the name of the prince they had chosen – and another two hours later, they did. They informed me that they had chosen Tipo Anei, the son of the Dinka mother, as the next Reth. The best choice would have been Othow Anei, they explained, but he had been born before his father became the Reth and he therefore had no claim to the throne. And the other Tipo, the one of the Shilluk mother, was a hotheaded man who all too easily resorted to violence to solve his problems. Tipo of the Dinka mother was not perfect, but of the three, he was the best. They did not expect his reign to last very long anyhow, they said, as the turn of the princes of the house of Anei never did. They were too rough.

"How will you announce the result?" I wanted to know.

"We are not going to call the people," they said. "We'll walk straight to the house where he is staying. He and his brothers and the Shilluk people will immediately know what has been decided."

They told me that they would spend the night at the place of the elected prince, and then take him to a place called Athodhuai, north of Kodok opposite Melut, on the western bank of the White Nile River, to bathe him in a tributary of the Nile. From there they would return, bypassing Kodok and sleeping over at Debalo. The next morning they would proceed to Fashoda, where they expected me to meet them. They asked me to provide extra guards to accompany them.

I duly went to Fashoda on the appointed day. It was larger than Ywodo, but like Ywodo, it stood separate from the other villages, some distance from the main Kodok - Malakal road. It consisted of thirty homesteads and a shrine – four beautiful tukuls built on very high ground, which I think had been raised by people for that purpose. From a distance it looked as if they had been built on a hill or mountain. The fence around them resembled the one at Ywodo. The homes were also fenced, but appeared old and neglected, falling apart.

It is worth mentioning that in Shillukland the houses belonging to the Reth are clearly distinguishable from those of ordinary people. They are constructed of very fine grass, known as *'ubuor'*, while commoners use an inferior type for grass, *'peeth'*. Tribes like the Dinka and Nuer use *ubuor* freely, but the Shilluk reserve it for use by the Reth only.

But it must be added that although the Shillluk use inferior grass to thatch their homes, once you enter a home, it looks much tidier and more beautiful than those of the Dinka and Nuer. They carefully construct a ceiling of *dura* cane so that the thatching cannot be seen from the inside. Moreover, the Shilluk tukuls have high walls that, together with the floors, are meticulously plastered with a very fine black soil. The Dinkas also plaster the floors and walls of their tukuls and homes with the same soil, but do so only once or twice a year. Shilluk women keep plastering their walls continuously. Every woman keeps a container of soil in her kitchen, and as soon as a slight crack appears in a wall or floor, she would repair it immediately. No tukul is allowed to form cracks before the next plastering.

Shilluks do not spit inside their houses. A woman would put some sand in a container to be used as a spittoon by anyone who needs to spit frequently, and she would regularly empty it in the grass or a field and then fill it with clean sand. The Reth himself avoids spitting altogether, even when outside his house or on a footpath. There seems to be something secret or taboo about his saliva.

Upon my arrival at Fashoda, I was taken to a room where the elected Reth was seated. Although there were many women in the other houses, not a single child could be seen anywhere. The two of us were served breakfast, brought in by a man. It was '*mongakelo*' with fish, a famous Shilluk dish. A local drink known as '*athobobo*' was also offered, but I did not taste it.

After the meal we joined the crowd that had gathered under three huge trees. Seven members of the Electoral College as well as all the head-chiefs and sub-chiefs and a number of other notables were there to pay allegiance to the new Reth. Most of them had travelled long distances to witness the rare occasion. The ordinary people sat in a semi-circle, whilst the VIP's had formed their own circle in front of them. The important guests sat on mats on the ground, but the commoners were seated on the bare ground. There were only two chairs at the open end of the semi-circle, for the Reth and me. The two of us were the only ones wearing shoes as no person, whether he is a chief or a commoner, is allowed to approach the Reth in shoes. They kept their shoes beside them, or left them at the edge of the compound.

Just outside the compound a good number of cows, rams and he-goats had been tied to stakes – gifts to the Reth. Some of his subjects brought cash instead. Latecomers kept arriving and sat down behind the others. To present a gift, one has to sit with folded legs and open hands in front of the Reth and say '*Who*' or '*Nyajwok*' or '*Kitkwan*' which mean 'Lord' or 'Son of God' or 'Symbol of our Ancestors'. When money is offered to the Reth, he does not count it. Likewise, when he gives money to anyone (a Reth is supposed to help his subjects), he just pulls out what he has laid his hand on and hands it over. All gifts to the Reth are presented in public. The Shilluk has a word, '*kumthok*', which they share with the Dinka, but whereas in the Dinka language it means 'bribery', the Shilluk do not see it as denoting any corrupt practice. Even when the relatives of a person, maybe a murderer, whose case is to be heard by the Reth, offer a gift to the Reth, it is not seen as bribery. A gift to the Reth is an offering to Nyikang.

The proceedings started with a speech by Kuanyreth Laa Adwok, the chairman of the Electoral College. He introduced the new Reth to the Shilluk nation. They had made the best choice, he said, and expressed the hope that the new Reth would lead them to prosperity. Then Jago Ajobwong spoke on behalf of the head-chiefs and the entire Shilluk nation, ensuring the Reth of their full allegiance and support. The third speaker was Kuanyreth Bol Acien, who was to be the new king's chief advisor. When he waxed critical about the previous administration, a police officer Richard (known as *Amaal Maruf*) from Raga leaned over to me and whispered: "Look at Kuanyreth Bol Acien! He does not look like a Shilluk at all. I think he is a Dinka who has camouflaged himself and has come to confuse the Shilluk people."

The new Reth, Tipo, took a new name, Ayang, and came to be known as Reth Ayang. He spoke next. He thanked the Electoral College for their good work, and the chiefs and the Shilluk people who had come such great distances to Fashoda to witness the historical event. Then he turned his attention to the previous administration and blamed it for not having maintained Fashoda to the expected standard. "The wealth of Fashoda has disappeared," he said. "What has become of the cattle? Only elderly women have been left at Fashoda, and they have not been able to take proper care of it." And he continued: "Where did that elephant tusk you used for the burial of Reth Kur Papiti come from? It was one of a pair. Where is the other one? I believe it was hidden by Kuanyreth Thabo and Prince Tipo Kur Papiti who accompanied the body of his father from Khartoum to Kodok. They will appear before me to answer the charges leveled against them." Prince Tipo Kur was a police officer, son of the late Reth, who had just graduated from the Sudan Police College.

It is true that some large animals like the elephant, hippo and waterbuck were in the past regarded as belonging to the throne, and no-one in Shillukland was allowed to kill one of them without the approval of the Reth. All elephant tusks belonged to Fashoda, and if any of these animals were killed with the approval of the Reth, their meat would be dried and the oil (especially that of the hippo) carefully prepared, and delivered to the Reth. Killing such animals without permission carried a heavy fine in the form of cattle.

This speech did not please me at all. When my turn to speak came, I reminded Reth Ayang that the people had just emerged from a war, and the fact that Reth Kur had maintained Nyikang's shrine and some of the houses and fences should be appreciated. I told him that everybody had lost their possessions during the war, and Fashoda was not exceptional. But, I said, wealth was already beginning to return to Fashoda, and that with the situation being stable, he would soon be receiving his share of it. The Shilluk people were ready to rebuild Fashoda.

As for the elephant tusks, I made it clear that there were no elephant tusks left at Fashoda, but that the late Reth Kur Papiti had realized that his health was deteriorating gradually, and requested the government of Sudan to provide him with an elephant tusk which he knew would be needed when he passed away. I myself had forwarded the request to the commissioner, who in turn had passed it to the government in Juba, and the Reth was issued with one tusk from government stock. I told the new Reth that, if he did not believe me, I could show him the remaining part of the tusk with the government stamp on it.

I added that there was no need to bring Kuanyreth Thabo and Prince Tipo Kur Papiti before him. "Let me tell you what happened to me," I said. "The government office at Kodok was not destroyed in the war, yet I had two colleagues who, when they left, used the war as a pretext to dump everything on me without properly handing things over. I had to pick everything up from where they left, but I coped with the situation. Perhaps you too can just take up things from where late Reth Kur Papiti left them, and go ahead."

Reth Ayang of course took exception to my words. "I am surprised to hear an outsider telling me that I should not call Shilluk citizens to appear before me," he said. "Don't interfere with the affairs of the Shilluk people."

I angrily informed him that I was totally neutral in all that was happening. I reminded him that I saw him only that day in Fashoda for the first time, while I knew his brother Othow long before the death of Reth Kur Papiti. I told him that, if I was not neutral he would not have been chosen Reth.

The young Reth appeared to be offended, but when we were alone in the tukul he told me that, according to information he had received from members of the Electoral College, it was true that he owed much of his success to me. "Don't take what I said seriously. I was joking," he told me. "But you should not have said what you said in front of my subjects!"

"Then *you* should not have made jokes about me in front of your people," I replied. "And remember, the government of the Republic of Sudan remains the supreme authority over the land – the Shilluk kingdom included."

I persuaded him to leave Kuanyreth Thabo in peace, and to allow Tipo Kur Papiti to return to Khartoum. Then I left for Kodok.

The struggle between Reth Ayang and his stepbrothers, however, was far from over yet. He was to be crowned in the dry season, and if anything happened to him before the coronation the rightg to succession would still remain in their house. So his stepbrothers might do anything to grab an opportunity to serve their own interests. And after the coronation the houses of Dak and Kur would be the ones to work underground to advance their cause. The throne could very quickly be transferred from the house of Anei to the house of Dak.

As for the house of Papiti, their position was not enviable. If the throne remained too long in the house of Anei and Dak, it might mean that the last children of the late Reth might grow old and die before their turn came. Should that happen, it would mean that the house of Papiti would lose it claim to the throne forever, because the Reth must be elected from princes born during their father's reign. For this reason the three houses were sure to continue struggling underground to assure quick circulation of the throne.

CHAPTER 9

Transfer to Renk

Before the coronation of Reth Ayang, a full local government inspector, Charles Ali Bilal, was transferred to Kodok, and I was told to go to Renk. I handed the office over to him, and left for Renk by steamer. My family and I arrived late in the evening, to be met by Enock Manyuon Malok who, like me, was an assistant executive officer. He took us to a newly built house with two rooms, a saloon and a veranda, where we spent the night. The next morning Enok accompanied me to the offices of the council and the assistant commissioner.

To my surprise the assistant commissioner was none other than Ajang Bior, who had been with me at Kodok. When he heard that my family and I had been accommodated in the new house, he disapproved. "That house was built for single administrative officers," he told Enock. "You can put Bol up in the house the clerk has vacated." The clerk had moved to a local residential area where he had built himself a private home. His former house was not nearly as comfortable as the one Enock had first taken us to. It consisted of two tukuls, built of baked bricks and thatched, with a tiny veranda connecting the tukuls. It had stood empty for a long time and I would have to do a lot of cleaning outside and inside before my family could move in. I was not happy! Enock occupied a very nice house, actually meant for a deputy executive officer. Ajang Bior was in the house that had been built for the assistant commissioner when he, Ajang, was still in Kodok.

Ajang allowed me two days to rest; then called me to his office and informed me that I was to work as Enock's deputy. Enock used to be an accountant, who, like so many other southerners, had been appointed to a post in local government administration. He was appointed in scale H, whereas I was in scale Q, so actually I was his senior. That argument did not impress Ajang. "You are both Range Three in local government terminology. Scale does not matter," he told me. "Enock has been here for a long time, ever since he arrived as an accountant. He knows Renk better than you."

After a month I was called to Juba for a three months' course.

When I returned I found that a number of changes had taken place. Ajang had left to attend a one-year course in Britain, and another assistant commissioner (grade 5) – Caesar Arkangelo Suleiman - had taken over from him. There was a new full executive officer (scale B) too. His name was Jut Ajobwong, and he had taken the council over from Enock, who remained as deputy executive officer.

It was the beginning of the rainy season. The house which Ajang had denied me was still vacant, but I did not mention it. I knew that it had a good fence, though, and I cultivated some maize inside the fence.

Renk was famous for its *dura* cultivation scheme, and, as Ajang had told me, Enock knew all the rich *dura* merchants very well. He was particularly good at building contacts between the top officials of the area and local councils and the merchants – in short, between the assistant commissioner and the merchants. Outside the surveyed area of the scheme, a large field was cultivated for Caesar. Everything was done free for him, because the merchants had a great deal to gain from their relationship with the top man in charge of the sub-province. Caesar received his produce ready in sacks, maybe hundreds of them.

It was not surprising that Renk was a popular posting. Senior administrators would compete for the privilege of being sent there. Our next arrival was Filberto Lolik (scale DS). He had been transferred from Juba to Malakal. Venasio Loro, the executive director at Malakal asked him where he wanted to work, and he chose Renk. So Loro wrote to Caesar at Renk, ordering him to appoint Filberto as deputy executive officer. The same letter stated that Filberto should be given Enock's house, and Enock was to move into mine. I was being transferred to Maban.

I asked Caesar whether it was the transfer or allotment of houses or both, which I knew were not the work of the executive director in the provincial headquarters in Malakal. "Both," he said. "But don't worry. You won't have to take your children to Maban."

When, a few days later, Venasio Loro came on a visit to Renk, I approached him and asked, "What is going on between the provincial administration and the area council administration? Why are you transferring me?"

Loro said that it was Ajang Bior's idea. He had stated in his handing-over notes that Bol (me) was to go to Maban in the dry season.

"Then why didn't Ajang transfer me before he himself got transferred?" I asked. "I'm not council property to be handed over, just like that! And why me only? Weren't any other officers mentioned in the handing-over notes? Anyway, Maban is a village council and should be run by a general services officer!"

"You are right," Vanasio said. "Why don't you write a letter to complain and send it to me in Malakal?"

That same evening I wrote my letter, and gave it to someone who was leaving on the same boat as Venasio. Venasio wrote right away to Caesar, telling him that I was a young graduate that should remain close to the assistant commissioner to receive the full benefit of his training. Caesar was to find another officer for Maban. Caesar, however, had no-one else except Enock to send – and, for obvious reasons he could not dispense with Enock. So he merely marked the letter "noted and put away", and filed it. He never even mentioned it to me. I enquired twice, but Caesar just told me that no reply had come from Malakal.

When I went for the third time, the head clerk in Caesar's office remarked, "You again! Why are you always coming here?"

"I have sent a letter to Malakal, and I must know whether Caesar has received an answer yet," I told him.

The clerk laughed. "Sorry, no reply yet," he said. But the expression on his face made it clear that it was not true.

"Please show it to me," I asked.

"I can't. I'll get into trouble with Caesar." He said

"Don't worry. I assure you there will be no problem between you and the boss." I told him.

The clerk then handed the file to me, and I read the letter. There was no doubt about it: Venasio had cancelled my transfer and it was Caesar who had a problem. I just laughed and went home.

The next day I went to Caesar. "Since the answer from Malakal has been delayed," I said, "I think it would be best for me to leave for Maban right away. The best time to get things done there is the dry season."

Of course Caesar was happy! "I wish I had more administrators of your calibre," he said, "men who are willing to work anywhere! I'm sure you will do well in Maban. But if I do receive contrary instructions from the executive director later, I will recall you to Renk."

Very early in the morning, two days later, I bade my family farewell and left for Maban. My driver and I had been given the use of an old Commer, known as Dungus. The office also had two new Toyota pickups, but these were reserved for the use of senior officials.

We took the road to Malakal, then turn southward at a place called Jalhak. There were no villages along the road, only sand or black soil, with a few trees. Maban is over two hundred miles from Renk. At midday we reached a place called Kitwa, about halfway between Jalhak and Maban. Kitwa was a small seasonal station, three tukuls, in the middle of the *toch*. There was only one petty trader who sold tea, pieces of soap and salt to the Falata nomads who were camping with their cattle near a small stream some distance away from the road. The driver and I took tea, rested for half an hour, and resumed our journey. Until we were approaching Maban town we saw very few houses along the road; the ones we did see were small single tukuls. It was very late when at last we entered the town.

Only outsiders and the government call this small town Maban. The locals know it as "Bunj". Members of the local Brun tribe refer to themselves as Maban, just like the Shilluk call themselves Sholo, and the Nuer call themselves Naath.

I was taken to a small but comfortable house, originally built by an Arab trader using permanent materials. All the shops belonged to northern Sudanese traders and were sturdily constructed. The houses, mine included, had baked brick fences.

In the morning I went to the office, about a hundred metres from the market. The building was U-shaped and built of permanent materials. It contained enough offices for the council's small staff. The police station was a square brick house, thatched, and measuring only about four by four metres. It was manned by a small number of policemen. There was no prison, and the occasional prisoner was kept at the police station. Prisoners were invariably from other areas. Crime, I was told, was very rare among the Brun people.

There was nobody to officially hand over the council to me. The two bookkeepers and the sole clerk that I found in the office, showed me the council's property which consisted of office furniture. There was a safe, but it was empty. The council staff in Maban, which included a few labourers and hospital staff, received their salaries from Renk – thanks to the *dura* taxes (called ushur and gibana) that the owners of the dura scheme paid.

There was a small hospital at Doro, a mile away from Bunj. It was built by an American missionary very long ago, but built of permanent materials so it was still sturdy. There were offices and a ward, and a good house that used to be occupied by a medical officer. There was a water supply system too. The pipes were of strong plastic, of a type you may see in towns today, but was not known in those days, not even in Khartoum. There was a large tank into which a machine pumped water, to be distributed through the pipes.

In order to carry out my duties, I needed some cash, but the bookkeepers informed me that only salaries were brought from Renk, and they provided no money for services or running expenses. To pay for services we were required to collect social service taxes locally – which the office had done, but the amount raised was small, and already spent. The area administered by the Maban local council was small and sparsely populated by the Brun and Barta tribes. There were not many registered tax payers, and the amount they contributed was hardly enough to pay the salaries of their own chiefs.

In the six months I spent at Maban, I never saw a large Brun village, nor did I visit any chief in his house. But I did get to know the people fairly well. The Brun have no cattle, but they do keep large herds of free-roaming pigs and goats. These animals sleep under trees, and when they give birth, the owner of the herd would go and cut his own mark into the ear of the new arrival. Occasionally a goat or pig would be caught and taken home to be slaughtered. Theft is unknown in that area.

There is no game in the area, no lions, no hyenas, not even snakes or rodents. They have all been killed and eaten.

It did not take me long to identify three potential sources of income. There was a dense forest to the south of the town, stretching to the mountainous area between Ethiopia and the Sudan. I discovered that two types of wood were being cut there by Arab traders, and smuggled out to the north. The logs of the *dom* trees were sawn into planks to be used for roofing in Jolus town and the villages. The other type of wood was similar to teak, and made into furniture. Three policemen accompanied me on the route the smugglers used, and they quickly arrested the drivers of six lorries with heavy loads. The lorries were brought to the town and only released when the wood had been paid for, and the fines paid. The smugglers soon got the message, and started coming to us for permission to cut the trees. Cutting was done in the presence of our supervisors, and the wood was paid for. As there was no forestry department at that time, I was the only authority in charge of the area.

The second source of income was the *dura* that was being smuggled out of Renk by traders seeking to avoid paying *ushur* and *gibana*. I placed policemen on their route to intercept their vehicles and make them pay their taxes plus a fine.

The Falata nomads were our third source of taxes. They spent eight months of each year in the Maban area, grazing their cattle, drinking the water, and availing themselves of the veterinary services and the hospital. Each year they spent only four months in the El Damazin area. This meant that we were entitled to their taxes. When I explained this to them, they understood, and started paying promptly. They came to Maban in large numbers to sell their cows and we collected a substantial amount in taxes from them. Instead of waiting for Renk to pay our salaries, we were now able not only to pay ourselves locally, but also to send some money to the main chest in Renk.

This did not please the authorities in El Damazin, though. When they learned that we were collecting social service taxes from the Falata, the assistant commissioner of Al Damazin, accompanied by police and army officers, came to Maban in two cars. I received them warmly, offered them tea and water, and we sat down to talk.

The assistant commissioner from El Damazin objected to our taxing their citizens, from whom they also collected the same taxes. It was not legal to collect the same tax twice from the same people, he said.

"Actually, they are not your citizens," I told him. "They are nomads who come from Niger or Nigeria and are scattered in many parts of Sudan. They are always on the move, from one area to the next. According to the law they are to be taxed by the authority in whose area they spend the greater part of the year. Since they spend eight months in Maban and only four months in your area, and receive most of their services here, it is here that they should be taxed."

"Yes, but the chiefs of the Falata have settled in the El Damazin area to work in the *dura* schemes," he told me. "It's their subjects moving with the cattle."

"I realize that I am a junior officer," I replied. "Why don't you go to Renk and talk to your own counterpart, Caesar Arkanjelo?"

The officers who were with him agreed with me. "I suggest we go back and arrange a trip to Renk," one of them said.

The assistant commissioner accepted their advice, and they returned. I continued collecting taxes, pending any contrary orders from Renk. I later learned that he did not go to Renk. I must have convinced him!

The rainy season was approaching, and I had no desire to spend it in Maban, cut off from Renk by the rains. The nearest town to Maban was Kurmuk, but that was sixty miles away! I asked for leave, and it was granted. I left for Renk in the first week of June, and less than a month later I went home, with my family. Before my leave ended, I was informed that I would be transferred to the Lakes Province. So, after collecting my belongings from Renk, I reported for duty to the Commissioner of Lakes in Rumbek.

CHAPTER 10

Cueibet

The commissioner of Lakes State was James Ajith Awuol, who, in 1975, had been director-general in the ministry of local government in Juba. When I arrived in Rumbek, I went straight to his office. "We have not met before," he told me, "but I am pleased that you have joined us. I know you through the confidential reports they have sent me. Your job is going to be to run the 1976 plebiscite of Jaafar Mohamed Nimeiri.

After completing the plebiscite, I received a letter informing me that I was being transferred to Cueibet. Cueibet had previously been a village council under a general service officer, Augustino Agai Dut, but had just been upgraded to rural council. When I went to see the commissioner for a briefing, I found a visitor in his office – The Paramount Chief Arol Kacuol Jok of Gok section of Cueibet, someone I had not met before.

The commissioner did not introduce me. "Sit down," he said, and continued to talk to the paramount chief.

"I want Augustino Agai to remain with us," the chief said. "We don't want him to be replaced."

"I know what I'm doing," the commissioner replied. "I know the administrators better than you."

"But Augustino Agai is the one I want."

"All right," the commissioner said, "I will send Bol Majok for six months to do special duty. Then I will return Augustino Agai to you."

The head-chief accepted the compromise reluctantly. When he left, the commissioner turned to me, "You have heard what he said. But I know what you are going to do in Cueibet – you are going to make them forget Augustino Agai."

The assistant commissioner, Gabriel Oywuac, provided me with a new Toyota pickup, and the commissioner added a Commer to be used for the transport of teak and bamboo from Rumbek to Cueibet. As soon as I got to Cueibet, I used the timber for the construction of two houses – one for myself and my family and one for the officers I expected to arrive soon. I also assisted the support staff with building materials so that they could build houses for themselves.

Then I sat down to plan the future of the new council.

We had no money. Neither did Rumbek Rural Council, and we were in arrears with the payment of salaries. But I also discovered that a substantial amount in social service taxes was owing to us, just waiting to be collected. I embarked on a serious collection drive and before long I managed to pay all the salaries and arrears, to both the chiefs and the council employees.

I also started registering all tax payers for the new financial year. The chiefs were happy and gave me their full cooperation. They had not registered people properly in the past, they told me, because the council authorities in Rumbek were not treating them fairly, compared to the chiefs of the Rumbek area.

At the beginning of 1977 I gave directives for social service taxes to be paid before the people were able to move to the *toch*, the river-flooded grasslands. During the dry season the inhabitants of Cueibet leave their homes to spend the dry season in the *toch*, to return only when the rains came. During the rainy season they would be cultivating their fields, and would be too busy to be concerned about taxes.

My instructions were ignored, however, and soon the tax-payers were gone, without paying – those living north of the main road had gone to the *toch* bordering Bentiu, and those living south of the road, to a place called Dingie, which was good for fishing as well as for grazing cattle.

Before they left for the *toch*, they stored their *dura* and other produce in their houses, sealing the houses with mud and stacking thorny branches against the walls. I sent the chiefs after them asking them to come back, but they refused to do so. So I went to the paramount chief and the other chiefs and informed them that I could not allow the people of Gok to do that. I told them that I was going to open the houses and remove one sack of *dura*, enough to cover the tax, from each house, and seal it again. "I don't think it will be necessary to open too many houses before they rush back to pay," I predicted.

We started at a place called Ayor. On the first day we opened three houses and took a sack from each. Then we sealed the doors and went back to the town. Three days later, accompanied by Paramount Chief Arol Kacuol, we returned and opened three more houses. Before we could repeat the exercise a third time, the people were back, some with cash, others with dried fish or *dura* to sell, all ready to pay. Forcing people to pay was not an easy decision, but it worked, and long after I had left Cueibet, the inhabitants would still remember it.

We were able not only to meet our financial commitments, but also to deposit part of the money in the bank to be used during the months when there would be no further collection of taxes.

Then the commissioner, James Ajith, sent for the paramount chief, Arol Kacuol, and reminded him of his promise to recall me after six months. "It's time for Bol Majok to come back to Rumbek," he said. "He has accomplished his mission. I'll send Augustine Agai back to you."

"But you can't do that!" the chief protested. "You'll destroy the good work Bol Majok has done in Cueibet! Augustino is a very good officer, but he would never have made that decision to compel the people to pay their taxes."

The commissioner laughed. "Don't be upset. I'm not serious," he said.

One day the paramount chief Arol Kacuol invited me to go with him to visit a very important man, Yuol Malual, twenty miles south of Cueibet, in the Gok area. We found Yuol sitting under a tree with three other persons, who left when we arrived. There were a number of huts scattered under some trees. They appeared to be new, as the grass around the houses had not been cleared yet.

Yuol greeted us; then disappeared among the tukuls. We heard the squawking of two cocks as they were caught and slaughtered for us. When Yuol returned, he and Arol talked, while I simply listened. Breakfast was brought, and we ate. Our guards and driver who were waiting under a tree, were also served.

Then Arol told Yuol Malual the reason for our visit. He referred to me as a child of Rek, despite the fact that I had always told him, I was from Twic not Rek. I told him that calling me Rek, was like calling him Agar, a name which Gok people of Cueibet always reject bitterly.

"He is the right person to develop our young rural council, people do not want him to go. What I have come to ask you is to use your spiritual powers to keep him in Cueibet." He told Yuol Malual.

I had never witnessed anything like this before! But I just kept quiet. If Arol had told me about this before we left Cueibet, I would certainly not have come. Yuol did not reply, and as Arol knew how Yuol handled such matters, he changed the topic. At about three o'clock in the afternoon Yuol got up and walked to an isolated hut where he remained for about thirty minutes. When he returned he sat down.

"The government is as pleased with Bol's work as you are," he told Arol. "If the Gok people are happy with Bol, we should also wish him well. But I can tell you that Bol will be promoted soon and be too senior for a rural council like Cueibet."

"If it's promotion that takes him away, I can't object," Arol said.

Then suddenly a woman appeared, bearing a long stick. I found it strange. Since morning I had not seen a single woman around the compound; only men served us. Now suddenly there was this woman. Yuol took the stick from her, and placed it across our path to the car. We had to jump over it to get to the car.

In the car on the way back, Arol asked me if I was expecting promotion soon.

"I have been in scale Q for almost six years now," I said. "I'm hoping to be promoted to DS, but that shouldn't take me away from Cueibet. Cueibet is entitled to a permanent officer, a DS. I'm only acting."

"Well, that certainly makes me happy," Arol said.

A month later rumours reached us that our batch was to be promoted, but the list had not arrived in Rumbek. Instead, I received a letter instructing me to report to Juba for a course. So I handed the office to my assistant and left for Juba – where I found that I had been promoted to scale B! There was no news about a transfer, though. After the three-month's course I returned to Cueibet, and simply continued with my duties.

Lakes Province, however, had a new commissioner – Hugo Dhol Acuil, who used to be a classmate of mine at Rumbek Secondary School. He knew me very well. In spite of fact that I was not the most senior officer in the provincial headquarters, Hugo posted me to Tonj as assistant commissioner. After a month in Tonj I was called to Britain to do a course there.

The real force behind my promotion, I realized later, was Caesar Arkangelo, my former assistant commissioner in Renk. Apparently he remembered with appreciation how some years before I had opted to go to Maban even after I had learned that my transfer had been reversed. The clerk in Renk must have told him that I had seen the letter from Malakal.

Caesar was particularly happy with my work in Maban, and with the confidential report he had received from James Ajith Awuol, the former commissioner of Lakes Province as well as reports from Kodok and Malakal.

I stayed in Britain from October 1978 to June 1979. As soon as the exams ended, I left for Sudan. Actually, I was supposed to wait another two months for the results, but I was confident that there would be no supplementary for me. In Khartoum I received the good news that I had been promoted again – to Grade Five. They informed me that I was being transferred from Tonj to Nasir in Upper Nile Province.

CHAPTER 11

Malakal

In Malakal I reported to the commissioner, Jashua Dei Wal, who had been my mathematics teacher at Rumbek Secondary School and remembered me very well. He did not have good news for me.

"When you get to Nasir, I'm afraid you will find that the people will not like you, simply because you are a Dinka."

"Then why are you sending me there?" I wanted to know.

"Nobody else wants to go. Nasir is the most difficult posting and no official, whether Nuer or non-Nuer has lasted very long there. It was the ministry, not the province that recommended you."

I immediately knew who I had to thank – my old ally Caesar Arkangelo, who had been responsible for all my promotions. He had chosen me for Nasir! Long before my companions who had gone to Britain with me were even back in the country, I moved to Nasir.

And the people were not bad at all! Throughout my stay they were kind to me.

Most of my colleagues were junior officials. The accounting system was in a mess. The officials used sheets of paper instead of books, and the bookkeepers who were mostly inhabitants of Nasir, were constantly quarrelling with the junior officials, whom they felt were not handling their money properly.

I told the administrator in charge of the council to put his books in order, but he could not and I had to do it myself.

The bookkeepers were willing but ignorant, and I had to train them – which they appreciated.

Then there was the self-help scheme which, long before I arrived at Nasir, had been initiated by the Lutheran World Federation. Their idea was to construct an elementary school at Nasir, as well as a drugstore in the market. But for this they needed the assistance of the people, and the people were reluctant to become involved. There were six large kilns where baked bricks had been produced by the community. The Lutheran World Federation now wanted the people to stack the bricks in thousands, so that they would be able to transport them to the site of the new school. The community was also given the task of carrying sand from the river bed and heaping it on the bank. The Lutherans were to supply all non-local materials such as cement, corrugated iron sheets, nails and wood.

It took a long time for the project to get off the ground, though. The community just did not seem interested. I realized it would be difficult to mobilize the chiefs and their rural subjects, so I concentrated on the town's population who would be first to benefit from a school and a store selling drugs at a reduced price. I closed the office and the market on Fridays and Saturdays and appealed to everyone to come and help. Our first job was to stack bricks, and I worked as hard as anyone else. I involved the organized forces, and the officers could not just stand by and watch me work. Soon everyone was hard at work, including some villagers who were rounded up when they came to town.

Next we excavated sand from the river bed and carried it to the bank. I wore shorts and a T-shirt, and worked long hours lugging sand up the slope in a bucket I had brought from home. No-one would stop working before I did. Within days we had a mountain of clean dry sand waiting for the builders.

The population seemed happy to have an assistant commissioner joining them in hard manual labour. The same individuals who I had been told would resent any non-Nuer official, especially a Dinka, took the news to the commissioner, who sent a letter to congratulate me, telling me that he and his colleagues in Juba had always known what I was capable of. I had proved to the Nuer of Nasir that not all Dinkas were bad! The representative of the Lutheran World Federation was equally happy – he was now able to build a large elementary school consisting of eight classrooms and two offices, as well as a drugstore. I was away on leave when he was transferred from Nasir, but he left a letter telling me that he had never before experienced such good cooperation anywhere. He gave my wife a small portable typewriter as a personal gift.

When I returned from leave, I was given first-class magisterial powers. Fortunately Nuer customs are similar to those of the Dinka, so I had no serious problems handling their cases. Where necessary, I consulted elderly persons for advice. Some Nuer citizens as well as the commissioner, Joshua Dei, used to tell me that they could not believe I was not Nuer. The commissioner was not on such good terms with other Dinka officials in Malakal, particularly those from Bahr el Ghazal. Whenever I paid a visit to Malakal and he saw me in the company of Lazaro Deng Atem Barac, Atillo Aguek Kuc and Dut Malek Arol, he would warn them not to try to influence me.

When it came to the payment of compensation for people killed or injured, there were some minor differences between Dinka and Nuer tradition. If someone was killed, the Nuer would pay fifty cows, of which ten went to the government, and forty to the relatives of the deceased. The Dinka paid only thirty-one cows, all of which would go to the family. For someone only injured, the compensation would depend on the number of days he spent in hospital, or under treatment in a dispensary or clinic – a goat for five days, a small bull for seven days and so forth, according to the gravity of the injury.

One case I will always remember is that of the head-chief of Wulang. He and a retainer were both attacked and beaten in a court by an angry opponent. The retainer sustained a broken elbow. I formed a special court to settle the case, under my supervision. The members deliberated, then came to give me their verdict before announcing it to the concerned parties. I was shocked to learn that the chief, who had spent two months in Nasir hospital, would not receive any compensation at all, whereas the retainer was awarded two cows. The chief did not have any broken bones, they explained.

I delayed the announcement of the court's decision and went to consult the head-chief himself. He told me that they were perfectly right. He did not expect any compensation as he had no broken bones to show. If he had been a Dinka, he would have received four or five cows.

Another task I was given in Nasir, was to run the elections. The commissioner, who came from Nasir, favoured some contestants over others and from time to time tried to influence me, but I remained neutral throughout.

After exactly one year at Nasir, I was informed that the people of Gogrial had requested the ministry to transfer me to them. The inhabitants of Nasir sent a delegation to Juba to protest against my transfer, but they were told that if I had served them well, they should also allow me to serve the people of Gogrial, where I was born.

So I handed the area council to David Deng Athorbei, and left for Gogrial.

CHAPTER 12

Gogrial

At my welcoming party in Gogrial the employees of the area council and many others talked at length about the difficulties they experienced. For months they had not received their salaries. The minimal amount they managed to collect from the market was given as advances to the administrative officers whilst others continued working, month after month, without any payment. Even the chiefs had not received any money for more than a year.

"I will collect the money," I promised, "and everyone will receive his salary plus arrears. They say that I am a good man, but I'm not easy to get along with. I have no patience with people who neglect their duties."

I was used to this situation. Every time I had been posted to a new area as administrator, I had found it in financial crisis. The only exception was Renk. My first and most urgent task had always been social service tax collection.

I did the same in Gogrial. I asked the accountants to furnish me with exact figures of arrears in each chieftainship. I discovered that some, such as Apuk, had collected no taxes at all for years. So that is where I started – in the Apuk section. I sent my deputy, Albino Mathiang Thiep (who came from Apuk), to Pathuon; and a junior officer, Ayii Deng Ayii, to Apuk Toch. A month later they were back – with very little money. I was not happy at all. I instructed my deputy to remain in my office and do my work. He could always consult me when necessary, and I left for Apuk Toch.

As soon as I arrived at Liet-Nhom, I called a meeting with the sub-chiefs and *Gol* leaders. "I want the taxes paid immediately," I told them.

"The people have no cash," they said, "but they do have cattle that can be collected and taken to Gogrial and sold at auction. Then they will have the cash to pay."

I gave them permission to collect the cattle, as I waited for them. After a week they arrived with a good number of cows and oxen, which we kept in a pen. But soon the owners of the cattle started playing the same trick they had played on Ayii Deng Ayii on me. One by one the cattle disappeared as they were taken out to graze. The *Gol* leaders were clearly not serious about collecting taxes. I told the *Gol* leaders and the sub-chiefs to assemble outside the cattle pen one evening, and had an accountant check how many heads of cattle had disappeared from each *Gol* leader's herd. Their punishment was one blow with a lash for each missing animal.

Not a single animal was missing the next evening. Within twenty-one days we had completed the collection of taxes in form of cattle and some cash in Apuk Toch and got back to Gogrial.

In Gogrial, I formed a committee under my deputy Albino Mathiang to sell the cattle at public auction. I told Albino to keep detailed accounts of the animals sold and if a cow or ox fetched more than the amount the owner owed us, the balance was to be refunded to him. As soon as a *Gol* leader brought the money from his section, both current taxes and arrears, he was paid his dues - ten percent of what he brought in. Each sub-chief was paid when all his *Gol* leaders had brought their money, and finally the head-chiefs received their percentage. The balance went into the council's chest.

Next I turned my attention to Luonyaker. On the afternoon I arrived there, I found all the sub-chiefs and *Gol* leaders in a meeting with Moudit Giir Thiik, the paramount chief of Apuk. I went to join them.

"You need a rest," they told me. "Relax, and we'll meet with you in the morning."

"I have no need to rest," I assured them. "Since I'm so lucky to find you all together, I'll explain the reason why I have come to you right away."

"We know why you are here," they said. "But we assure you that we will work hard to obtain some money to hand over to you. You can go home to Gogrial. We'll do the job for you."

I pointed to my car. "I'm in no hurry to leave," I said. "I've got enough food in the car to last me while I'm here. And here's my gun. I'll just kill some of those wild ducks flying overhead for broth. I've brought my new wife to cook for me." I had indeed brought my newly-wedded wife, Veronica Nyanut Elario, with me. She was waiting in the car. "I am fully prepared to stay as long as the collection of taxes lasts. Take as long as you wish over it."

They just looked at me. "Could you show me to my accommodation?" I asked.

The chiefs did not spend the night at Luonyaker that night. They all walked back to their areas, and in less than twenty days, the collection was completed. Those who could, paid in cash. Others brought cows and oxen. No-one tried to repeat the trick of making cattle disappear, as people had done at Apuk Toch. We all left for Gogrial together, so that everyone could be paid their dues.

While we were waiting for the tax collection, something strange happened. There was an evil-smelling dog, covered with sores, that used to come around whenever we were taking our meals. I asked the owners of the house if they could get rid of it by killing it, but they said dog was their traditional totem and that in their family they didn't beat a dog, let alone kill it. I asked my guards to get rid of it but they were equally reluctant. One day when the dog again came through the compound and went behind the building, I took it upon myself to kill it. I loaded my shotgun and went to the other side of the building and waited for it to appear. It emerged at very close range and I short at it, but insteadof hitting the dog, the cartridge exploded in the barrel of the gun, filling it with a black substance, something that had never happened to my shotgun. The dog escaped unharmed. I went back to the house to clean the gun and wanted to try another shot but my wife stopped me, telling me that what these people were saying about the dog might be true, so I dropped the idea and we tolerated it until we left the place. Although I don't believe in traditional totems, I found this particular incident rather strange.

There was another hitch on the morning we left Luonyaker with the cattle, I was informed that there was a group of students who were not happy with what I did. They threatened to intercept the cattle as we herded them towards Gogrial. In the presence of the paramount chief, and in a clear voice, I gave firm orders to the policemen: "If anyone interferes with the cattle this morning or on the way to Gogrial, you are to use the appropriate force to stop them. I'll be following behind you." I kept two policemen with me and sent the rest ahead with the cattle, but nothing happened on the way.

Upon our arrival in Gogrial, I was told that all the *Gol* leaders and sub-chiefs of Apuk Toch had completed payment of all their taxes, and had received their dues. Many of them had received so much, that they were waiting for the cattle to arrive from Pathuon so that they might buy some to take back home. Once again, Albino Mathiang Thiep's committee was in charge of sales.

The same day I received a visit from some Apuk intellectuals and other officials from Wau headed by Madut Manoon.

"Could you tell us exactly how you collected the social service taxes in the Apuk area?" they wanted to know.

"You have come at the right time," I said. "The chiefs and *Gol* leaders from Apuk are still here; they haven't gone home yet. Why don't you talk to them first, and also to Albino Mathiang, the chairman of the committee, and then come back to talk to me."

They did as I suggested. They went to see Albino, and then went to the market to meet the chiefs and *Gol* leaders. And they never even came back to my office! I was told that the chiefs and *Gol* leaders had accused them of coming from Wau to spoil the good work done in Gogrial – work that had nothing to do with them.

Back in Wau, however, they did manage to find out how much money we had in our bank account. They went to the commissioner and told him how much had been collected from their area, and asked for part of it to go to their rural council for development. The commissioner instructed me to deposit twenty thousand Sudanese pounds into their account, and to provide a car for the junior officer, Adriano Nyiel Abot, who was to establish the rural council. This was a lot of money, because at that time a first class bull or ox, hardly fetched ten Sudanese pounds.

I did not go out again to any section to collect taxes, nor did I send an administrative officer. The head-chiefs, sub-chiefs and *Gol* leaders of every area gave us their full cooperation, and came to Gogrial to pay all taxes plus arrears to the area council.

The second thing I did in Gogrial Area Council was to stop the sectional conflicts that were claiming lives of many people in the area. Amakiir and Lual sections were fighting in Apuk and Kuac was fighting Aguok. In Twic, Amiol was fighting Adiang to the west and Akuar to the east. The Cuar and Thon sections in the Akoc area were fighting Noon. Awan Mou was also fighting Amiol; and Awan Pajok was fighting two sections – Ajuong and Lou of Aweil Area Council.

In the first security meeting I held, I asked how the people of Gogrial could be killing themselves so recklessly, while there were police stations in every area. "They just keep fighting in the presence of the police," I was told. "Whenever the police fire rounds of bullets into the air, you hear the fighters shouting, 'A cow mooing!' as they advance towards each other. The police know that their own lives are in danger, so they just leave the two sides to clash."

A fight always ended with one side retreating, leaving hundreds of dead and wounded behind.

"That can't be allowed,' I told the security committee. "The law is very clear when it comes to the role of the police in separating fights and dispersing riots. No guns are to be fired in the air. Especially not if they sound like mooing cows! When the fighting gets out of hand the police have the authority to shoot at anyone disregarding their orders. They can't just stand by as people kill and get killed. Their job is to be more than just witnesses!"

"Yes, but the police are not protected," someone said. "Not long ago a policeman shot a person in a fight at Mawut Apuk. The policeman was arrested, tried, and sentenced to imprisonment! No policeman will want to kill anybody and run the risk of being punished for doing his duty."

"Well, I will authorize the police in writing to shoot to kill when separating a fight," I promised. "If anybody considers that a crime, I will be the first to be taken to court."

"They say that if two sides are fighting, the police should shoot at an equal number of persons on both sides," I added. "That is not correct. If one side obeys the order to fall back, and the other side continues to advance towards them, then the police should shoot at the advancing side only."

The first fight after our discussion in which a person was killed by a policeman, was between Aguok and Kuac. A police sergeant came to my house at midnight and informed me that the Kuac and the Aguok were gathered in huge numbers and that they were ready to attack each other early the next morning. I went to my room and fetched a document. It was an abstract of the law dealing with the dispersal of fighters and rioters. It was a bright, moonlit night, and we sat down on two chairs.

"You will be protected by this letter," I said as I handed my letter of authorization to him.

"Yes, but the law mentions only 'officers'", he said. "What if you are not a commissioned officer?"

"In this context 'officer' means the senior policeman among those present. Even a constable can be regarded as an officer in the eyes of the law." I added: "In our job we always have to choose the lesser evil to avoid total disaster."

At about ten the following morning I received a report that one man from Kuac had been shot dead by a policeman. The fighters had dispersed immediately. I ordered the police to pull back, assuring them that the two sides would not attack again.

The head-chief of Kuac complained to me about his person killed by the police and wanted the policeman to be arrested and charged but I refused, he went and complained to the province judge Donato Mabior Mawien in Wau. Donato asked me to explain what took place, which I did and he was satisfied with my explanation and the policeman was not charged.

When someone is killed by the police, we Sudanese stop talking about fighting. But if the men kill one another, even if hundreds have been killed, they would start planning the next confrontation – to take revenge.

I have been told that since 1981 up to this day, as I'm writing, the Aguok and the Kuac have not fought each other again.

Other tribes continued the custom, though. There was a second incident, this time between Thon and Cuar on one side, and the Noon on the other. Again one person was killed by the police.

The third confrontation was between the two sections of Aweil Ajuong and Lou against Noon. I was on my way back from a visit to Akoc, accompanied by Captain Edward Wol Laang and three policemen, when I was informed of the warriors preparing to attack. We left the road and went to the *toch* to see what was going on. A huge crowd was gathered under a big tree. As I approached, they ran away, leaving behind a goat they had just slaughtered. I put it on my car, and went to the next group, where the same thing happened again. They ran away, leaving a slaughtered goat. In both cases the goats had just been killed, they had not been skinned yet.

The third group that I found under a tree in a nearby village turned out to be soldiers and policemen.

"What are you doing here?" I wanted to know.

"We have been sent to prevent the tribes fighting. But they won't listen to us. In spite of our presence, they continue fighting. Every time the sides clash people get killed. To make things worse, we have run out of ammunition. What can we do? We fear for our own lives. All we ask is to be allowed to go back to Aweil."

"What has become of your ammunition?" I asked. "What have you been shooting at? Is that what you have been trained for – shooting at nothing?"

"We fire shots in the air to deter the fighters, but they just shout, 'It's the mooing of a cow!' and continue to advance."

I told them to line up, as for a parade. "You are ignorant of what you are supposed to do when people ignore you," I told them. I produced a copy of the law and started reading it to them, explaining what their role was in such a situation. Before I had finished, the women in a nearby village started shouting that Ajuong and Lou were coming.

"Oh, good!" I responded. "I'm glad the fight is going to take place in my presence. I'll show you how to separate the fighters."

Telling the driver to follow in the car, I accompanied the policemen and soldiers to where the warriors were gathered. The Lou and Ajuong had crossed the Amatnyang River. We walked past the first group and stopped before the middle group.

"Who are you?" I asked.

"We are Lou and Ajuong."

"Well, I'll tell you who I am," I countered. "I am the assistant commissioner of Gogrial and a first-class magistrate. I have the authority to shoot anyone fighting."

After talking to the Lou and Ajuong group, I asked them to cross the river back to their territory. They hesitated. An elderly man among them told them to heed to my orders but still they wouldn't. I then told the elderly man to cross the river back alone and leave them behind. When the man crossed, they all followed suit.

Then we returned to the group we had passed, and asked them to cross the river as well. They were about to comply with my order, when those who had crossed the river before them, started to insult them, warning them not to cross. They had got up and were approaching us in a roundabout way.

Meanwhile we became aware of a third group advancing towards Awan, whom they thought were running away from them. What actually happened, was that the people of Awan had recognized me, and they knew what had taken place in the two previous fights in the Gogrial area. They knew I would order them to be shot at if they continued to advance. As they withdrew to a nearby forest, however, I noticed a very strong left-handed man holding a large shield made of buffalo skin firmly to his chest, and moving to the edge of the crowd.

"Watch that left-handed man," I told the Arab soldier standing near me. "Shoot when he tries to raise his arm." I noticed that the other warriors were holding their spears ready to follow the example of their leader. As the left-handed warrior raised his arm to throw a spear at us, the soldier fired at him. And the whole force followed suit. I had to shout at them to stop. The warriors retreated across the river, leaving four wounded men on the ground. I told the wounded that I was taking them to Gogrial hospital. They were reluctant to allow me to, but I said that it was I who had ordered them to be shot and as a responsible person I could not leave them in the middle of the *toch*. They were from Aweil, after all! I promised that I would take care of them throughout their treatment. One of them had a broken thigh and died in Gogrial hospital. The rest recovered and were sent back to Aweil area through Wau.

The fight was over.

Much later, in 2008, when the governments of Northern Bahr el Gazal and Warrap met at Ameth, the inhabitants of Ajuong and Lou told them, "Since the time Bol Majok Adiang ordered police to shoot at us at Amat-Nyang, there have been no problems between us and the people of Awan Pajok."

Later I defused another fight, this time between the Amiol section and three other sections (Adiang, Akuar and Awan Mou). I made a solemn promise that my people would not kill themselves again as long as I remained in Gogrial. Whenever I received news of trouble brewing between Amiol and another section, I went there as quickly as possible and rounded up all those behind the problems and brought them to Gogrial with me.

One thing I appreciated about our people was that once the trouble-makers were arrested and taken away, they would not fight again. The reasons they gave for fighting were often very simple. Some of the culprits were tried and punished. In the event of simple disputes I returned with those arrested to their areas and sat down with the chiefs and elders to find the root cause of their problem. In one fight between Akuar and Amiol a person was killed, but I managed to resolve the problem without the two sides resuming their battle.

It did not last though. Only months after I had been transferred from Gogrial, there was a major fight, in which Amiol lost hundreds of its people.

There was another senseless custom that I put an end to in Gogrial. The young men used to leave the elderly, the women and children at home to cultivate the fields, while they themselves would stay with the cattle in the *toch*, drinking so much milk that they became repulsively fat. They would stay from May to August, and then come back from the *toch* to attend dancing competitions, at which the fattest man of the year was chosen. On their way home from the cattle camps, the young men would move in groups from village to village, hungrily stuffing their fat stomachs with the good food the villagers had worked so hard to produce. They argued that they were tired of milk and needed better food.

I was determined to stop the way the able-bodied portion of society who should be doing the heavy work, was exploiting the weak.

I also stopped people cultivating their plots in the town of Gogrial. During the wet season Gogrial would look like any ordinary village. It would also attract mosquitoes. So I called a meeting with the administrators of the town, including the head of departments, the organized forces and the chiefs of the areas bordering the town, especially Chief Wek Kuanyin Agoth, who had a number of tribesmen living in the town's residential area. We all agreed that the town should not be cultivated.

The residents of the town were all informed of the ruling in February, and again every month. Yet when the rains started, the people of Gogrial began cultivating as usual. "The white man who ruled Gogrial in the past did not prevent us from cultivating our fields. The Arabs who took over from him had no objection either, nor did the Southerners who succeeded him. Who is this Bol Majok Adiang to think he can stop us? He comes from Wunrok. What makes him think he is better than us?"

So I left them to cultivate their plots, and waited until their *dura* stood about a metre high. "What should we do now?" I asked the members of the administrative committee. "It's too late to do anything now," some said. But I told them that we needed to take tough decisions. "If we let them get away with this, we will never succeed in doing anything difficult in the future." I told them that we were still waiting for the town to be surveyed. When the town planners came, houses would be knocked down to make space for roads. "How can we expect them to accept that if we do not take a stance now? We have no option but to cut down all the *dura* in town," I said.

Next I spoke to the security committee. "You are the right hand of the administration," I said. "To implement such a very difficult decision you'll have to persuade your men to cooperate fully. Tomorrow we'll begin with the fields of the soldiers, then of the police and the prison warders. Only then will we move to the fields of the ordinary people."

The information was sent out in the evening, with a warning that any attempt to challenge the decision would be met with dire consequences. Many people did not sleep well that night. Everyone was up talking about what would happen the following morning.

I put on a *jalabiya* and went out to asses the reaction of the people. Those who welcomed the decision were about equal in number to those who opposed it. Some friends of mine, including my close friend William Majak Kur Maloc came to me with a request to change my mind. "I'm convinced that I'm doing the right thing," I said, "And it is lawful."

"Well, we're leaving for Wau in the morning. You can do your ugly work in our absence."

"I don't need your support," I told them.

The next morning the organized forces assembled in front of my office and, led by the members of the security committee and Chief Wek Kuanyin Agoth, we marched first to the fields of the soldiers, then to homes of the police and the prison headquarters some distance away from the town centre, cutting and removing their crops. When we reached the residential area, the residents admitted that they could not object, since they were not the only ones to be targeted. School children poured out of their classrooms uninvited and began to uproot the young dura shoots. They ran from field to field, shouting "We are cows! We are grazing!"

Within four hours the whole town was cleared of vegetation, in my presence. There was no resistance. "We have now cleared the town of dura, which is a useful plant." I told my depuy Albino Mathiang Thiep. "Now we won't tolerate wild and useless grass taking the place of the crops we have uprooted."

That year cases of malaria were greatly reduced in Gogrial. Even those who had initially opposed soon congratulated me.

I had been in Gogrial for about a year, when the 1982 elections came. Some members of the Sudan African National Union (SANU) in Juba hoped that I would support them for election to represent Gogrial, but they were uncertain of my political stance, so they decided that I should be removed from Gogrial and be replaced with someone who would be certain to support their candidates.

They enlisted the support of the minister of local government of Southern Sudan in Juba, Major General Joseph Kuol Amuom, himself a member of SANU. Kuol ordered my transfer to Tonj, and in my place appointed Mabior Acuil Agoth, whose brother, Deng Acuil Agoth was one of the candidates for the Gogrial constituency. In Tonj I was not involved in the elections, as the election officers had been appointed long before my arrival. As an assistant commissioner I was not supposed to run elections anyway. There were junior officers to undertake the task. As administrators we were trained to be totally neutral in any elections. We were not allowed to belong to any specific party, although we could vote. Not all administrators, however, complied.

Even though Gogrial had got rid of me, all SANU candidates for that constituency lost their seats. It was also after my departure that the great battle between Amiol and Akuar, which I have mentioned earlier, took place.

The 1982 elections were the last to be run by the autonomous South. The legislative assembly elected James Tombura as the president of Southern Sudan. Under Tombura, the people of Equatoria rose up against the people of Bhar el Ghazal and Upper Nile and asked for the South to be spilt into three regions. This coincided with the plans of the central government which also wanted to abolish local autonomy in the South. The Addis Ababa Agreement was made under Nimeiri but most of the influential Northerners blamed him for having given the South local autonomy, allowing them to grow stronger, more aware of the benefits of democracy. They feared that this would lead to the separation of the South. This pressure from the North and the demands of the people of Equatoria encouraged Nimeiri to cancel the Addis Ababa Agreement, which he said was not a Qoran nor a Bible. He abolished local autonomy in Southern Sudan and upgraded the three Southern Provinces of Bahr el Ghazal, Upper Nile and Equatoria into states with their headquarters in Wau, Malakal and Juba respectively. He also turned the six Northern Provinces into states to put the whole country into the same status.

Bahr el Ghazal was then divided into three provinces – Lakes, Western Bahr el Ghazal and Eastern Bahr el Ghazal. Lakes, was composed of Tonj, Rumbek and Yirol Area Councils with their headquarters in Rumbek. Western Bahr el Ghazal, was composed of Wau and Raga Area Councils with their headquarters in Wau and Eastern Bahr el

Gogrial

Ghazal, was composed of Aweil and Gogrial Area Councils with their headquarters in Aweil.

I was promoted to grade three deputy executive director, and transferred to Aweil as an executive director. I had to rush to be there in time for a visit of President Nimeiri to Aweil. When that was over, I went back to Tonj to collect my family and belongings.

While I was away, my deputy in Aweil, Justine Jok Ayoc, agreed with two Falata brothers, Ali and Suleiman Goni, to rent a house in Aweil residential area (*malakai*) from them to be used as offices for the area council, as most of the offices of the area were occupied by provincial staff. The rent they had agreed on was one thousand Sudanese pounds per month, to be paid annually in advance. Residents of Aweil working in the area council did not approve of the contract, and purposely delayed payment, pending my return.

On the day I arrived in Aweil with my family, two officials came to my house to inform me of the contract. I agreed with them. "One thousand Sudanese pounds per month paid annually in advance! That is a huge amount!" I said. "We cannot do this without informing the commissioner. I'll talk to him."

Meanwhile a messenger arrived from the Falata brothers with a ram for me. "Listen, I told him. My family is exhausted after the long journey from Tonj. Take it back. I'll send for it when I want it."

Then I went to see the commissioner Major General Joseph Kuol Amuom, who was the minister of local government in the government of Southern Sudan. He had just been appointed as the first commissioner of the newly created Eastern Bahr el Ghazal province. I explained what had happened, and gave him an alternative. There was a very good brick house in the area belonging to the police. Its roof had been blown off by the wind and it was in a neglected state but it could be renovated for about twelve thousand Sudanese pounds – as much as we would otherwise have had to pay the Falata brothers every year. It had a good floor that did not need plastering, and the house could be divided into four good offices, enough to accommodate the staff of the area council. And when we built new offices, this house would be of good use to the police.

The contract with the Falata brothers was cancelled. The ram was not brought back, and I did not send for it.

CHAPTER 13

Family

My son Bol Bol Majok, who was born in Cueibet in 1977, had since birth suffered from a disturbing medical condition. I took him to see many different doctors, and each time he was sent away with antibiotics.

Then one day we consulted a Northern Sudanese doctor, Salah in Wau, who diagnosed him with congenital heart condition that prevented normal development.

"You are wasting your money and your time going from one doctor to another," he said. "Your son was born with a heart defect that no medicine can cure. What he needs is an operation. And for that, I would strongly advise you to take him to Egypt."

I followed his advice and went back to Aweil to prepare for our trip to Khartoum where I would obtain travel visas to Egypt for the three of us – my second wife Veronica, my son Bol and myself. In April 1983, we travelled to Khartoum and I proceeded with my son Bol Bol to Egypt and left my wife in Khartoum.

The Egyptian hospital told me that, due to the young age of the child (he was only seven) an operation and treatment would be costly – the equivalent of sixteen thousand Sudanese pounds. But the hospital would charge me only half the amount. Major General Joseph Kuol Amuom had given me a thousand US dollars when I left, but the medical tests alone soon exhausted that amount.

I called my wife Veronica back in Khartoum. "You'd better come back to Sudan with Bol, and try to raise the money here," she suggested.

"No!" the Egyptian doctors said. "Further delay will not be in the interests of the child."

Still, I was about to book a seat on a plane to Sudan, when I ran into a student from Twic studying in Egypt. "There is something you could try," he said. "The deputy governor of Bahr el Ghazal, Aldo Ajou Deng Akuei, is in Cairo. Why don't you go and see him about your problem?"

I was reluctant. "How? Will he be prepared to see me?"

"The African students are playing a football match this afternoon. We expect him to attend."

So I took my son Bol with me. At the football stadium, we found the deputy governor already seated, and I was allowed to go and greet him. Ajou Deng Akuei immediately recognized me. We had been classmates at Rumbek Secondary School! He greeted me warmly. He held my son between his legs. "There is a problem with this child," he said. "What is it?" I told him everything and he invited me to come to his hotel the following morning. He and his wife welcomed little Bol and me and offered us tea, cold drinks and food.

"I'll help you with some money," he promised. "But you will have to go to Khartoum to collect it."

"Thank you," I said. "The problem is that I will have to spend a lot of money just to get to Khartoum and back. But my wife Veronica is there already. Perhaps we can arrange for her to receive the money and bring it to Cairo."

Ajou Deng Akuei agreed, and when he got back to Khartoum he directed the minister of finance, Cornelio Koryom Mayiik, to give a certain amount to my wife. Koryom, however, told my wife that she would have to follow him to Wau.

I had a better idea. My third wife, Acol Ayuel Rehan's millionaire cousin Cypriano Cyer Ayuel Rehan, was in Khartoum. She fell ill once, and had to be taken to Egypt for treatment, Cyer was the one who lent me the money I needed – which, within a month of my return, I paid back. Cyer trusted me. So I suggested that I would ask Cyer to lend us the amount, promising that the minister of finance would refund his money in Wau. It was agreed, and a document was drawn up. My second wife Veronica whom I had left in Khartoum was asked to collect the money from Cypriano Cyer.

"All right," Cyer told my wife Veronica, "even if the state fails to honour the agreement, I know that Bol will pay." My wife exchanged the money for US dollars, and joined me in Cairo.

We waited for two months at Kasr El-Aini Hospital. It was arranged that Prof. Jaafer Hussein would perform the operation, but some visiting American doctors studied Bol's case and recommended Prof. Anwar Balba instead, and the Egyptian doctors took their advice.

At last one evening we were told that the operation had been scheduled for the next morning.

"This evening you are not allowed to eat anything," I told my young son. "Your operation is tomorrow."

"That's good, Dad," he said. "I'm tired of waiting. I want to go home."

I knew how much he missed his mother and brothers and sisters.

I could not eat either, and tossed our dinner into the bin. My heart was beating fast. They came to inform us of the time of the operation. "You stay here in the ward," I told Bol. "I'll quickly go to the hotel to tell Veronica about this." The hotel was in Manila, not far from the hospital, and I knew the area, but in my disturbed state I walked past it four times without recognizing it. I was about to turn back, when I realized that I was at the entrance. It was very late when I got back to the hospital. The security guards knew me, and allowed me through the gate.

That night I could not sleep at all. Unlike Bol, I was aware of what had been happening at the hospital in the two months we had spent waiting. I knew that half of the patients who were pushed into the theatre, died there. "Please don't tell Bol about it," I begged the nurses. But Bol was wondering about the patients who were not brought back to the ward. "Where is Mohamed?" he asked me one day. "Why hasn't he come back?" Mohamed was Bol's age, a boy from a small town near the Libyan border. His case was simple compared to Bol's, but he did not survive the operation. "Don't worry about him," I said. "His was a simple operation and has gone home." I was thankful that the relatives of the deceased did not wait in the ward and that Bol never saw them weeping.

"Will they also discharge me immediately after the operation if my case is a simple one, Dad?" Asked Bol

"We'll accept God's will," I replied, lamely.

When Bol was wheeled to the theatre, almost everyone in the ward got up from their beds and accompanied him up to the door of the theatre. He was pushed in, and I remained on the veranda, sitting alone, clutching some of his clothes. My wife joined me after an hour. I thought the operation had started by that time, but then we saw Prof. Anwar Balba arrive with a large team of doctors, some carrying cameras. We sat there all day, watching the doctors emerging from the theatre, and going back again. The expression on their faces told us nothing.

It was six o'clock in the evening when Prof. Anwar Balba at last appeared. "Your child is okay," he told us.

"Go home, and get some sleep. You have nothing to be concerned about."

That was all! After waiting for so many hours!

"Can we please just see him?" I begged.

"No, not yet," he said. "But why are you so upset? Is he your only child?"

"We have more children, but that does not mean that going home to Sudan with a dead child will not be very painful!"

"You will be the sick ones if you do not go home now and rest," he said.

We took his advice, but could hardly sleep that night. Before six o'clock we were back at the hospital. We had not eaten for twenty-four hours. When, at midday, we accepted that we were not going to see Bol, we went to have breakfast, then returned to wait.

At last, on the fourth day, we were allowed into the intensive care unit. We saw many wires attached to him, connected to computers, so many tubes for different functions! Bol recognized us, but was unable to speak. He tried, but choked in his saliva. He closed his eyes, and we were asked to leave.

Three days later, Bol was moved to a ward for patients who were less severely ill, and after another three weeks, to his original ward, where he spent four months. The wound took a long time to heal. When at last he was discharged, we waited for another month before returning to Sudan. But we were happy. Before the operation, I used to carry Bol upstairs – he could not climb a single step. Now he was still looking pale and weak, but he was able to run upstairs and wait for us there.

Prof. Jaafer Hussein, who first examined Bol in his private clinic and referred him to Kasr El-Aini Hospital, explained

Bol's operation to us. He said that the condition was referred to as 'total anomalous pulmonary venous connection'. Normally pulmonary veins return oxygenated blood from the lungs to the left atrium of the heart from where it is pumped to the rest of the body. But in Bol's case all four pulmonary veins were malpositioned and made unusual connections to the systemic venous circulation. During the operation the veins were removed from their position and attached in the proper position in the left atrium.

"Your son's operation is only the second of its kind in the history of Egypt," the professor told me. "The first case was in 1957, and the patient did not survive."

We were finally back in Sudan and travelled to Aweil in October 1984. In our absence, my wife (and Bol's mother) Acai Ayuel Dual had left Aweil with four kids, Wal, Ajal, Ngor and Abuk for Wunrok where she gave birth to a son, Deng. Her eldest daughter, Aker was left at Commissioner Joseph Kuol Amuom's house as she was already attending school. My third wife, Acol Ayuel Rehan was in Gol village with her parents, where she had gone with her baby boy, Ajal.

CHAPTER 14

An Attempt on my Life in Aweil

Only four of us were left in the house in Aweil after the rest of my family had travelled to a village in Twic - the three of us who had returned from Egypt, and my daughter Aker. War had broken out between the Sudan government and the SPLM/A while I was in Egypt. In Awiel, every local government officer but me had a guard or guards. Although I was the most senior administrator in the province, I was not given guards and I did not ask for any. After I had been in Awiel for less than a month, some soldiers from Mathiang garrison came to my house at exactly eleven o'clock one night. They arrived in a car. We had just put off the lights and gone to bed. I thought that they were guests from Wau and both of us, my wife and I, came out to the verandah.

The moon was very bright and we realized that they were soldiers, not guests. They got out of the car and ran round the house, meeting in front of the main verandah. My wife and I stood on the verandah, on one side of the door. They were on the other side. The soldiers saw us and shouted, "Come out, come out," all of them shouting at the same time.

"Who do you want?" I asked.
"You, the one speaking."
"And who am I?"

They just repeated, "Come out!"

"Who sent you to my house?"

The soldiers ignored my question and continued to shout at me to come out.

"I won't come if you don't tell me who wants me!"

One of them said, in Arabic, "Nal el din-nak."

This was an offence against my religion!

"Nothing good will come of talking to you if you are going to insult me," I said.

I took my wife's hand and we went back into the bedroom. We locked the door behind us. One of the soldiers cut the wire netting of the veranda with a knife and pulled back the bolt, and another entered and tried to open the bedroom door, but he found it locked. He left and ran back to his comrades. The soldiers continued threatening me, telling me that it would be in my own interests to come out. I did not reply. I put on my clothes and my wife did the same. The children who were in the other room woke and joined us. The house was an English type of building; all the rooms, including the kitchen and bathroom, were interconnected.

I cautiously moved from the main room to the kitchen, to see see if the path leading from the kitchen door to the gate was open. My wife held on to my shirt, telling me not to leave the room without her. The children followed, clinging to their stepmother. We all moved through the dark room to the kitchen, knocking against beds and tables in the dark.

Very slowly I opened the outer door. There was a soldier pointing his gun directly at the door! I closed the door very quickly and we went back through the rooms the way we had come, and entered the bathroom. The bathroom had no door leading out. I opened the window and found that the soldiers' car was parked right in front of the window.

The officer in command was still sitting in the car close to the window. We could just stare at him. Our movement through the rooms apparently alarmed the soldiers. They did not know that the rooms were interconnected and thought that the movement inside was of many people, possibly bodyguards taking positions. Some soldiers who had been listening from the front door, went to the officer and told him that there was a lot of movement in the house.

I stood in the bathroom listening to them talking. The officer instructed the soldiers to guard the house well, while he went back to the garrison for further orders. I watched and listened as, on his way, he stopped at the officers' mess, less than a hundred metres away.

"Did you say that there were no guards in the house?" he asked the officers.

"Yes, there are no guards."

"Then how do you explain the number of people moving about in the house?"

"We don't know," they replied.

The officer proceeded to the garrison. When he returned after fifteen minutes he used the car's white and red lights to signal to the soldiers. Standing at the window, we saw them run trom both sides of the house and get into the car very quickly. They drove off into the direction of the garrison.

When the car was gone, my wife Veronica and my daughter Aker ventured out through the main door. The two of them ran in different directions round the house to make sure that all the soldiers were gone. Then together they ran to the commissioner's house. They bypassed the guards, crept through the fence and knocked at the back door.

Minutes later I saw the commissioner's car coming out of his gate and driving away in the direction of the army commander's house. Commissioner General Joseph Kuol Amum, as I heard later, asked Brigadier Martin Kejeboro, who was a southerner, what the soldiers wanted in the house of the executive director at midnight. Brigadier Martin told the commissioner that he was not aware of what had happened. He called the officer on duty and told him to go to my house to find out what was going on. I saw the commissioner's car returning to his house.

After a while, the officer on duty came out and got into into an armoured car. But instead of coming to my house, he drove north to the residential area of the rice scheme workers. There he fired several rounds of ammunition into the direction of the *toch*.

I was sitting on the veranda with my son Bol as the armoured car passed very close to us. We were caught in the headlights, but remained seated. The car did not stop, but went back to the commander's house. After a few minutes, my wife and my daughter Aker were brought back home by the commissioner's guards. We closed the doors and went to sleep.

I was not afraid. Everything passed as in a dream. On Saturday morning news spread of what had happened to me and my family during the night and a number of citizens came to visit us. The commissioner of police, Colonel Abdel Jubar Wed Thiep, allocated to my house eleven policemen to guard us. He issued stern orders that no-one was to be admitted to my compound at night –certainly no soldiers.

"If any soldiers arrive in the night and try to enter by force, I want you to stop them by force. I will listen for the sound of gunfire, and come to your rescue."

The policemen would be on duty from five o'clock every evening until six the next morning. And they were to continue doing that until they were relieved by another team.

The army security officer visited me that afternoon and asked me what had happened. I told him everything. He tried to convince me that the soldiers who had come to my house were rebels. The ground around my house was wet and I showed him where the car had parked and where soldiers' bootprints were.

The police guards spent the night in my house and on Sunday morning they carried their bedding to the store and left for their homes. Immediately afterwards, at about nine o'clock, the soldiers came back under the command of a sergeant. They found me in a *jalabia*.

"We are looking for the owner of this house," they told me.

"I'm the owner."

"Okay. We need to search your house."

"Will you show me your search warrant, please."

"We are doing this under emergency law. We don't need a search warrant."

"All right," I said. "Go ahead."

"Come with us."

They proceeded to ransack my house. We first entered my bedroom and they saw my shotgun in a corner and took it. The soldiers also found a pistol under my pillow. They then searched the rest of the house and stacked all the boxes, including those that contained the belongings of my other wives, on the verandah. My wives who had travelled back to Wunrok village in Twic had locked the boxes in which they stored their clothes and other belongings and left them in the house. The soldiers ordered me to open all the boxes. Veronica, the only wife present, opened her box, and the children and I followed suit. I told the soldiers the rest of the boxes were locked because they belonged to the wives who had moved to a nearby village and I had no spare keys.

"Well, then force them open," the sergeant ordered. "If you don't, we will."

"Go ahead," I said.

But one of his men, a corporal who looked like a Southerner or a citizen from Western Sudan, called the sergeant, an Arab, aside and talked to him. When they returned, they told me to take all the boxes, including the locked ones, back to the store. The sergeant told me to relax while they went around the house searching everywhere, using sharpened iron points to probe for whatever we might have buried. They even searched the rubbish heap.

Then Lt. Colonel Charles Riak Yak, the deputy commissioner of police, arrived and found the soldiers in the house.

"What are you doing here?" he asked them. "What do you want?"

"We have been sent from the garrison to search this house, and to take the owner – and whatever we find - back with us."

"I'll take him to the garrison in my car."

"No," they replied. "Our orders are that he accompany us on foot."

Charles was annoyed and objected. But I told him to just leave them to carry out their orders. "What was really bad, was what happened last night. If there is anything the army wants me for, you had better not get involved."

So Charles went off to the provincial commissioner's house to tell him what was going on and we set out for the army garrison. We passed between the commissioner's house and that of the army commander. The commissioner saw us and he sent a police corporal to tell the sergeant that he wanted them to stop at his house.

The sergeant refused, saying that he had a lot to do at the garrison and had no time to go to the commissioner.

During the war, the Northerners regarded Southern officials as rebels and had no respect for Southern leaders. So, the corporal went back and we continued our walk to the garrison.

When we reached Aweil Civil Hospital, Lt. Colonel Charles came in a car with a single policeman sitting in the back. He stopped us and told the sergeant that I was not going to move one inch from that spot. It was an order from the provincial commissioner of Eastern Bahr el Ghazal and the chairman of the provincial security committee.

"Listen I have orders to search this man's house and to take him and whatever we found in the house back to the garrison. We're operating under emergency law and I take my orders from the army commander, not from you – or anyone else."

He turned to me. "Move," he ordered.

"Don't you move one inch!" Charles said.

By this time a huge number of people had gathered around us. Patients who had come to the hospital left the queues to come and see what was happening. People came running from the market. Policemen, prison warders and even soldiers joined them.

The civilians were very angry and ready to riot. They said that if I had escaped death at night, then they would not allow me to die during the day. An army captain also dropped by and asked the sergeant what was happening.

"It's this police colonel, Charles Riak, who thinks he can stop soldiers on their way to the garrison and who wants to release someone the commander of the army has ordered me to search and arrest," the sergeant said.

The captain then turned to Charles, who informed him that he was executing the orders of the provincial commissioner.

The army captain remained silent for a moment scrutinizing the sergeant from head to toe, then asked what my position was. Some bystanders told him I was the executive director of the province. He again kept silent for a while, looking at me in the same manner he did at the sergeant. He then turned to the sergeant and said, "Let him go, but take the pistol and the shortgun to the garrison."

I got into Charles's car and went with him to the commissioner's house. My wife and children who were following me returned to our house and the crowd dispersed. While I was still in the commissioner's house, the police commissioner Abdel Jubar heard the news of my arrest and went directly to the garrison to find out if I was still under detention or released. He brought my pistol and the shortgun back to me from the army garrison.

I suggested to both commissioners - of the province and of the police - that they call a security committee meeting to find out the reason why the army was after me. Monday came and the security committee meeting didn't take place. On Tuesday the commissioner sent for me very early in the morning. He told me he was called to Wau by the governor and added that it was not safe for him to leave me in Aweil as acting commissioner in his absence. He asked me to accompany him to Wau and back again. I went home and told my wife and children that we were leaving for Wau together with Commissioner Joseph Kuol Amum for security reasons. We arrived at Wau at midday and my family and I proceeded to Gogrial and reached my home at Wunrok that same day. I stayed for three days and returned to Wau.

When I got back to Wau, I received news from Aweil that Deng Deng Akot, a citizen of Aweil and a university graduate, was arrested by the army in the market area a day after we left. He was taken to the army garrison and killed.

An Attempt on my Life in Aweil

Many people from Aweil said I was lucky to escape death. They said it was the death which I escaped that had taken Deng Deng Akot. Many friends wrote to me asking me not to return to Aweil. It was in Wau, when I heard of Deng Deng's death, that real fear gripped me. For the first time since the incident, I spent an entire night sleepless. I realized, for the first time, that I had escaped imminent death.

In the history of Southern Sudan, from Anya-Nya I to the SPLM/A, it had never happened before that soldiers went to the house of a Southerner with orders to arrest him and came back without that person after they had found him in the house. My case was the first.

There is a well documented case of a prison officer in Rumbek during Anya-Nya I. Some soldiers went to his house to arrest him. They found him with his bodyguards. All of them resisted arrest and the soldiers ended up killing them all. The officer and the guards also killed a number of soldiers. The Northern Arabs believed that once an attempt was made to arrest a Southern official for any reason and failed, the official would immediately leave for the bush to join the Anya-Nya rebels. Their only alternative was to take that person to the military garrison or kill him on the spot. I would have died like the prison officer in Rumbek, if Providence had not ordained that, for some purpose, I should live.

CHAPTER 15

Growing Unrest

My transfer to Aweil was cancelled due to complications when the director of local government in Wau, Samuel Ater Dak, was purged from the Bahr el Ghazal local government. The director general, Caesar Arkangelo, told me not to go to Aweil, but to Rumbek instead, as executive director. Paul Marial Dot would be sent to take over from Samuel Ater.

I dispatched my wife Acol to Aweil to collect our furniture, and when she arrived back, I got onto the same lorry and we headed for Rumbek. Paul Marial Dot took me to the house he had been occupying in a good location, and we moved in.

That very evening there was an attempt on the life of the commissioner, Gabriel Mathiang Rok by a police officer, 2nd Lt. Enock Manyuon. The two of them had quarreled and Enock swore vengeance. When he saw Gabriel sitting outside a policeman's house in the police residential area, discussing some matter, he rushed to his own house and fetched his gun. The moon was shining brightly, but nobody saw him as he approached the house. And Enock was not aware that Gabriel had finished what he wanted to say, and that the owner of the house was showing him out through another gate in the fence. Three other people were now occupying the chairs. Without bothering to find out if Gabriel was still one of them, Enock opened fire and killed two of them. Then he ran away, in the direction of my house.

I had heard the shots being fired, and then I saw someone running, passing through my compound. Enock must have been unaware that the house was occupied, but when he saw the children inside (I did not have any guards yet), he disappeared very quickly.

Enock escaped to the forest that night and joined the rebels (SPLA), informing them that he had killed Gabriel Mathiang Rok. Soon Gabriel's relatives came running to the town, only to discover that Gabriel was alive and well, and that two innocent men had died in his place.

Both Gabriel Mathiang Rok and Paul Marial Dot left for Wau that same day. I had to take over right away. The only problem he mentioned to me was that of the primary school teachers threatening togo on strike because they had not been paid for many months.

"Look for the ringleaders if they go ahead with the strike," Gabriel said to me.

"Maybe you should do something to solve their problem when you get to Wau," I countered.

The following morning the teachers called a meeting at one of the schools. "We've heard what the commissioner said," they told me. "Perhaps you would like to repeat it to us in the tone he used."

"Listen, I'm only one night old in Rumbek," I replied. "Give me two weeks, and I'll see what I can do for you. And I'll urge the commissioner in Wau to make an effort too. But I can tell you one thing: what is between you and the government is a contract. You are to teach the children, and they are to pay your salaries."

"If we receive no response from the commissioner," I promised, "I will allow you to remain in your houses while you look for other sources of income to feed your children. I certainly won't force you to work if I can't pay you."

Gabriel Mathiang Rok remained in Wau for six months.

Meanwhile more trouble was brewing. The SPLA's Rhino Batallion under commander Daniel Awet Akot had invaded the area and captured Yirol. Some employees from Yirol escaped to Rumbek and I had to take care of them.

The Sudanese army commander of Lakes Province was an Arab, based at Malou, about ten miles from Rumbek town. He would come into Rumbek from time to time to check on the forces in the garrison. I disagreed with him on two issues. Firstly, whenever there was a night attack on the town, the soldiers from the garrison would concentrate their bombardment around the commissioner's house, even if there was no shooting from that direction. One day two cars were damaged in the commissioner's compound, and a seven-year-old boy was killed. The commander disregarded my protests.

Secondly, the commander failed to attend the security committee meetings, sending a junior officer instead. This was not allowed. The rule was that he could only send a representative if he was outside Rumbek or Lakes Province. Moreover, the committee members were his seniors. He was a colonel, whilst I was a grade three director and the commissioners of both the police and prisons were brigadiers.

One day the commander sent me a message that the regional security committee was coming to Malou, and we were expected to meet them there before ten o'clock. How could I trust the commander? When members of the security committee came to me to make arrangements for the trip to Malou, I told them, "We are not going. I think it is a trap. They are going to ambush us and blame it on the SPLA."

"What if the commander did tell the truth, and the regional security committee members do come from Wau?" they replied.

"I'll be the one to answer," I assured them. "I am the head of the security committee here. The governor of Wau is the head of the committee that is supposed to visit us, and whenever he is planning a visit to Rumbek, he must first inform me by radio. I have received no such message."

The commanders of the police and prisons, however, did not want to fail their bosses, so I allowed them to leave for Malou the next morning without me. The Arab commander of the town's garrison also left for Malou early in the morning, accompanied by a number of soldiers. That was not right, I told them. I was the one who was supposed to be accompanied by the forces when I travelled – not they.

Anyway, the other members of the security committee stayed with me. And the security committee that was supposed to come from Wau, never turned up. The incident was never mentioned again.

It was now six months since the provincial commissioner Gabriel Mathiang Rok had travelled to Wau after the attempt on his life. There was no other convoy from Wau to Rumbek. The first convoy to come to Rumbek in six months was for the commissioner and for Paul Marial Dot who was coming to collect his family. The convoy spent the night at Kuarjina, and that same night Field Marshall Nimeiri was overthrown, which meant that by the time Gabriel Mathiang reached Rumbek, he was no longer the commissioner.

The commander from Malou came to Rumbek. He told me that he did not want to be involved in the affairs of the province. "I know nothing about civil administration," he said. "Please carry on with whatever you are doing." He would drop in every morning just to say hello and to enquire how I was doing, and then he would go back to Malou.

The convoy remained in Rumbek for seven days.

Paul Marial, who had been my predecessor in Rumbek, had already packed his furniture, ready to leave with the convoy, when he received a message from the residents of Rumbek asking him to remain there as their acting commissioner. He was from Rumbek, they argued. I wasn't. He accepted the call of his people. Rumbek had representatives in Wau, and they petitioned the minister of local government, Andrew Kuac Mayol and the director-general to allow Paul Marial to stay in Rumbek. They agreed and one day before the departure of the convoy, Paul received a personal message asking him to remain as the acting commissioner of the Lakes Province. There was no mention of me, Bol Majok. No-one even bothered to send me a copy of Paul's assignment or to explain to me what was going on.

I went to Paul. "You will not be using that lorry anymore," I said. "May I please use it to carry my family and my belongings to Wau?"

"But you are not being transferred!" Paul replied.

"I am a senior government officer. I know the rules and regulations governing local government. When I came to Rumbek, it was not as your deputy. I was appointed executive officer in your place. We cannot have two executive directors in one province."

Paul handed the lorry over to me to take my furniture. I myself intended to travel in a Landrover station wagon. When the convoy left for Wau I joined it with my family. That afternoon, when we reached Gel River, the military car leading the convoy hit a landmine and overturned. The passengers were badly injured, but alive. Soldiers jumped from the other cars and bombarded the surrounding bushes, but there was no response from whoever had planted the mine. They did find a letter, though, stating that there were no ambushes along the way, but that the road was mined up to Tonj.

When the wounded soldiers were being collected I noticed something very strange, something that I had heard of, but never witnessed before. The Northerners and Arabs attended only to fellow Northerners, treating them with whatever drugs they had. The Southerners were left to attend to their own men – which they did. To me it confirmed the reports that Northerners would abandon a Southerner hurt in a convoy and leave him to die if there were no Southerners to help him. The travellers in the convoy searched their boxes for vials of penicillin which they handed over to their own people only. The convoy was a large one, with many civilians travelling in it, mostly Southerners. "Don't let the Northerners have any of this!" the wounded soldiers would say as we handed them our contributions.

We spent the night at the spot where the mine had destroyed the vehicle. My family and I put down a mattress near our car and lay down to sleep. My daughter Aker chose to remain in the car. About ten metres away, a group of Arab military officers were sitting, roasting meat and drinking *siko,* a local alcoholic drink brewed of sugar and yeast. They spent the entire night drinking, talking and pointing at me. My wife and daughter were not happy at all. The two insisted we all sleep in the car, so the whole family ended up sitting in the car – three of us in the front seat, and the children in the middle seat. By this time the Arab officers were drunk and walking about. My wife and daughter would alert me whenever they came close to our car.

In the morning the mine-detection team went ahead on foot and the convoy followed. The sun was very hot. The injured soldiers complained that their wounds had started smelling. "We are going to die of these wounds," they told the convoy commander. "At this rate we'll never get to Wau alive. Please take us to the front of the convoy – and tell all those people to get into their cars so that we can move faster!" The officers were about to refuse, but the wounded men threatened to shoot. So the cars carrying the wounded men were allowed to go ahead up to Tonj. To everyone's surprise, in spite, the warning, there were no landmines on the road.

At about eight that same evening, the convoy reached Wau. The next day I reported to the director-general, Caesar Arkangelo. He did not ask why I had come, but he found temporary accommodation for me and my family in the Riverside Rest House.

After the fall of Nimeiri, it took about a month for a new government to be formed. When the government was in place, Brigadier Andrew Makur Thou was appointed governor of the Bahr el Ghazal region, and Makur Cagai became commissioner of the Lakes region.

The next group to arrive in Wau was the council employees who had fled to Rumbek after Yirol had fallen to the SPLA forces. They complained bitterly of the bad treatment they received after I had left Rumbek. Makur Cagai and Caesar Arkangelo tried to persuade me to return to Rumbek, but I refused. "It was not my choice to leave Rumbek," I told them. "It was the decision of the sons of Rumbek, who appointed Paul Marial Dot in my place. I was not happy at all with the way it was done. Now they will just have to manage on their own. Perhaps it was God's will for me. Rumbek is becoming a very difficult area. I've been lucky to escape."

So they just left me in the ministry's headquarters.

When I came back from Egypt, I had already made up my mind to join the Liberation Movement. My financial position, however, would not allow me to. My son's treatment had drained the little money I had saved. I would have to continue working until I had saved enough to sustain my family who would remain behind at home. But delay had almost cost me my life in Aweil. The security situation was not good in Wau, either. So I decided to go to Gogrial, from where I thought I could easily take my children home and prepare to join the movement. I persuaded the director-general to approve my transfer to Gogrial, although the position there was a junior one.

Then came the news of the death of Commissioner Makur Cagai in a helicopter crash, shot down over Rumbek by the SPLA forces. The commissioner and others in two helicopters had been on their first visit to Rumbek. They landed smoothly at Rumbek. The first helicopter carrying military officers took off again safely. On board the second helicopter were, among others, the commissioner and Bishop Malou Apaac. When they took off, the SPLA forces, who were waiting very close to the town, fired an SA-7 at it and hit it. The helicopter crashed killing everyone on board. Only God knows what would have happened to me if I had remained the executive officer of Lakes Province.

CHAPTER 16

Trouble with the Arab Cattle Raiders (Marahliin)

Things in Gogrial did not work out as I had hoped they would. I found Gogrial and the whole of Twic devastated by the Arab cattle raiders known as *Marahliin*. I had hoped to take my family to the village, but was compelled to take my elder wife, who had been at Wunrok with me, back to Gogrial town. That was in September 1985. In December the *Marahliin* crossed the Lol River at Pakor and looted a great number of cattle. There were some SPLA soldiers in the area under Captain Deng Dau. They tried to rescue the cattle, but were overwhelmed by the much larger *Marahliin* force and ran out of ammunition. Captain Deng Dau sent me Chief Mayuol Wol Agany, requesting my help.

I called a very urgent security meeting so that we might explore ways of solving the problem. I did not inform the people in the meeting about the chief who had brought the message. The commander of the army garrison was Lt. Colonel Zubeir Mohammad Salah, who was later to become the First Vice President under Omar-al-Bashir. He told me that the army had written orders from their general headquarters in Khartoum not to engage in any battle with the *Marahliin* when they entered Southern Sudan to loot cattle. "It's the cattle that are enabling the SPLA to fight the war against the North," he said. "The *Marahliin* are being used to deprive the SPLA of a food source. An army effort to rescue the cattle would be contrary to orders from Khartoum. It would mean assisting the enemy of the state, and of God. So, I'm very sorry I can't help the local people. You could try the police and the other organized forces."

So we decided to forget about the army, and at least visit Panliet to assess the situation the people were in. Early the next morning I left for Panliet, with a force of seventy men, made up of police, prison and wildlife officers. At Panliet we found that the *Marahliin* had already crossed the river with the cattle, and we proceeded to Wunrok and stopped at my house, south of the Lol River, then went to the town to gain information. The residents were still in their houses, hoping that they would be safe. After all, the action was about twelve miles away from them, and the *Marahliin* were known to return by the same route they had come.

There were some SPLA soldiers on the southern side of the river, and when they saw our cars some of them crossed the river to Wunrok and some went along the river to the east of the crossing point. Adhar Majic, who had been imprisoned with me in Abyei years back when I was on my way to university in Khartoum, came to my house and informed me that the SPLA force was a very small one, and that their commander, 1st Lt. Kuol (also known as Dr Kuol) was in a house at Wanatiop not far from my house.

Leaving the policemen who had come with me at my house, I went with Adhar Majic to meet the 1st Lieutenant. When the soldiers hiding in the grass saw that I was alone, they came out and took me to their commander. I was dressed in my local government uniform, with a pistol in a holster strapped to my belt. Kuol received me warmly and offered me his only chair, the one he had been sitting on. He found himself a seat on a piece of wood lying on the ground. I explained to him why I had come, and that the seventy men with me were composed of southerners only, from the police, prison and wildlife services.

"You were lucky not to catch up with the *Marahliin* at Panliet," he said. Your force of only seventy men would not have stood a chance against them. They are tough! It would have been a disaster! My men and I try to avoid direct contact with them."

"We don't want direct contact, either," I assured him. "But if we are able to reach the crossing point at Alal before them, we could perhaps lay an ambush on the other side of the river. From there we will be able to attack them at long range. We have mark 4 rifles and some Magnum guns. They have a longer range than their AK47's."

There would be no way for the *Marahliin* to attack from the flank as they usually did, I thought, because there was no crossing point besides the one they would have used to enter the area. Any attempt to cross through the tall elephant grass would be disastrous as the grass was thick, and mixed with thorny trees known as *'peth'*. Their thorns are curved like fishing hooks.

If we could put them in disarray, maybe some of the cattle would escape and disappear in the long grass before the *Marahliin* could cross the river to where they would expect to find us.

"We'll be heading for Pan-Nyok," I told Kuol. "We've left our cars unguarded."

"Your cars will be safe," he assured me. "No-one will tamper with them."

So I collected my men, crossed the river and we left for Pan-Nyok, where we stopped at the house of a spiritual leader, Cyer Cyer-dit (also known as Cyer 'Majok Lol').

"Yes, the *Marahliin* have passed this way with a lot of cattle," Cyer Cyer-dit told us. But they are much too strong for your small number of men. You'd better just allow them to take the cattle. Any attempt to fight them will be disastrous, and they will keep the cattle anyway. It's better to lose the cattle only than so many human lives as well."

I told him what I planned to do, but he remained unconvinced. "Please just show us the shortest route to the crossing point," I asked, "so that we can reach it before them."

"All right, he said," I'll send for a man who knows the route and the terrain very well. You can ask him." When the man came, Cyier Cyier-dit took him aside and talked to him in private first before he introduced him to us. We later learned from this man that the route he sent us on was the longest one, because Cyier Cyier-dit did not want us to clash with the *Marahliin*.

When at last we reached a place called Ataak about three miles from Alal River, it was eight o'clock in the evening and we were very tired and hungry. All the way from Wunrok to Pan-Nyok, and then to Ataak, we had been wading through water and mud, making our way through tall grass and thorns. We decided to spend the night at Ataak. We were trying to find accommodation in the few houses scattered around the village, when we saw the fire. The *Marahliin* had set fire to the houses at Wunbol, on the other side of Alal to provide them with light to gather their cattle.

It was not difficult to guess what had happened. The *Marahliin* must have captured a villager and made him show them the shortest way to follow to the crossing point. We gave up.

We spent the night at Ataak and walked back to Pan-Nyok in the morning. We were extremely exhausted and hungry by the time we got there at midday. A small bull was slaughtered for us, but it was not enough so satisfy the hunger of my men who needed more than just meat. I decided to return to Wunrok that same day, taking with me those men who could make it, and leaving behind those who would not be able to, to spend another night at Pan-Nyok and join us the next day. It was a relief to find our cars intact. I and the men with me spent the night in my house.

It was late evening when the men we had left behind, caught up with us. That same evening we were informed of another wave of *Marahliin* coming from the direction of Mayen Abun, heading for Wunrok. We decided to wait at Wunrok. At nine o'clock they had reached Atiok Kuel, a village about five miles away. Again they set houses and tyres alight, and people fled. We took position to help the people cross the river to the southern side. "Slow down and walk once you have crossed the river," I admonished them. We brought our cars to the riverside and switched on the searchlights, hoping that the Marahliin would realize that there were government forces at the river. The few SPLA soldiers we had met at Wunrok before we left to follow the raiders, had all gone. It may have been the searchlights that did it, but the *Marahliin* did not advance to Wunrok. They left Atiok-Kuel in a hurry, without any cattle. That same evening we also left, for Gogrial.

On my arrival at Gogrial, I was met with rumours that I had defected to the SPLA. Members of the security committee told me that it was 1st Lt. Akol Kuol Agok who had told them about me joining the freedom fighters. The lieutenant was called and he said that he had been brought the news by a man who had come from Wunrok on a bicycle. "Who is the man?" I asked. "I don't know his name, but I will be able to identify him if he comes to the market," he replied.

Three days later Akol had not found his informant yet. I blamed the members of the committee for not telling Akol to bring that person to them immediately after he had spoken to him. The information given to Akol was dismissed as a fabricated lie.

CHAPTER 17

Joining the SPLA

In February 1986 Major Deng Ajuong Malual, commander of the Nile Batallion of the SPLA, arrived in eastern Gogrial. It was the largest force to reach northern Bahr el Ghazal since the beginning of the war. Upon his arrival he visited the spiritual leader of the Adiang section, Cyer-dit Deng Thiapduok, also known as 'Ajingdit', a stepbrother of Cyer Cyer-dit whom we met at Pan-Nyok when we pursued the *Marahliin* cattle raiders. They met at Maker Cattle camp in Apuk area to discuss his strategy. Ajingdit was able to give him exact details of the devastation caused by the *Marahliin* in Gogrial and Twic in particular. He told the major that the *Marahliin* had adopted a new strategy - killing the men and elderly women and carrying away the young women and children, besides the cattle. Many children had been brought to Gogrial town for safety. He told the major that if he attacked Gogrial town, the children would be forced to return to the villages where they would be exposed to the danger of being carried away by the *Marahliin,* besides the hunger now sweeping the countryside. He added that March and April would be very hot and water would be scarce, which would make it very difficult to flee with the children when the *Marahliin* came. He therefore begged the major not to attack Gogrial town, but to concentrate on the danger posed by the cattle raiders in the countryside. The Arabs in Gogrial town should not pose any danger, he said. And he advised him to leave the running of the town to me, Bol Majok.

"If you fight the *Marahliin* and report to John Garang how many Arabs you have killed and how many guns you have captured, I'm sure he will be pleased," Ajingdit said.

"I'm sorry," Deng Ajuong replied, "but I have been sent to liberate Gogrial town. I have to obey orders."

So Deng sent only one company to Twic, while the rest of his force advanced on Gogrial town.

On 27 February my father-in-law, Ayuel 'Manyang' Rehan Nuer, sent me a message from Mangol Apuk, urging me to make up my mind whether to stay with the government or join the SPLA. If I was staying with the government, I would have to get out of Gogrial fast, as the town could not possibly withstand the attack. I immediately arranged for my family to leave.

The time had come for me to join the movement.

"Get into the car, quickly!" I told the children. "You are not going to spend the night here."

Just then we heard the first gunshots. The army reconnaissance had collided with the SPLA. My children stood there, confused. "Get into the car!" I shouted. "Move!" More people than a Landrover was meant to carry jumped into it, and it pulled away towards Twic. I remained standing outside the fence, watching them drive away. Then a bullet hit the wire netting of the veranda. I fell down flat and crawled back into the house.

My family drove right into the advancing SPLA soldiers, but as they were women and children, they were allowed to pass. I was already regretting my decision to allow my children to move off while the battle had already started. My whole family could have perished if caught in the crossfire. There was no guarantee that the SPLA would spare the lives of families and allow them to pass.

The fighting continued into the night. Most of the

residential area was set ablaze. The entire population was fleeing into the countryside. The prison was overrun, and only the police and army garrison held out till morning. The police lost two men, and the army three, including 1st Lt. Akol Kuol, the man who had accused me of joining the SPLA when I had gone to Twic. The SPLA lost more men, because they had not surveyed the town before they launched the attack. Unlike other towns they had attacked before, they found Gogrial empty when they moved in. I remained alone, an assistant commissioner without any personnel.

In the morning, two of the citizens who had left during the fighting came back to the town to speak to me – Rosario Deng Bek Bol and Aguan Nyuol Aguan, the son of my maternal uncle. I told them to inform Deng Ajuong that I was joining the SPLA, and was trying to persuade a police officer, Major Col Mayen from Gok to join me with the whole police force. Major Col Mayen, however, was not yet ready to defect. Aguan took my message to commander Deng Ajuong, and when he returned I sent him back again with a message that I would be coming in a car the following morning. On that morning, I left the commanders of the army and the police on my veranda, while I left with my bodyguards ostensibly to inspect the market. As I expected, many policemen who saw me driving off towards Twic, also decided to defect. I spent the night at Wunrok, then drove to Deng Ajuong's base near Gogrial town. I spent two days with him, after which he told me to return to Wunrok and wait for him there.

Gogrial had received government reinforcement from Wau, and Deng Ajuong was not able to capture it. Meanwhile, the *Marahliin* had stepped up their devastation in the Twic area. One day Deng Ayuong came to Wunrok and spent the night at my house. That morning we were attacked by the *Marahliin*, and I narrowly escaped with my family. My house and everything I had prepared for my family were burned to the ground. Only the cattle remained. Ajingdit's warning to Deng Ajuong had come true. He was not able to capture Gogrial town, nor could he stop the *Marahliin*'s attack and looting. Life became extremely difficult. I had to reroof two huts and I went in search of *dura* so that my family wouldn't starve when I left for Bilpham in Ethiopia for SPLA training as advised by Deng Ajuong.

I left my house at Acol Village on 1 June 1986. I took with me my third wife Acol Ayuel Rehan, her brother Maror, my two sons Ajal and Wal, and the sons of my brothers and sisters and other close relatives. My other wives and children remained.

I was going to spend a month at Mangol Apuk to assemble the recruits I was to take to Bilpam and collect some bulls for the journey, as all the cattle of Twic had been moved to the Mangol Apuk area to avoid *Marahliin* raids. By the end of June I had over a thousand men and sixty bulls (besides what we had already slaughtered for food at Mangol). Managing so many men at Mangol was complicated, so I decided to move on.

Our next stop was at Maker Apuk cattle camp, where I knew I would find Ajiingdit Deng Maduok, our spiritual leader. "I'm on my way to Bipham with a large number of recruits," I told him, hoping for his blessing.

"There will be many problems and obstacles on your way," he said. "But you should still go." He turned to the men with me. "Whenever you get into difficulties, call my name, and God will protect you on your journey."

I am a Christian and I do believe in God and Jesus Christ, but I was brought up in a society that always looked to Ajiingdit (or Cyerdit, as he was also called) in difficult times, and believed that he would help them overcome their problems. If someone from our section, especially from Adiang, walked alone at night and was suddenly overcome with fear, he would pray to Cyerdit. I am no exception. I call on God, Jesus and Cyerdit in turns.

Among the huge number of recruits were the three former government officials, my maternal uncle Donato Madut Kon Awan, Piol Ngor Majok my nephew and myself. That night at Maker we were joined by another large group of recruits, over a thousand young men led by Diing Malong and Diing Aher from Aweil. The recruits from Aweil had no bulls with them and were already showing signs of weakness. The next morning all of us moved together towards Bilpam. On the second day we decided to divide ourselves into two groups, because it was difficult to manage three thousand people spending a night at one place. The recruits joining from Aweil were more than us, so I brought some of them into my group. We called the groups battalions, naming the first one, commanded by Ding Aher, Najda. The second was called Gerger. I was the overall commander, and led the way, with Najda. The bulls were divided equally between the two groups. The second group followed a day's distance behind us. We followed the *toch*, avoiding the towns on our way, so that the people were largely unaware of our movements. If the enemy found out where we were, we knew we would be a soft target.

It was July, the season of heavy rains. We slept in the open grassland or at the cattle camps of Tonj and Rumbek. The local population contributed no bulls and we had to make do with those we had brought from Twic. About ten SPLA soldiers on their way to Rumbek joined us, but we could not rely on them for any support. As the enemy could attack at any time, we spent the rainy nights sitting up, covering out heads with small plastic sheets, clutching our belongings on our legs.

The route through the *toch*, the grassland, was a long one, and some of us fell ill due to the cold wet nights spent in the open. Hardly any of the recruits – mostly students and young men from the villages and cattle camps – had mosquito nets. My own family had to make do with what my wife had brought with her.

It took us two weeks to get to an SPLA base east of Rumbek town. We were warmly received by commander Bona Bang Dhol, who supplied us with enough bulls to last for three days. "Keep the few you have left for the journey ahead," he said. "But having so many recruits massed near Rumbek is not advisable. Yirol is a liberated town. It would be better to go there." It took us three days to reach Yirol.

1st Lt. Marial Chanuong welcomed us at Yirol, telling us that we had arrived at the best possible time – harvest time. "Spend at least a month here," he invited us. "In Bor the people are still hungry. Why don't you send your men out to help the people with the groundnut harvest? They will pay you in kind. The most difficult part of your journey is still ahead of you, and you will need the food, so be sure to save some of it."

The inhabitants of Yirol, in particular the ones from Atuot, were extremely kind. They said that they understood what had brought us so far from our homes, and did not complain about the inconveniences our presence caused them. Moreover, Marial Chanuong was a son of their own area, and they were satisfied with his administration. They even killed an elephant or two for us. My family refused to eat elephant meat, but the recruits who did soon recovered from their illnesses, and those who were weak, became strong again.

But we received bad news too. Starving survivors returning naked from Bor area urged us not to think of continuing our journey. They told us frightening stories about conditions on the islands of the Nile and the way they were treated by the people of Bor, who could only be persuaded to provide them with a little food in exchange for their clothes. Many of their comrades had died along the route, they said. Their stories affected our own recruits badly, and about a quarter of them escaped and followed the returnees from Bor back home.

Those who stayed consoled themselves: "Remember, they were there during the hunger gap. When we get there it will be harvest time. Anyway, we have some money with which we can buy food. And we have clothes to exchange."

In September 1986 we set off for Bor. The terrain between Yirol and Bor was the worst distance I have ever covered in my life. We left Yirol in the morning and arrived at a village called Tot, east of Yirol, in the evening. There were huge swarms of mosquitoes, and they did not go away in the daytime. You might be standing in the sun, and they would still bite you. The recruits who did have mosquito nets were no better off. Even if they lay down under their nets before sunset, they would find hundreds and hundreds of mosquitoes already in the nets. Those of us who did not possess nets, lit a big fire and stayed close to it all night. The mosquitoes would get into your mouth when you were speaking. You had to keep your eyes half shut and cover your ears and nose with your clothes.

We spent two days at Tot waiting for some members of our Najda group, who had stayed behind at Yirol, to catch up with us. We wondered whether they would ever come – perhaps they were having second thoughts about undertaking the journey, we thought. In the end 1st Lt. Marial did manage to persuade them to follow us. When they arrived, we moved to an evacuated cattle camp on high ground at the edge of the forest, from where a deep *toch* stretched all the way down to the Nile.

The people of Tot had warned us: "You'll only be taking more skulls and bones – your own – to the place, to add to the ones of the recruits who have already perished there." And it was true. We found skulls and bones scattered all over the camp.

On our way down to the Nile very early in the morning, we waded through cold water, so deep at places that shorter recruits had to be supported by taller ones. Some places you stepped on thick water weeds and papyrus, only to have the plants give way under you, and you had to be pulled out of the water by your comrades. At midday we arrived at the first proper branch of the Nile, as wide as the Jur River, but very deep, with a very swift current. We stood on a narrow wet piece of land surveying it, gathering the courage to cross. Then we went ahead. It took us the remainder of the day to cross to an island the size of a football field and constantly wet, on which there were three huts.

We found some men with two women but no children living on the island. They grew maize there, but when they heard of our approach, they had quickly harvested it. There weren't even any maize stalks left for us to chew. The first recruits to cross the river ahead of us had finished them. At home no one would dream of chewing maize stalks, but we were so hungry we would have eaten anything.

In Yirol I had warned the recruits to take proper care of the groundnuts they received, as there was a long hungry journey ahead of us. Some listened, keeping the raw nuts, or crushing them into a paste. But most of them did not take my advice seriously, and the careless ones finished the nuts they had before we even left Yirol. The inhabitants of the island had hidden what little they had for their own use.

As for my family, we still had some milk powder cans filled with fried or roasted nuts that my sons had brought back from working in the fields at Yirol, as well as some paste.

We had been told that a cement boat would come on the day we arrived to transport the recruits from the island to Bor mainland east of the Nile. We waited in vain. Most of the recruits were starving, and they began to cook a wild plant locally known as *apat* into a porridge. Back home *apat* was never eaten in any form.

My family and I spent the day without eating anything. That evening, like every evening after that, when everyone else had lain down to sleep, my wife would produce one can from the bag she had held securely in her lap all the time. To each person in turn she would hand a spoonful of paste. Sometimes she would refuse to eat anything herself. "You can't do that," I told her. "You are not the one finishing the paste. We are all in this together, struggling together. We don't want anyone to perish. We'll share what we have to the end. And we don't want you to be the first to starve to death!"

On our fifth morning on the island, some recruits failed to wake up. The cause of death: starvation, combined with disease! I made up my mind to offer the little money I had to one of the inhabitants of the island to take six members of my family to the mainland, a trip that would take six hours. They were my uncle Donato Madut Kon, as well as Piol Ngor Majok, Anguei Majok Anguei, Bol 'thii' Majok Adiang, Mayar Majok Adiang and a young man from Amiol named Garang, who used to carry my belongings for me and look after my children when they went to the villages at Yirol. They would have no problem finding food on the mainland, I hoped, so I kept the paste we had left to keep me and my immediate family alive for some more days. My wife and children refused to go without me. I decided that the next trip would be theirs.

When we first arrived on the island I thought that I would be the last to leave. At Yirol we were led to believe that the boat was ready and waiting to transport us to the other side, and I did not expect to spend more than three days on the island. But the fact that people were already dying of hunger, gave me second thoughts. If I could only get to the mainland, I thought, I might meet responsible people who would come to the rescue of the recruits on the island. The other option was to return to Yirol, but some of the recruits were already too weak to cross that difficult terrain again.

I waited impatiently for the canoe to return. At last, at about six o'clock that evening, it came – with the news that the cement boat was on its way and would be there in the morning. This raised our morale. Some sick recruits got up from the ground where they were lying to hear the news. I realized, however, that the boat would have to make several trips, taking at least three days to take all the recruits to the mainland.

I went to the owner of the canoe. "Do you think you could take me and my family early tomorrow morning?" I asked.

"No, I'm sorry," he replied. "It will be too risky. The rain is still coming down heavily and those stormy conditions combined with a very strong current, are very dangerous. Your relatives and I caught the storm close to the landing point. We narrowly escaped disaster."

I would just have to wait for the boat.

That night we lost three recruits. They died of malaria coupled with hunger.

When the sound of the approaching boat was heard around nine o'clock, everyone ran into the water and waded to the bank of the main Nile River, three hundred metres away. As the boat anchored some distance from the shore, the pilot shouted, "Please organize yourselves! Let the most vulnerable people get on first!" The request fell on deaf ears. No-one wanted to be left behind.

"Then form a line! Let's do this in an orderly manner!"

That also failed. When the pilot brought the boat to the shore, it hit the bank and immediately pulled back. About two hundred men had already got onto it, clinging to the side. Some fell back into the water. Only a few of them managed to swim to the shore.

I just stood there, confused, with my wife and children. When the boat left, I shouted, "Please bring us some food when you come back!" I do not think they even heard me. It took the boat two hours up the river, and one hour back. They did not bring any food. The stampede of the morning was repeated, and the boat left, to return only the following morning.

I spent the night wondering how I was going to save the lives of my family. We had no food left at all, and went to bed without the usual spoonful of groundnut paste. Before daybreak, I had the solution. I paid the owner of the canoe to take me and my family some distance into the Nile, and anchor his canoe close to where the boat would pass. We were hoping that the crew would stop the boat and call for us to come to them. It worked! We were called, and helped on board.

"Let's try it again," the pilot said. "Let's use the canoe to bring the recruits to the boat, instead of having them all rush on board. We have lost too many lives already. And if we don't limit the number of passengers, the boat is going to sink."

But it proved to be impossible. Everyone wanted to get onto the canoe at once, several times sinking the canoe. So the pilot resorted to his old trick, hitting the bank and pulling back. My family and I stood on the deck, watching men falling into the water and drowning.

I was sick when we arrived at the jetty. My wife and I stayed behind as the children left for Paliau with the rest of the people. The village was about six miles away, and the path was flooded, but, like in any normal *toch*, there were dry spots too, here and there.

When I had rested for a while, and was able to walk the distance, we continued. I sat down on every piece of dry land. By the time we got to Paliau, another load of passengers had arrived and passed us on the way. The children had meanwhile found their relatives who had been taken to the mainland in the canoe. They had exchanged a bed sheet for dura, and were waiting for us with food. We were very hungry, but had to force the tasteless amak (a Dinka word for food prepared from undried newly harvested sorghum) down our throats that for many days had not swallowed solid food. We ate as much as we could without broth and lay down to sleep.

I could not stop thinking of the recruits that were still left behind on the island. I knew that they were the most vulnerable ones. I tried, but in that village I could not find anyone willing to take responsibility for them. I did not even know where to find the crew of the boat. It was obvious that no food was taken to the island at any time during the evacuation. When the evacuation was complete, I looked in vain for many familiar faces. Those comrades of mine must have perished.

CHAPTER 18

A Life of Hardship

At Paliau, there were no rations for us. The villagers told us that we were going to be supplied with food when we got to Kongor. All we could do meanwhile was to exchange some of the clothes we still had for *dura*.

In most of the houses there were SPLA soldiers who had returned home with their guns, and they grossly mistreated us. Some of our hungriest recruits were lashed for entering a field to chew some *dura* canes without permission.

Kongor was the district headquarters, but no-one was taking responsibility. The unfortunate recruits who had arrived before us, with no clothes to exchange for food, were left to die, and their corpses were dragged to an open plot the locals called "the grave of the people from Bahr el Ghazal". Before we left for Poktap the following day, we visited this grave to pray.

Like everyone on the Bor mainland, the people of Kongor made it very clear that recruits from Bahr el Ghazal were not wanted there. That was why they were so reluctant to send a boat to the island to bring us over. They had received a request from 1st Lt. Marial Chinoung to evacuate us from the island, but failed to respond until the canoe I sent over arrived conveying our urgent plea. The crew of the boat showed no sympathy at all with the sick and dying on the island of Dhiam-dhiam, or those who drowned. They carried out the evacuation at their leisure, making only two trips a day whereas they could easily have made four.

At Paliau, I tried to find out who was in charge, but the responsible persons in the movement were nowhere to be found. "Where do these people from Bahr el Ghazal think they are going?" was what everyone was saying. "Don't they know that the liberation is over? "Baai aci tom ben bei?" They said.

"Over? Aren't there any Arabs left in Bor town?" we asked. They admitted that there were. "Then what war is over?" we wanted to know. "The Arabs are still occupying all the towns of Bahr el Ghazal, except Yirol and Thiet. *The Marahliin* are still devastating the whole Bahr el Ghazal region," we told them.

It took us two days to reach Poktap, east of the Jonglei Canal, where we found some abandoned houses built by labourers digging the canal. The doors and window shutters had been removed. There was no village, but we found clean water. We waited for two days to make sure that all the recruits had caught up with us. Then we lined the men up for roll call.

When we left Maker Apuk there were one thousand five hundred men in each of the two groups, Najda and Gerger. By the time we left Tot, the Najda battalion had lost two hundred absconders, leaving a thousand three hundred. Now, at Poktap we found that the number had been reduced to one thousand two hundred and seventeen. The rest had disappeared on the island, most of them in the rush to get to the boat. It is possible that a few had remained behind at Paliau or Kongor but I received no report to that effect.

From Poktap it was another day's walk to Duk, where we were received with great kindness. The people provided us with our first "free" food since we crossed the Nile, recognizing us for what we were – legitimate members of the SPLA. They slaughtered bulls for us, and issued us with *dura*. Three days later, when we had to resume our trek, they sent a guide with us. Our next destination was the village of Pan-Gatwic, inhabited by members of the Nuer tribe – the only Nuer group that had remained loyal to the SPLA. At midday we reached a spot where the path split into three. Our guide showed us which path to take, and explained to us what to do when the path separated again. "I will have to leave you here," he informed us. "I have no-one to accompany me back, and the distance is too long for one person."

So we continued on our own. At about six o'clock that evening we reached a deserted village – a large Nuer village. There were fields of *dura*, almost ready to be harvested, and pumpkins and beans aplenty; also water and firewood for cooking. Since we did not know the distance to Pan Gatwic, we decided to spend the night at the village. We wondered uneasily about the whereabouts of the villagers. Were they in the neighbourhood? What if they came back to check their houses that night? We had no option but to sleep there and take the consequences. There were pounding facilities and we made some *dura* flour and cooked it with pumpkins.

Thank God we spent the night without trouble. We left early for Pan Gatwic, which we reached late in the evening. We were well received and given rations. Our next stop would be Tiergol on the Akobo River. We were told that another battalion of recruits, Petrol, had left for Tiergol a few days ahead of us, and had arrived safely. We were too exhausted to move on and decided to spend another night.

The next evening a person arrived from Muor, a section of Nuer that was hostile to the SPLM/SPLA. He told the authorities at Gatwic that the Nuer of Muor had heard of our arrival and gone to Akobo to obtain ammunition. "You'd better leave early tomorrow morning," the commander told us. "I'm afraid I do not have enough men to accompany you to Tiergol and defend our village as well. But I've given a cow to someone who knows the way. He will take you to Tiergol." One of the recruits with me, Ajuet Atem Gitbek, had an automatic machine gun. We sold it for six cows, which we intended to take to Tiergol with us.

We left very early in the morning. At about seven o'clock we came upon the route that the Petrol battalion had taken. "Do you want to follow the same route?" our guide asked.

"No, we'd rather not," I replied. "But tell me, how far will this route take us from the Nuer villages on the left, and the Murle villages on the right?"

"The Nuer villages are fifteen to twenty miles from the route," he replied, "but those of the Murle are very far from here."

So we decided to walk southwards towards the Murle area for about two hours, and then take a shortcut through the grassland. (This grassland is sometimes mistakenly called the Akobo desert, but it is not a desert at all. The terrain is covered with thick grass, but treeless.) It was the first week of October, and we expected to find plenty of water, but we were wrong. The land turned out to be flat, without potholes or streams. By midday we were very thirsty. "That's the way it is," our guide said. "There is no known source of water ahead of us. In the wet season you may come across some stagnant water."

We should have learned our lesson on the island. By this time it had become clear that the people on our route would not tell us of the conditions ahead. They did not want us to stay. They wanted to get rid of us as quickly as possible. I proposed that we turn back to Pan Gatwic. We could reach it by nightfall, and it would get cooler as we walked. No-one would die of thirst, whereas it would take us three days to get to Tiergol. It would be disastrous to depend on stagnant water, I argued. But Diing Malong and others insisted that we continue. So we dragged on.

In the afternoon the men leading the way came upon a very small pond of water. Instead of finding containers like cups or dishes to scoop up the water carefully and drinking it, they repeated the mistake that had killed so many of our comrades on the island – they all rushed into the pond to drink from their cupped hands, turning the pond into undrinkable mud. Not even the recruits immediately behind them got anything to drink, let alone the others.

At nightfall we found a small open area and decided to spend the night there. When we woke up in the morning we realized that this spot was even dryer than the area we had left behind. And I knew, if any water at all was to be found, it would be spoiled again by those in front. It would be a waste of time to talk to the recruits in the state they were in – and I regretted ever undertaking such a long and dangerous journey with such a large number of uncontrollable men.

Among us there was a small group of young men who had joined us from the cattle camp of the spiritual leader, Cyerdit. Cyerdit had admonished them to pray every evening before they went to bed, and every morning when they started the day. That evening the young men prayed longer than usual. They prayed and sang songs, and then lay down to sleep under a cloudless sky. Two hours later we were woken by rain pouring down on us. We jumped up and put out everything that could possibly catch the water, even the plastic sheets on which we were lying. Nobody complained of getting wet, or of the cold. We drank and drank and saved as much water as we could for the coming day.

A Life of Hardship

The problem was a lack of containers. My family and I used the dish we all shared to eat from. Many others did not even have a cup to carry at least some water. We walked on across the parched land. At midday we spotted some *lalop* trees on low ground. When we reached them, we found a reasonable amount of water – enough for all of us to drink, and even to cook with. The trees also provided dry firewood, and for the first time since we left Pan Gatwic, we were able to cook. We slaughtered all six of our cows, and I told the recruits to save some of the meat for the remaining part of the journey.

There is a very strange thing that always happens during warfare. Whenever a large number of people move together, they are followed in the air by swarms of vultures. The birds seem to know that these people will feed them in two ways. They expected some cattle to be slaughtered and they would be able to feed on whatever they could grab. They also knew that there would be fighting, resulting in corpses strewn over the battlefield. And even if there was no fighting, on a journey like ours people were bound to die and be left unburied. We were afraid that the enemy would spot the vultures and know that we were there.

We quickly finished cooking and eating and moved on. At about seven that evening we came to a good place to spend the night, with enough water for all. As we sat down to eat some of the meat we had saved, our guide warned us: "Don't light a fire tonight. Don't use any kind of light. The enemy is not far."

At two o'clock in the morning we started to move. It was the toughest and most dangerous day yet. We had to move fast, often running rather than walking. At midday a helicopter on its way from Akobo town to Malakal passed over us. "Sit down!" I shouted. "Keep your heads down!"

The helicopter was flying low, and our route was like an open road. It would not be difficult for the pilot to see us. We saw the passengers in the helicopter quite clearly. But they continued on their way, and we on ours.

That afternoon as we reached the road from Akobo town to Malakal we found the wreck of a military vehicle that had been hit by a land mine. Near it was a large water hole. We were very thirsty, but feared that the water might have been contaminated. "Look!" someone said. "There are insects in it. They are swimming. They are alive." That was the sign – the water was not poisonous. So we just filtered it through our shirts, and drank. The recruits in the rear were still a long way from us, but we crossed the road and continued.

By that time some SPLA soldiers on their way to Ethiopia, including three officers from Bor had joined us. I put ten of them in front, and seven at the rear. They were welcome, but not a force we could rely on if we were attacked by the Nuer. About a mile from the road, the men in front arrested four Nuer soldiers who were moving in the direction of Malakal, and brought them to me. The Nuer soldiers carried arms – two automatic machine guns and two non-automatic guns of the type known as '*Lout*'. Our soldiers had disarmed them and tied their hands behind their backs. I was not sure who they were loyal to, so I asked, "Where are your departure orders?" These orders were a must for every SPLA or SPLM soldier when they left their battalion, even for a short distance. They had none, so it was obvious that they either belonged to the Arab militia or the section of the Nuer who were hostile to the SPLA.

I nevertheless decided to release them. "I know that you do not belong to the SPLA," I told them. "But you haven't done us any harm. So take your guns. You are free to go. Move away from our route if you like."

A Life of Hardship

That evening we came to a spot where some very tall grass known in Dinka as '*ayai*' grew. Our guide told us that the Tiergol SPLA base was near, and that we would be able to reach it early the next morning. So we flattened the grass, and slept on it, with empty stomachs, but at least not thirsty, for a change. The first recruits reached Akobo River around nine o'clock.

There were many villages along the western bank of the river. As we walked through the fields of *dura*, a strange thing happened – in each village we passed, the people started to blow on horns, from house to house. We did not understand what was going on. But it was disturbing to find human skulls and bones scattered on the river bank. I knew that this was the spot where a group walking from Bahr el Ghazal to Ethiopia had been ambushed and attacked by the Nuer. It was here that Valentino Akol Wol Agany of Awan Mou and eight members of his immediate family and all those who had accompanied him from Gogrial had lost their lives.

We expected to find Tiergol SPLA base on the banks of the Akobo River, but when we got there, they had gone. There was no sign of the presence of our army. And the Nuer on our side of the river continued to blow their horns. Were they the ones who had killed our people, whose skulls and bones we had found, we wondered, or were they friendly to the movement?

We walked on. The first recruits to reach the river did not wait for orders or pause to rest. They poured into the river and swam to the other side. By the time I got there, four of them had drowned.

My family was as terrified as the others and we decided to cross to the eastern side as quickly as possible. My wife and my uncle knew how to swim, but they were not strong swimmers. My wife panicked when she saw that the only other woman in our convoy was among those drowned. I was alarmed, too. But then I remembered how I had watched small boys at Nasir bundling water hyacinths into rafts on which they rowed themselves across a river.

So seven men from Wunrok, myself and my stepbrother Mayar Majok Adiang, went down to the river and collected a huge heap of the water hyacinths which grew there in abundance. My wife sat down on the heap, holding our belongings on her lap, with Uncle Donato next to her. Eight of us who were strong swimmers, pulled them safely to the other side. I had told my two children to swim, because they were good swimmers, but when we reached the bank, I discovered that my son Wal was still standing on the western shore. The sight of the drowned people had terrified him, and he refused to enter the water without me.

I was exhausted, but jumped back into the water. When I was halfway through, I suddenly found that I was too tired to continue. I could not lift my arms – they had become heavy and numb. My shoulders hurt badly.

"Relax," I told myself, "just relax and float on the water and resume swimming when you have rested." But I sank like a piece of iron, as if something was pulling me down. With all my strength I pushed myself up. When I came to the surface, I cried, "Cyerdit, my Lord Jesus!" I turned onto my back, and found that I could move forward in that position. At last my hands touched the shore. I stumbled up the bank, and sat down, shivering with exhaustion, alarmed at what might have happened to me. Wal stood quietly near me.

You may be wondering, dear reader, if Bol Majok is a true Christian. Well, from day one, the first day of creation, God has sent certain people to the world, to every nation under the sun, and given them special powers, not found in

A Life of Hardship

other members of their communities. The Dinka people are no exception.

When I say "God of Abraham", it does not make me less of a Christian, though Abraham lived long before Jesus. From the first Cyerdit up to the present one, they have been the religious leaders of our people, during times of epidemics and times of war and famine, and even at times of peace. They are the people who have pulled us together and urged us to raise our voices as one body to God the Creator, asking God to have mercy on us, to bless us and grant us whatever we requested of Him. So, when I pray to "God of Cyerdit" there is nothing wrong with it. It does not make me any less Christian.

After a short rest, I asked Wal to go down to the river with me and to swim to the other side. He reached the eastern bank before me. When I reached the shore, I found only my wife and the two boys waiting for me. The other recruits had disappeared into the huts. The villagers must have heard of our approach, because they had brewed a lot of the local *dura* beer known as '*merisa*'. Those of us who still had a little money to spend, or clothes to exchange could not wait to taste the beer. We were told that the SPLA base had been moved away from the river, two or three miles from where we were. Some of the recruits had already left for it. Danger was imminent. For the sake of my family I could not wait to see if everyone had arrived safely. They would not go without me, so, without delay we followed the men to the base.

At Tiergol we were shown to a spot under some trees that would serve as our accommodation for as long as we remained there. I asked the leaders of the different groups (called 'companies) to assemble their men for roll call and to let me know how many had crossed the river. The report was not good – we had lost seven men, including a certain Macar from Apuk. Macar was a strong man, not anyone, one might have expected to drown. Those who knew him told me that when they were at the cattle camp, he would put a newborn calf on his shoulders and swim with it across a river wider than the Akobo. Those who were drowned were not necessarily the ones who could not swim. They were just too tired and hungry to make it. Perhaps we should all have taken a rest first.

The base commander was Cdr. Peter Panhom Thanypiny. I was on my way to report to him, when I met him coming towards our place. One of the soldiers who had accompanied us, had already told him how many men had drowned, and that the person responsible for the recruits was Bol Majok.

He came towards us, calling, "Where is Bol Majok? Where is Bol Majok?"

I stopped before him. "That's me," I said. "I'm Bol Majok."

"Well, Bol Majok, why have you killed your people?"

"What people have I killed?"

"Those who drowned in the river." He was hitting the ground with a long whip he held in his hand.

"I did not kill anyone," I said angrily. "You did!"

"And how did I kill your people?"

"You were aware of our coming and you did not send anyone to the river to receive us. Secondly, there was not a single canoe in the river for our use, and, thirdly, why haven't the remains of the men killed at the crossing point been removed? It was when the recruits saw those skulls and bones, and heard the horns being blown in the villages, that they jumped into the river. Nobody waited for orders. They crossed in a hurry and got drowned. If nothing is done about those human remains and the Nuer blowing their horns, many more of those following us will still be drowned."

Cdr. Peter relaxed and told the captain with him to take me to the mess for breakfast. My family were relieved to see me when I returned. They were alarmed when they heard the base commander shouting for me.

On the second day Cdr. Peter sent for me. "I hear that you met four armed men on your way and that you released them," he said. "I'll tell you what happened afterwards. These men were soldiers of the Sudan government in Akobo. About two miles from where you crossed the road they encountered the Muor Nuer running towards them on the road. The Nuer had been to Pan Gatwic and learned that you had already left, and deduced that you must have taken a different route, not the one on which they were waiting in ambush. They were running because they were hoping to catch up with you before you crossed the river. But the four men you had released were very happy with you, especially with the fact that you had returned their weapons. So they told the Muor that you had already crossed the river – early that morning. The Nuer turned back."

"The Petrol battalion was attacked by the Nuer of Muor, and they lost some men. That goes to show – even a wild beast will be thankful when he is treated well. They sent a woman to tell me that on the same day you released them they returned your favour."

Some of my comrades had blamed me for setting *Nyigat* free. Now they congratulated me. "You have prevented real disaster," they said.

Cdr. Peter told me, however, that we would have to move on the next day, to make room for the Gerger battalion which they expected to arrive the next day. "It's not far to go," he said. But he did not tell us how many days. Two or three days, some soldiers said, and told us that there would be nothing to fear on the way, as the Nyigat had been defeated and had gone to Akobo town. (In the Nuer language the word *Nyigat* means robbers – those who loot the property of others by force.)

CHAPTER 19

Itang, the End of our Journey

In 1972 the south was granted regional autonomy under the Addis Ababa Agreement, but in 1982 President Nimeiri, in violation of this agreement, dissolved the southern government again, prompting a renewal of the civil war, the Second Sudanese Civil War. Southern Sudanese soldiers in two regions of Bahr el Ghazal and Upper Nile formed the Anyanya II movement to fight the Sudanese government after President Nimeiri violated the Addis Ababa Peace Agreement.

In Upper Nile the Anyanya II movement was led by 1st Lt. Col. Samuel Gai Tut, Major Abdalla Cuol and Akuot Atem.

In Bahr el Ghazal the Anyanya II forces stepped up their activities, but lacked good leadership. This resulted in infighting for power and leadership.

The Anyanya II of Upper Nile were better organized under 1st Lt. Col. Samuel Gai Tut, Major Abdalla Cuol and Akuot Atem. They had a base at the village of Bilpam in Ethiopia and in a refugee camp at Itang. Although the regime in Ethiopia was socialist, they were not hostile to the Anyanya II who were supported by the West.

When Lt. Col. Kerubino Kuanyin Bol and Southern soldiers mutinied in Mading Bor on 16 May 1983, a new armed resistance movement was formed. He and his newly formed force, now called the SPLA, immediately went to Itang in Ethiopia, where they found the Anyanya II under Samuel Gai Tut. They made an effort to combine the two forces into a united front, but could not agree to share power. Fighting broke out between them, and Gai Tut's Anyanya II were dislodged from Itang and Bilpam and forced to retreat towards the Sudanese border, followed by the SPLA. When the Anyanya II found themselves trapped between the SPLA and the Sudan army, they decided to ally themselves with the Sudan army to fight the SPLA. It was these same Anyanya II soldiers who came to ambush the SPLA recruits making their way from Bahr el Ghazal to the SPLA training base in Bilpam. In consequence of the battle, they lost their leaders 1st Lt. Col. Samuel Gai Tut, Major Abdalla Cuol and Akuot Atem but they remained organized under new leadership. The Anyanya II of Samuel Gai Tut and Abdalla Cuol were called *Nyigat* by the SPLA. Those who defected from the Anyanya II and joined SPLM/A were always highly received and given due consideration. In most cases they were not stripped of their Anyanya ranks.

The Anyanya II soldiers of Bahr el Ghazal disintegrated when they heard of the newly formed SPLM/A and joined it in smaller groups or individually. Those who joined the SPLA as early as 1984 were given due consideration but those who went late like Diing Malong, Diing Aher, Ajuet Atem and Bol "Maluk" Bol Chol, who were Anyanya II officers, were treated as mere recruits - like us.

Today most of the Anyanya II officers of the Upper Nile who were mainly from Nuer make up almost half of the South Sudanese army, and many of them occupy top positions in the government and the army.

To return to our journey:

We left Tiergol for Itang in Ethiopia the next day. Although there were no *Nyigat* armed men on our route, the

Itang, the End of our Journey

terrain was very difficult. One river (I think it is called Gilo) in particular posed a risk. We crossed it in canoes because it was teeming with crocodiles. When we threw a stick into the water, more than one crocodiles would leap up from the water to catch it before it fell and break it into pieces. At least they did not try to attack the canoes. And we fired shots into the water to disperse them.

After this river there were several more streams to cross. Along the path the elephant grass grew so tall that for long stretches it was interlocked above our heads and we had to walk head down. It took us seven days to reach the Red Army base called Abolo in the Anyuak area.

The base commander came to talk to us, but said that there were no rations for us. Luckily we still had some of the maize meal we had exchanged for clothes when we came through the Anyuak villages.

At about three o'clock that afternoon Dr John Garang de Mabior, the chairman and commander in chief of the SPLM/SPLA, arrived at the base with three Toyota pickup vehicles. The leading car had a big machine gun mounted on it, then came John Garang's vehicle, followed by one carrying heavily armed soldiers. The convoy stopped in front of the office and the soldiers jumped off and took their positions. Some went through the office and lined up behind it. Others pointed their guns in the direction of the Red Army's huts, and others in the direction they had come from. Most of the guns were aimed at us. Our large number must have caused them concern. Dr John Garang alighted and the base commander hurried to meet him. The two of them entered the office with two officers.

Three officers from Bor who had joined us at Kongor went to talk to some other officers near the cars, then came back to collect their belongings. When Dr John Garang emerged from the office, he stood at the door and looked in all directions, including ours. Then he greeted the three officers and allowed them to get into the vehicles. They drove off.

The commander told us that the chairman was very happy that we had arrived and that he wanted us to leave very early in the morning for Itang as there were no rations for us in Abolo. It was one and a half days' walk, he said. For the first time an officer told us the truth. It took us exactly one and a half days to get there.

It took very long for everyone to cross the Baro River in a canoe, however, and by the time I had crossed, it was almost dark. We were taken to a place called New Wunrok, named after my own village, on the eastern side of the camp. I was happy to find members of my own family there, men only, mainly from Adiang section, including Macam Atem Barac, the son of my sub-chief. It was good to spend the night with them.

In the morning Macamdit asked a young man to take me to the house of Lt. Col Victor Bol Ayuolnhom Kuol. He was my wife Acol's maternal uncle, so she was happy to see Bol's wife and also the wife of Lt. Philip Ajak Bol Ajak by the name Akuek Malual Awak. Victor himself was not there, though. A small boy told me that he was in prison.

That evening I called Biem Ring Panek, the wife of Victor Bol to ask her about her husband. She told me that Victor was arrested after he returned from Bahr el Ghazal where he and Kawac Makuei brought the recruits who made up Muor-Muor division. Both of them were arrested and imprisoned by the SPLM/A. She could not tell me why.

When we arrived at Itang, we were told to "control our tongues" as newcomers, especially the intellectuals, were considered to be Arab or Sudanese government spies sent to destroy the Movement. Security in the refugee camp of Itang was very tight. Anyone accused of being against the Movement would be arrested, tortured and sometimes condemned to death without proper investigation or trial. People imprisoned for committing minor offenses would languish in custody for a very long time without trial. I therefore, decided not to talk about Victor Bol's imprisonment as that alone was likely to cause me problems.

The young men who came with me were accommodated at a youth centre a kilometre away from the main camp. Those who came with wives like me remained in the camp but used to report to the youth centre for parade every morning.

The youth centre served as an assembly point for those to be sent for army training. The Zalzal I division had also stayed at the same youth centre, but were taken to Bonga for training a few days before our arrival to make way for new recruits to assemble. After three days, the Gerger battalion arrived in Itang and they too were accommodated in a youth centre.

I was taken to the UN office with all the members of my family for registration and issued with a tent, two blankets and cooking utensils. The soldiers at Tiergol had persuaded us to leave them our old mosquito nets, assuring us that we would receive new ones at Itang – but there were none. We received food from the group office. The whole camp was divided into groups called "teloons" and I was in Teloon Seven where the house of Victor Bol was. The food items distributed in the camp included maize, beans, "jenjaro", sugar, salt and vegetable oil. Powdered milk was also provided in big bags that looked like cement bags.

I went to the administrative centre where I found the base commander Dr Amon Wantok. The office was located inside a fence, it was old and in bad shape, thatched with grass and with grass walls. There were four tables including Dr Amon's. He welcomed me into his office and told me to come back to see him in a week's time.

Itang refugee camp looked like a modern village although the houses all had grass roofs and mud walls. Most of the houses in the camp were well built, especially the houses of the army officers and the Movement's leadership. The houses of the army leaders had sturdy grass fences around them. Whenthe Muor-Muor recruits arrived at Itang from Bahr el Ghazal, they found the people in the camp sleeping on the bare ground. Most families were accommodated in tents. It was the Muor-Muor recruits that constructed good houses and equipped them with beds and chairs made of wood only. No nails were used.

Life in Itang was not bad. There were grinding mills and boreholes. Officers could afford to eat meat frequently, and fish was available for all who could afford it. Not all the SPLM/SPLA leaders were in Itang, but their families lived there. Only Dr John Garang's family had been sent to safety elsewhere. He himself lived in the largest house, which was heavily guarded.

After a week, I went back to see Dr Amon Wantok. I found in his office some intellectuals whom I had left in Yirol when I was travelling with the recurits. They included Isaac Kon Anok, Eli Acol Deng Hot, Kau Akol Dhieu and Cagai Matet Guem. Dr Amon gave us some minor assignments. Eli Acol, Kau Akol and I were to settle land disputes in the camp - but we had no cases to settle, as we were all refugees, and there was no struggle for land. There were no land cases to settle until we left for army training.

The officers and soldiers working in the centre were issued with extra food as well as non-food items like bedsheets and blankets. But as we were new recruits, we were not included in the distribution of the non-food items.

A month later Dr John Garang, accompanied by Commander William Nyuon, stopped at Itang on their way to Bonga to open the military training centre for the Zalzal I Division. Cdr William Nyuon invited me to go with him, as evidence that the flow of recruits was not stopping, that I had brought three thousand men to fill the places of those in training when they left.

CHAPTER 20

A Cold Reception by Dr John Garang

In Bonga, Cdr William handed me to a captain who took me to the junior officers' mess for the night. In the morning I accompanied Cdr William to the place of celebration, where ten battalions of recruits and all the other forces were assembled. Dr John Garang was waiting behind a fence for the ceremony to commence.

Surrounded by bodyguards and officers, he stood with his hands behind his back, holding a small stick in his left hand. Cdr. William took me by the hand to introduce me to Dr. John. I put out my hand to shake his, but Dr John merely nodded. I withdrew my hand and stepped back, ashamed. Cdr William was not happy either with the cold reception accorded to me by the chairman and commander in chief of the SPLM/SPLA. When I was the assistant commissioner of Nasir, Cdr William served as a captain there, and he knew and respected me. But he requested one of his guards to take me to the place of celebration and find a seat for me among the junior officers.

When all the preparations were complete and every officer had taken his seat, Dr John Garang de Mabior and his high command made their appearance. I expected to see Cdr Kerubino Kuanyin and Cdr Salva Kiir, but they were not present. The ceremony was opened by the base commander, Alternate Commander Martin Mawien, also known as Agangrial. He introduced the members of the high command and other guests, most of them Ethiopians. He then handed the floor to Cdr William, who did not say much, but did explain why he had brought me to Bonga with him.

Next Cdr William introduced Dr John, who spoke at great length, explaining why he had delayed coming to open the military training centre. He told the trainees about the influx of new recruits, but failed to mention me by name, as the one who had led them from Sudan to Ethiopia. Why he did not mention me, became quite clear to me at a rally that took place a month later in Itang.

That same evening, back in Itang, Dr Amon instructed us to report very early every morning for parade and some preliminary military training. We were trained to stand in line, at ease and at attention, and to march. After breakfast every morning I was to go to administration to wait for people who might come with land claims.

Exactly a month after Dr Garang had opened the training centre at Bonga, he came to Itang to attend a rally, accompanied by all the members of his high command, Kerubino Kuanyin Bol, William Nyuon Bany, Salva Kiir Mayardit and Arok Thon Arok. We were instructed to report to the youth centre very early in the morning on the day of the rally.

At seven we arrived in battalions, marching and singing military songs. We were told to sit down and wait. When Dr John and the rest arrived at eight, the recruits stood up and sang revolutionary songs. When the chairman and his team had taken their seats, we were ordered to sit down again.

The ceremony was opened by the base commander Dr Amon Wantok, after which William Nyuon and Kerubino Kuanyin gave short speeches in which they expressed their happiness at the arrival of the new recruits. Then Dr John

Garang de Mabior spoke for a full two hours. He was equally happy about the new recruits, six battalions of them, he said. Then he gave a brief summary of the movement's manifesto. "The intellectuals among you will receive details from Dr Amon in due course," he added. He then turned his attention to the formation of the high command, and the problems they encountered. "We were able to put together the high command just in time to prevent the movement from being hijacked," he said. "When we first came to Itang, the majority of soldiers in the force were from Nuer and together with a number of *marasiin* from Nuer they tried to seize power. They are marasiin!" ('Maras' in Arabic usually means a debased person who does dirty work for the rich and powerful, such as bringing to them other men's wives or daughters to satisfy their wicked needs.) "Then the Koryom division arrived. The majority of them were from Bor, and the marasiiin from Bor tried to seize power. After them ten battalions arrived from Bahr el Ghazal, and the marasiin from Bahr el Ghazal tried to seize power. But they all failed to hijack the movement. They were detected by our security network, and their plans were nipped in the bud."

Now I understood why Kawac Makuei and Victor Bol Ayuolnhom were in custody. Dr John then turned to us. "There are some among you who tried to destroy the movement when you were serving the Sudan government. You failed. Now you have come to infiltrate the movement and destroy it from within. Let me tell you clearly: If you are looking for ranks, then you have come to **THE WRONG CAMP!**"

The message was clear. We, the former officials of Sudan, especially the university graduates, were not wanted. We were blamed for all that was wrong in the old Sudan. And the simple, ignorant soldiers listening to John Garang were led to believe that it was the educated persons who had caused the problems.

Present at that rally, for instance, was William Nyuon, a simple, uneducated man. This kind of talk had caused him to view the intellectuals with suspicion. At the rallies that followed, he would raise his gun and shout, "This is my qualification! If anyone wants to replace me, I'll deal with him through the barrel of my gun."

When the rally ended, we went back to the youth camp and dispersed. That night I could not sleep properly. I connected the cold reception I had received from Dr John Garang de Mabior on two occasions – at Abolo and at Bonga – with his words at the rally, and came to the conclusion: I had really come to the wrong camp.

When I left my home at Wunrok, I thought that people of my caliber would be needed to fight the war, to lead the army and to plan strategy. We could bring brains to the movement. It had never occurred to me that I would have to struggle for power with those who had joined the movement before me. That, I thought, was what John Garang meant when he referred to ranks.

I consoled myself that I would gain my position through good and hard work. The movement also needed diplomats, and that role could only be fulfilled by educated persons. I continued to do whatever I was told to. Sometimes Dr Amon asked Eli Acol Deng, Cagai Matet and me to go with him to meet UN personnel or donors when they came to Itang. We recruits were, however, not allowed to talk to them directly. I, an intellectual and highly educated person, found it degrading to pretend not to understand what a white man was saying, and to talk to him through an interpreter. The people we talked to knew from our expressions that we understood what they said, and clearly failed to understand why we did not talk directly to them.

For more than two months no land dispute came to my attention. Dr Amon now told us to start building houses in which to leave our families when we were called for training. The houses of important officers and all SPLA offices were built by recruits who brought the building materials from the forest and supplied the labour. We however, were recruits ourselves, and were not entitled to any free services. I found a very good plot about two hundred metres from my wife's uncle Victor Bol's house, and constructed a sturdy hut. We brought the materials ourselves from the forest, but I paid a Nuer woman from one of the villages a sack of maize to do the thatching for us. My two sons were still very young, and collecting building materials was hard work. My wife could not come with us, because in Ethiopia, unlike Sudan, the cutting of grass was men's work. And I knew that one hut without a fence would not be enough for my family.

One day I went down to the river where some men from Aweil used to sell fish. I knew I was a great fisherman – and thought that if I could do some fishing myself, the fish I caught might provide the means of finishing my house.

"Where do you get the fishing nets?" I asked them.

"Oh, we collect the nylon sacks no-one is using, and use the treads to make nets. We'll show you how to do it."

My children helped. They collected nine empty nylon bags from Twic neigbours, and unravelled them. Together, following the example of the fisherman, we produced a very good fishing net.

When I was a student I learned to make nets and cast them from a standing position in a canoe. We used to attach pieces of lead, 'rassas', to pull the net down over the fish, but at Itang I could not find any lead so I made use of broken bits of metal from old tents. I then asked a young man from my village, Malang Col Dut, to do the fishing. He caught a lot of fish. We ate some and sold the surplus for cash. This enabled me to complete my house and a fence around it. There were two small trees inside the fence, providing welcome shade.

Some of the cash I used to acquire real nylon twine from Gambella, a town some distance from the refugee camps. I made a proper fishing net, and earned so much from the sale of fish that I was able to buy six cows from some soldiers who had brought them from the front.

Dr Amon next arranged evening classes which we were required to attend. He explained the manifesto of the SPLM/SPLA in full detail. At times he talked to us about his own experiences in Sudan before he joined the movement. He was constantly being imprisoned for being a Communist, he said. "Now, in the movement I can keep repeating 'I'm a Communist, I'm a Communist!' and no-one will imprison me – because I am in a position of power." He launched an attack on religion. "What you call God, is a myth," he said. "There is no God." He turned round and shouted, "Where is God? If there is a God, let Him kill me here and now! Here and now!"

"You may be quantity, but you are not quality," he told us. But I'll brainwash you thoroughly! He pointed at the white shirt he was wearing. "Only when your brains are clean and white like this shirt, will you be accepted in our ranks."

Under normal circumstances his statements would have elicited vigorous argument. We all knew very well why he had been imprisoned in the former Sudan. And we were Christians who strongly believed that there was a God, the creator of the world and everything in it. But, as Dr

Amon so aptly put it, he was in a position of power. Any disagreement with him could land us in serious trouble. It could be taken as criticism of the movement. We had heard enough stories of what happened to people who dared to disagree with the base commander.

Two batches of recruits were sent to political school in Addis Ababa while we were at Itang, but we were not included. Our brains were not considered clean enough yet to be trusted. While the Zalzal I battalion was under training at Bonga, Cdr Salva Kiir Mayardit came to Itang to arrange for our group to be trained at Bilpam as Zalzal II. He told me that I was to attend cadet training or political school. He was right, I was an intellectual who was destined to be an officer and to lead the army, and therefore, it wouldn't be a good idea for me to attend general military training together with the recuits. So we remained behind and continued our classes with Dr Amon.

But even for him, in his position of power, things went sour. On his way back from Gambela one day, not far from his house, Dr Amon's car overturned. He sustained major injuries and was taken to Addis Ababa for treatment. In his absence his son shot and killed the brother-in-law of Cdr Daniel Awet Akot. Soon after he returned to Itang, Dr Amon was arrested and sent to prison.

Alternate Commander Samuel Ater Dak, a former local government administrator in the Sudanese government, took over from him. He maintained the administration centre and built storerooms for the food that was to be distributed to the soldiers in Itang and Bilpam. This was something Dr Amon never did, in spite the fact that he was free to use the labour of the recruits. When he was in charge, food would be distributed in the open air, and in the rainy season it was often spoiled.

In collaboration with Madam Nyandeng Col, the wife of Col. Kerubino Kuanyin who had by then also been imprisoned, Samuel Atar Dak built huts for the sick trainees who were referred back to Itang for medical treatment. Madam Nyandeng organized the women from Bahr el Ghazal, including my wife, to take care of the patients. In Dr Amon's time the sick trainees were abandoned. Those who had diarrhoea were left to lie on the floor in their own defecation. Madam Nyandeng, in contrast, would wash them with her own hands. The other women (mainly from Twic) followed her example. When Ater Dak provided the centre with bedding and food such as sugar, tea, milk, maize meal and cooking oil, the women, organized by Madam Nyadeng, made porridge for the sick and washed their clothes and bed sheets. A medical officer was posted to the centre to care for the sick. The result was that they soon recovered and could return to the training centres.

Dr John Garang used to pay only brief visits to Itang – his family was not there. One evening the base commander informed me and four others that the chairman wanted us to report to his house at eight o'clock the following morning. That night I did not sleep well. I could think of several reasons why we were being called by the chairman for the first time since we arrived in Ethiopia. Others like Colonel Dominic Dim Deng and Colonel Salva Mathok Geng had arrived after us, and were met by the chairman upon their arrival and received in his house as guests of honour. But he did not have the courtesy to include us, or even to acknowledge the fact that we, who had brought a large number of recruits to the camp, were former high-ranking officials in the Sudan government, university graduates like himself, and senior to the two colonels who were so well received in the movement.

"He must have summoned me for one of two reasons," I finally told my wife. "Either he wants me to go for training or to do one of the SPLM/SPLA courses, or I have done something wrong." My wife and I were both disturbed, but at least happy that I had at last been summoned. I was happy to be able to talk to the chairman for the first time.

All night long it was raining heavily. At seven it was still pouring. But I was ready, and dressed in my best clothes and the shoes I reserved for such occasions. My house was about three hundred metres from Garang's. At ten to eight I set out through the rain and thick mud. I found the other four gentlemen waiting for me at the gate. It was eight o'clock sharp.

We were expected, and a soldier took us into the outer fence. The chairman's compound was very large. There was an outer fence and an inner one in which there were some houses. Big cars were parked in the open space between the fences. There were also huts for the guards. We could not see the gate through the inner fence. It was to the left, I suppose, and we were taken to the right. "Stand there, against the fence," the soldier said, and disappeared through a small door in the inner fence. We expected him to return soon and lead us in, for we were getting wet. There were many guards between the two fences, but they were all wearing raincoats. We were growing impatient, but the soldier did not appear. The rain stopped and we were still standing there. As long as we did not move, the soldiers did not talk to us, but only whispered among themselves. The sun appeared and our clothes dried and the cold went away. Now we were feeling the heat of the sun.

By ten we were tired of standing, and squatted for short whiles. At a quarter to eleven an officer came and searched us thoroughly. He found nothing but wrist watches, pens, handkerchiefs, keys and scraps of paper as well as some cash.

Everything was handed to a soldier. The officer went back into the inner fence, to emerge again fifteen minutes later with three soldiers carrying three wooden chairs. They placed the chairs against the wall of the inner fence and left. Another officer came and inspected the chairs, then covered them with heavy blankets which he folded, and thick bed sheets.

Finally three men emerged and took their seats. John Garang de Mabior sat in the middle, with William Nyuon on his right and Salva Kiir Mayardit on his left. I was the first to be called. I stood before them at attention. There was a table in front of them. John Garang de Mabior did all the talking – and the writing.

"Bol Majok Adiang?" he asked.

"Yes, Comrade."

"You are Bol Majok Adiang?"

"I am Bol Majok Adiang," I replied, wondering why it was so important to him to confirm my identity. What had he been told about me?

"How old are you?"

"In my late forties, Comrade."

Garang then asked me about my education, my occupation in the old Sudan and when and where I defected from the Sudan government service to join the SPLM/SPLA. He wanted to know about my arrival at Itang.

"Were there any recruits coming with you?" he asked. (Surely he knew! He had seen me with Najda at Abolo! And when William Nyuon introduced me to him at Bonga he told him that I had come with Najda and Gerger!)

"Why did you not go with those batallions for training?" he asked.

"I was going to," I said. "I was present when they were being organized to go, but I was left behind by Cdr Salva Kiir Mayardit."

"And why would he have left you behind?"

"Cdr Salva did not tell me, Comrade. I didn't ask him." I did not add that Salva Kiir had told me that I was an elder and was going to do cadet training or military school rather than general military training. Salva Kiir was present, and I wanted him to explain his reasons to Dr. Garang himself.

"Bol is an elder," Salva Kiir said. "I thought that other courses would suit him better."

"An elder? Bol is younger than me. He is stronger than me!"

"I am strong," I agreed. "But the conditions under which you and I are living in the bush are not the same."

Dr. John pulled out a handkerchief and wiped his face. "You can go," he said. "I'm done with you."

Then he called Eli Acol Deng Hot and after him, the others. At last our belongings were returned to us and we were ordered to go back to our houses. We had no idea what would be required of us next.

CHAPTER 21

The Death of an Innocent Man

When Kerubino Kunyin Bol, SPLM/A deputy chairman, was accused of plotting a coup against Garang and jailed, some people from other regions in the movement adopted a very hostile attitude towards the people of Bahr el Ghazal in general, and of Twic in particular.

Soon after Kerubino's arrest a member of the high command, Cdr Arok Thon Arok, called a rally at Itang, a major refugee camp in Ethiopia. He made a very irresponsible statement at this rally. "We have done everything good for the people of Bahr el Ghazal," he said. "There is nothing we have not done except that we have not given them our mothers to be their wives." "*We* have…" could only mean the people of Bor. We, the people of Bahr el Ghazal could not think of one good thing the people of Bor, or any other group of Southerners, had done for the people of Bahr el Ghazal.

After Kerubin Kuanyin Bol's arrest, any crime committed by anyone from Bahr el Ghazal, and particularly from Twic, was connected with him. One day Sergeant Aguek Bith who came from Adiang in Twic, was charged with a crime that under no law on earth could have carried the death penalty. On their way back from the front he and Captain Col Deng Majak stopped at the house of one of their relatives. At about eleven they decided to go to the house where they both lodged when they were in Itang. It happened to be Kerubino's house. On their way they knocked at my door and my wife opened it. "I'm back from the front, and I just wanted to say hello to Bol Majok," Aguek told her. She told him that I was asleep, and the two men left. They stopped to greet Victor Bol Ayuolnhom's family in his house, and then headed for Kerubino's house, south of the road that divided the refugee camp into two.

Near Kerubino's house there was a market where the Sudanese sold items like the vegetable oil, sugar, salt and maize that they received from the UN to the Ethiopians. It consisted of a large fence with one wide gate opening to the main road. When Aguek and Col crossed the road, they were stopped by a soldier who was standing in front of the gate. "Who are you?" the soldier wanted to know.

"Soldiers returning from the front," they replied.

"Stand at attention!"

He called another soldier, who came from inside the fence and asked Aguek and Col again who they were and where they were going. They told him everything, but he ordered them to put down their guns. They refused.

"You'll get them back in the morning," the soldier said.

"Sorry," Aguek said, "I cannot hand my gun to a soldier I do not know."

When Aguek and Col realized that the two were going to call more soldiers, and that they would be disarmed by force, they walked away, following the road towards an open space from where they would turn to Kerubino's house. Meanwhile more soldiers had arrived, and they ran after Aguek and Col, who also started running. The soldiers fired some rounds of ammunition above their heads. There was an Ethiopian police post on the other side of the open space, and as the shots were fired in their direction too, they returned fire, shooting low. An Ethiopian bullet struck Col. It entered his face close to the nose, and passed through his neck. He fell. When the pursuing soldiers saw him fall, they stopped shooting and took cover. The Ethiopians stopped firing too. The soldiers returned to the market, and Aguek ran to Kerubino's house, while Col remained lying on the road. There were some soldiers in the house, mainly relatives of Kerubino who had been wounded on the front. They came with Aguek and carried Col to the hospital. Col was in a coma, and Aguek stayed with him all night. In the morning, Aguek was arrested at the hospital, and taken to prison.

This was the time when Dr Amon Wantok was the base commander at Itang. He reported the incident to Dr Garang de Mabior who immediately formed a major court under the presidency of Honorable Bullen Pancol to try Aguek Bith. The court stripped Aguek of his rank, and sentenced him to imprisonment. Garang rejected the verdict right away and ordered a retrial. It was of course illegal for the same court to try a person a second time for the same crime, but they did and this time sentenced Aguek Bith to death by firing squad. The second verdict was approved at once.

Cdr William Nyuon was ordered to carry out the execution. When Cdr William arrived at Itang, he ordered all the refugees in the camp, men, women and children, as well as everyone at the youth centre, to come to the administration centre for a very important rally. Dr Amon opened the rally, and handed the floor to Cdr William Nyuon. I quote Cdr William's words: "We have given orders that no-one should fire a bullet in the refugee camp. Now somebody has disobeyed our orders and fired some shots in the camp. We are now going to shoot this soldier as an example to any soldier who shoots again in the refugee camp in the future."

For some reason I do not understand, Cdr William Nyuon added that, although Aguek Bith had been sentenced to death, there were people in prison in Itang who had committed graver crimes than he. Some of these crimes included murder, he said, but they had not been investigated and no court had yet tried the criminals. Some of them had remained in custody for more than a year. But Aguek's case was a special one, he said.

William Nyuon then told the people to move to the open space behind the fence of the administration centre.

Up to that moment, it had not occurred to me that it was Aguek Bith who was going to be executed. Cdr William Nyuon had just said "a soldier" without mentioning his name. It was now exactly eight days after the shooting incident. Col was still in a coma in hospital. But I knew – it was not Aguek who had fired a shot. It was the soldiers at the Sudan market who had shot at him, and the Ethiopian police who had returned fire. Besides, one would have expected them to wait for Col Deng Majak to recover before their case could be heard!

About ten prisoners were brought with their arms tied behind their backs at the elbow, and chained together. Martial music was played. An Anyuak man who had committed a murder managed to pull his hands free, and tried to run away. He was caught and brought back. Some of the prisoners collapsed, and some were crying, especially those who had committed major crimes. Among them was an Arab. I did not know what crime he had committed, but he fell down even before they were told to sit. Aguek Bith was in the middle. He was among the two or three who did not show any sign of fear. The rope was untied on both sides of Aguek and the other prisoners were taken back to prison.

Aguek alone remained sitting there. His hands were tied behind his back, but his legs were free. He made no attempt to get up and run away. William Nyuon ordered the verdict to be read out aloud. It ran: "Aguek Bith is found guilty of shooting in the refugee camp of Itang and has been sentenced to death, to be shot by a firing squad until he is dead. This sentence has been approved by the Chairman, Cdr Dr John Garang de Mabior."

"Is there anything you wish to say before you die?" Aguek was asked. There was! He began by insulting both the chairman, Dr John Garang and Cdr William, calling both of them thieves. "You and Garang will not remain on earth forever," he told William.

He then turned to the members of the firing squad. "I hold nothing against you," he told them. "You are only executing your orders. But don't give up the struggle! Fight until the whole of Southern Sudan has been liberated!" He then started to sing war songs as he used to when going into battle.

"Shoot me in the chest, not in the head," he told the soldiers. He was sitting cross-legged. He threw his head back and did not look at them again.

"Ready, aim, fire!" The soldiers poured bullets into Aguek, almost burying him in the mud.

Many women and children who had never witnessed such a cruel act before, fainted and collapsed. Pregnant women had to be rushed to hospital for fear of miscarriage.

Throughout that day my mind never rested. Did Aguek's death have anything to do with the case of Kerubino Kuanyin Bol, I wondered. I also remembered that some years back when Aguek was in the Sudanese army, he had killed a certain army sergeant major from Gok after a disagreement at Girinti Barrack in Wau. This sergeant major was said to have been a close relative of Dr Amon Wantok's. Of course! Dr Amon had got his revenge!

Aguek never fired any bullets in the refugee camp, but even if he had, it did not warrant the death penalty. The bullets fired that night (by others) were not the first after the order referred to by William Nyuon, nor were they the last. And no-one else had ever been punished. Let alone received a death sentence!

The SPLA soldiers were responsible for security in the camp, and they all carried guns. From time to time drunken soldiers would shoot in the air. And whenever the SPLA captured a town, there would be random celebratory shooting in the air, in all the camps, some soldiers emptying a full magazine. Up to the time of my writing, this has not stopped. During the May 16 annual celebrations SPLA soldiers and others continued firing shots for hours, wasting their ammunition. I cannot remember any of them being punished.

Aguek Bith was a very brave soldier when danger threatened, and a very kind person in times of peace. Only God, who created him, knows why he was killed for no convincing reason at all. His friend Col Deng Majakdit survived and when he was discharged from hospital nobody mentioned the shooting incident to him. He was certainly never charged for his role in it, and no-one was charged with firing that near fatal shot at him either. The whole affair ended with the death of Aguek Bith.

CHAPTER 22

Military Training

After our meeting with the chairman and commander-in-chief, Dr John Garang de Mabior, we remained in Itang for another four months. Batches of soldiers were sent to political school but we were always omitted. Then one day Cdr Yusif Kowa Mekki came and organized us to go for military training at Bilpam.

We were formed into six battalions, plus a company for girls. Each of us was ordered to carry or transport two sacks of maize containing thirty *malwas* each (total of about 200 kgs), to Maker, a halfway station between Itang and Bilpam, about ten miles away. This had to be done within a week, after which the maize would be carried the rest of the way to Bilpam.

To transport sixty *malwas* of maize in a week, one had to carry ten *malwas* per day. They were very strict - the maize was weighed at Itang, and again when we reached Maker. Ten *malwas* was very heavy, and difficult to balance on your shoulders as men do at home. On my first trip I had to rest several times. The weight was pushing my neck down into my chest. Very late that evening I was one of the last to get back to Itang, very tired and hungry. The only good thing was that the path to Maker followed the river, so finding water was not a problem.

My wife rebelled when she saw the condition I was in. "You can't possibly carry such a load again tomorrow," she said. "I'll do it for you. Or at least I can carry half of it. If we carry five *malwas* each, it'll be much easier."

"They will never let you do it," I said.

But she insisted, and the next day she followed me to the youth camp, carrying her half.

When we reached Maker, a soldier looked at her, and said, "Very good! You are welcome to carry as much maize as you can. It'll help all of us. I wish more women would follow your example. But that doesn't mean that your husband can carry any less. Carrying maize is part of the training. Everyone going for training must do it. We cannot make an exception."

So my wife went back home, and the next day left it to me to carry the full load. There were also stores of sugar, vegetable oil, salt, beans and powdered milk. But these were left behind in Itang.

When we eventually arrived in Bilpam, it was April, and the rains had started.

In Itang men from the same area were generally left in the same company, platoon and squad. Now we were reorganized, and found ourselves grouped with people from different areas. I was in Battalion 1, named Munir, first company. Reorganization took the whole day. In the evening we were shown our centres. My battalion was situated in the best location, near the river and a small market named Linglaad.

When we reached our centre, we were told to line up. "Squad!" the sergeant-major ordered. He then pointed at me and told me to move out of the line to the front of the battalion.

"March," he ordered. Then he stopped me. "About turn! Face the battalion!"

He told the battalion that I was to be their regimental sergeant-major. He then appointed sergeant-majors for the companies and other divisions. When we had been registered, he took me away with him to the compound of the second company and showed me a small '*kurnuk*'. "This is where we store food for the battalion," he told me. "You will be responsible for issuing the rations daily. You will also sleep here." There was a wooden bed, and a mattress filled with grass. "I'm afraid it's full of bedbugs," he said. You will have to remove the grass and bring fresh grass."

His name was Kuac, and was also known as 'Abu Hajash'. "Don't you recognize me?" he asked.

"I can't recall seeing you before," I replied.

"Well, when you were the assistant commissioner of Nasir I was a corporal in the old Sudan army, and a driver. I used to see you going to the officers' mess with the army commander of Nasir, Col Alfred Deng Aluk."

"You will take your meals at the trainers' mess of Company 2," he told me. The trainees received only maize ground into meal and cooked as sida throughout the training period. The trainers also had beans for broth, and sometimes oil and salt. I was given some sugar and tea, too. Abu Hajash said I would be allowed to listen to my radio, using earphones, unlike the trainees who were not allowed to. My appointment as regimental sergeant-major and the special treatment accorded to me by Abu Hajash was indeed a piece of luck!

Training started immediately. The exercises were difficult and within only a few days the trainees had become very weak. The little food they received was of poor quality. The girls were given their own sleeping quarters, but they joined the male battalions for training. They at least received better food – beans, salt and oil besides maize meal.

Soon the trainees were dying in disturbing numbers. The base commander was A/Cdr Cagai Atem Biar, who used to be a petty trader in the old Sudan. Why he did not make an effort to save the situation, was beyond me. When I was in Itang, I used to see food items like oil, sugar, milk, and beans included in the rations intended for Bilpam base – enough for everyone. Items such as oil, sugar and salt had market value, and army officers would sell them at the Sudanese market. But there were no buyers for the beans and milk powder that were supplied in what looked like cement bags. The refugees in Itang did not want them either, and at the time when Dr Amon Wantok distributed food in the open air, these items remained on the distribution ground. When they got wet, they gave off a horrible smell. So why on earth were these items not allowed to be brought to the training centre, especially as the recruits themselves provided the transport? The beans alone would have made a great difference.

Did it have anything to do with the fact that over half of us were from Bahr el Ghazal, and the rest from the Nuba Mountains, I wondered. Most of the girls were from the Nuba Mountains.

The death rate did not seem to alarm Cagai Atem Biar. I never saw him making rounds to find out what was happening, or why the trainees were dying at such an alarming rate. I could not tell whether he wanted to be rid of them, or whether he just was not capable of running such a large training base.

The chairman and commander-in-chief, Dr Garang, had openly stated that he would rather work with people of less ability and experience, in whom he had confidence and faith, than with highly experienced intellectuals he did not trust. He used the Arabic colloquial term "*ne mang-mang wanamshi gi dam*" – we shall mess up and still push ahead. What the chairman might have ignored is that he would pay dearly for his *mang-mang* attitude. Many significant assignments were given to people who were simply not capable or carrying them out. This caused the war to be drawn out, causing great losses of lives and materials.

After nine months Dr John Garang de Mabior came for the graduation ceremony. For the first time Cagai Atem also visited the various battalions. The soldiers were now going to the battle field, they announced. But not me. Cdr William Nyuon took me out of the line, saying that I would remain behind, together with some other intellectuals and some elderly people. The girls were all taken back to Itang. It is worth mentioning that not a single girl died during the training, although they underwent exactly the same training as we did. To me it was proof that it was lack of food that had killed the male trainees.

A month later Cdr Salva Kiir Maryadit came to organize those left behind for cadet training. We were to receive our departure orders the next morning, but when we went to the administration centre we were told that Cdr Salva Kiir first wanted to brief us. So we returned to our centres and waited. When Cdr Salva eventually came to our centre, he called me with a few others. "You are not going for cadet training," he told us.

"May we ask why not?" I asked.

"A decision from above."

"You also left me behind when Zalzal II went to the field for general training," I said.

"This is not negotiable. You are going to attend a political school."

No use of arguing about that, so we all just kept quiet. But when Cdr Slava Kiir was about to leave, I raised my hand.

"Yes?" he said.

"Some of us have left our wives behind at Itang. Will you give us permission to go back to them and see our children?"

"All right. You may go to Itang and remain there until you are called for political school."

I then understood that I was not wanted for military service, although by now I was a trained soldier. People older than me, men like Dr Justin Yac Arop and Victoria Adhar Arop had also been included among those going for cadet training. Both of them were from my area.

CHAPTER 23

Mistreatment and Victory of the Malou Ci Guak Recruits

The next group of recruits after us from Bahr el Ghazal arrived at Dimo Refugee Camp late 1988. Most of them were from Northern Gogrial. This was to be the last group of recruits to join the Movement voluntarily. The stories they told when they arrived at Dimo were terrifying.

The great famine of 1987/8 coupled with the devastation caused by the Arab cattle raiders (*Marahliin*) had forced the communities bordering Northern Sudan to split into two main groups. One group moved northwards and settled in the Northern cities up to Khartoum. The other group which was composed largely of those who still had cattle, went southwards up to the border of Gogrial with Tonj. This group encountered new problems. The host communities were sometimes hostile to them. Their arrival with large numbers of cattle caused great congestion over grazing areas and the water points and caused quarrels between them and the host communities. There were several outbreaks of disease, both human and animal, and the blame was always put on the newcomers for allegedly coming with cattle and human infections.

At Dimo, the recruits talked of their intention to go back to Bahr el Ghazal after their training to fight the Arab cattle raiders. This was an open secret which reached Dr John Garang very quickly. The members of the movement from Northern Bahr el Ghazal had repeatedly complained to Dr John Garang that their people were neglected and left to be destroyed by the Arab cattle raiders. Dr John Garang therefore decided to open a base in Dimo for the training of those recruits instead of taking them to Bonga as usual. He then appointed Cdr Abu Lela Adam as base commander of Dimo Training Camp and A/Cdr Marko Col Maciec as his deputy.

Cdr Abu Lela Adam was an officer in the Sudan army and commanded Khartoum forces against the SPLA forces under Kerubino Kuanyin Bol. Abu Lela Adam and others were captured by the forces of Kerubino in a battle around Blue Nile area. This was when Kerubino was the SPLA sector commander for Blue Nile before he split from the SPLA. Cdr Kerubino spared the life of Abu Lela Adam and sent him to the SPLA detention centre as a prisoner of war (POW) and gave the report to the Commander-in-Chief of the SPLA, Dr John Garang. Dr John then ordered that Abu Lela Adam be transferred to his headquarters. Abu Lela Adam was a Funj from one of the most neglected areas in Sudan.

Dr John hoped to orient him and make him understand the reasons why the SPLM/A was fighting the Khartoum government. He would then use him to bring the Funj youth into the movement. Very soon Abu Lela was given the rank of Commander (Cdr). While Abu Lela was still at the headquarters of the Commander-in-Chief, he was appointed Commander of Dimo Training base. Being the commander of the training camp, Abu Lela Adam decided to feed the trainees boiled maize grain - and maize grain only - throughout the training period, unlike our case in Bilpam where we were allowed to pound the maize into flour before cooking it. They also had no health services. A number of trainees died of stomach complications and malnutrition.

A/Cdr. Marko Col Maciec who was a Southerner and a Dinka for that matter did not intervene to alleviate the mistreatment of his own people. I fail to understand why both men, Cagai Atem in Bilpam during our training and Marko Col Maciec in Dimo, cared so little about the lives of the trainees. It may have been coincidence, but both of them were promoted to the rank of Commander (Cdr) soon after the graduation of those trainees.

Dr John went to Dimo to graduate the trainees. They were armed with G3 rifles which had been confiscated from the Sudan army. This was the first time the SPLA soldiers received G3 rifles and they were not happy about it, but when Dr John told them that they were all going back home to Bahr el Ghazal, they were extremely excited and wanted to move immediately.

They were given Cdr Agasio Akol Tong as their commander as they returned home to Bahr el Ghazal. Meanwhile, Abu Lela Adam went back to Dr John's headquarters. He did not stay long. Before he could be deployed to the frontline to persuade his people to join the Movement, he escaped to Khartoum. In Khartoum, he openly confessed - and boasted about - what he had done to the SPLA trainees. He said that the SPLA was a strong army but lacked good military intelligence, otherwise, they would have discovered what he was doing. The rate at which the trainees died, should have alarmed any person, particularly the leadership. Maybe I was the only one to consider what was going on at Bilpam and Dimo as abnormal.

The newly graduated soldiers should have rested for at least two weeks in Dimo with good food to prepare them for the long journey back home, but instead they were instructed to leave immediately.

Cdr Agasio went ahead and arrived in Yirol in Bahr el Ghazal long before the last man under his command passed the Murle area in Upper Nile. The rear was not well organized. The soldiers broke into very small groups and in the rush to reach water points some weak soldiers were left to follow unassisted. The people of Murle had a reputation for ambushing such small SPLA groups and kill the soldiers for their guns. This time, they simply followed the weak soldiers and found them lying by the roadside with their heads resting on their rifles, too weak to offer any resistance. So they collected the rifles and offered the men walking sticks with which they could support themselves for the rest of their journey. Not all of them made it to Yirol.

The journey from Yirol to Gogrial took about a week through the *toch* as the soldiers had to avoid the government-held towns like Rumbek and Tonj in the south. There were a number of Dinka cattle camps on their route, where they were offered bulls and milk for sustenance.

The Dinka refered to these men as "Malou Ci Guak" meaning the "pale thin soldiers" or "Malou Giim", after their G3 rifles.

When they arrived at Mangol Apuk, about thirty miles from the River Lol, they were told that the Arab cattle raiders had reached Twic. The following morning they left for Twic. When they reached halfway, they met other SPLA forces grouping up for a fight with the Arab cattle raiders (Marahliin). They were told that the Arab cattle raiders had already crossed the river and followed it eastwards. When the Marahliin reached a place called Akuac Ariem, they halted for the night. They believed that they would be secure because to the north the river Lol was too deep for anyone to cross. If they were attacked, they reasoned, it could only be from the south or west.

Anyway, there were so many of them – more than ever before. A battle they had fought earlier had given them a rough idea of how many SPLA soldiers there were in the area, and they were confident that they would easily overrun them in the morning, after which there would be nothing to stop them from penetrating deep into the south, where people still had cattle. What they did not know was that Malou Ci Guak had arrived in the area, and had moved into position to the west, up to the Lol.

In the morning, as they were moving southwards, they were engaged in battle by the forces they had expected to find there. But then Malou Ci Guak launched a surprise attack from the west. The Marahliin attempted to push back the SPLA forces on both fronts, but failed. When they realized that they were overwhelmed, they ran into the swampy Sudd because the river Lol at that point was too deep to cross. They left behind their dead and wounded, and their food. They hoped to find an escape route from the swamp, but the Sudd extended for miles and miles and was getting deeper and deeper. What with the swarms of mosquitoes and other insects pestering then, the snakes and crocodiles – and hunger – it would be impossible to remain there, let alone reorganize from there. They attempted to fight their way back to dry land in smaller groups, but the SPLA forces were waiting for them at the edge of the Sudd, killing the men as soon as they emerged. Nobody could tell how many of the cattle raiders escaped and returned to the north.

This was the famous Battle of Akuac Ariem, the one that finally put an end to Arab cattle raiding. All the SPLA forces were subsequently moved to the border with Northern Sudan, and many of them returned home with the cattle they had lost. When the Marahliin realized that cattle raiding had become too dangerous, they signed a peace agreement with the Dinka people, whereby they were allowed to come to Dinkaland - unarmed - with their cattle for grazing and to access water points. Peace markets were soon opened to which they brought their goods for trading.

CHAPTER 24

Distressing News

One evening Cdr William Nyuon called Taupiny Malek Aguek and me to his house in Itang. Unlike my experience at Dr John Garang's house not so long before, we were well received. A soldier at the gate escorted us to an officer waiting inside the fence. The officer offered us chairs to sit on and went to announce our arrival to Cdr William Nyuon. When he came back he asked if we had pistols, and we assured him that we did not. He did not search our pockets but ushered us in right away. Cdr William Nyuon received us very warmly. We sat down and the officer who had brought us in served tea.

Cd. William Nyuon chatted to us about Nasir. But after we had finished our tea, he took a deep breath. When he spoke again, his voice had changed.

"I'm told that you are close relatives of Victor Bol Ayuolnhom Kuol," he said.

When we had each explained how we were related, he said, "There is a very important matter I must talk to you about. Victor Bol has passed away."

We just looked at him, without uttering a word.

"Victor Bol died of a disease," he said. "He has not been killed. He died of a disease. Sudden severe diarrhoea."

Cdr William Nyuon kept talking, on and on, repeating his statement that Victor Bol had not been killed by anybody. He had died of a disease.

"Have you got any questions?" he asked.

"How long is it since Victor Bol died?" I asked.

"He died about two months ago."

"Victor told us that there were no medical facilities at the place where he was held," I said.

"Where did he die?" Taupiny Malek wanted to know.

"I'm afraid I don't know the exact place."

"All I know is that he died in prison." Cdr William Nyuon replied.

"There is something very important I want you to do," Cdr William Nyuon said. "I need you to explain to his family that he died of a disease and has not been killed by anyone."

"We understand your message, and we'll pass it on to the family," I said.

We left Cdr William's house in a gloomy mood. We decided not to go to Victor's house that evening because it was already very late. We'd break the sad news to his wife and the rest of the family in the morning.

The next day I walked to Victor Bol's house accompanied by a number of other people to break the news to the family. His wife Biem Ring Panek was distressed when she saw so many people approaching. She gave us a very difficult time. We conveyed Cdr William Nyuon's message, to her, but she did not believe it. She insisted that her husband had been killed by the leadership of the movement. If he had not been imprisoned, he would not have died. If he had received medical attention, the diarrhoea would not have killed him. It took a month for emotions to calm down in that family. All the efforts made by Biem Ring Panek to know or see where her husband was buried were in vain.

Then it transpired that the two men, Victor Bol Ayuolnhom and Kawac Makuei who recruited and brought to Ethiopia a very large number of recruits that later became the Muor-Muor Division, were among the people whom Dr.

John Garang referred to in his speeches as the *"marasiin"* from Bahr el Ghazal.

It is worth mentioning that Victor Bol was very popular among his people, he was in the last parliament of 1982 in Juba. He came as unopposed member from our consistuency in Twic West (Wunrok, Pan-nyok and Akoc). His death was a great loss beyond his immediate family.

CHAPTER 25

Tharpam to Kapoeta

While we were in Itang, a small problem cropped up between the SPLA soldiers and the Ethiopian Anyuak militia in which there was an exchange of fire, but no-one was killed. Soon after this incident we heard talk that the presence of the intellectuals in Itang was a security risk. Whether this was connected with the shooting incident, we did not know.

Whatever the reason, we were told to report to a place called Tharpam, three miles away, on the northern side of the road from Itang to Gambela. When we arrived there, the base commander, A/Cdr Bol Kong, showed us a single big tree. "That will be your accommodation," he said. It was the rainy season. The grass around the place had been burned down, and what was left, had rotted. But we managed to gather enough grass from it to construct three small *kurnuks*, each to accommodate forty of us. When it was not raining, we slept outside. Rainy nights we spent sitting up in the kurnuks, as there was no space for us to lie down.

One evening we were ordered to go to a small village between Itang and Tharpam, where some Ethiopian Nuer people lived. We had to search the Nuer houses for guns – while we ourselves were not armed. When we asked the base commander for arms, he just said, "You did not come from Itang with arms. I can't arm you now. These are orders, and must be executed."

It was getting dark, and as we approached the village, we divided ourselves into groups of four. As we neared two huts, the four of us split into two. There was no gun in the house I entered with Cagai Matet Guem, but next door my comrades did discover one. When they ordered the occupants to hand over the gun, a heated argument broke out. They called out to us to come and help, but when the Nuers heard us coming, the owner of the gun shot both of our comrades in the chest, and ran away. We found them lying unconscious on the ground. We sat down with them, fruitlessly waiting for help. After a few minutes one of them passed away. Shooting was intensifying throughout the village. We noticed that the rest of our comrades were running for their lives, some in the direction of Tharpam, others to Itang. We followed the group running towards Itang. We spent the night in our own houses and returned to Tharpam in the morning. The only casualties turned out to have been our two friends. Realizing that we were unarmed, the Nuers had shot into the air - to deter us, not to kill us.

We used to go to Itang for food rations, and carry the items back to Tharpam on our heads. One morning it was my turn to go to Itang with some others to fetch our food. As my companions had some private business in Itang after we had received the food, I decided to return by myself, without going home to my family first. Men usually carry loads on their shoulders, not on their heads, but six gallons of vegetable oil was too heavy for that, so I put the carton on my head and followed the main road to Tharpam, which happened to run past the Sudanese market. A friend of my wife's, Madam Ayak Gol, the wife of A/Cdr Salva Mathok Geng, was behind me on the road, on her way to the market. She was astonished to see me, well dressed, and carrying a carton of oil on my head, walking towards the market, where the Sudanese sold such items to the Ethiopians. Knowing me well, she could not believe that I would do such a thing. It was beneath my status. If I had anything to sell, she thought, I should have got someone else to do it for me. She stood watching me, puzzled, until I had passed the market and disappeared from her sight on the road to Gambela.

She immediately went to see my wife, Acol Ayuel. "What has become of Bol Majok Adiang?" she asked.

"He's been taken to Tharpam," Acol told her. "With the other intellectuals."

"Did he come home this morning?"

"No, he wasn't here."

"Well, I have just seen him carrying oil on his head. The state he is in makes me extremely sad. Is this how low the former senior officials of Sudan have fallen in the movement?"

In Tharpam, the bad treatment given us was worse than that meted out to Arab prisoners of war - they were issued with mosquito nets unlike us who never received any. We also used to carry food for them, from Itang to Tharpam.

Two months later we were taken to Bonga to wait for Dr John Garang. It took him another two months to arrive and order us to be taken to another SPLA base called Zink between Gambela and Bonga. Here we spent a short while until Dr John Garang came back to organize us for political school.

After a thorough inspection – everything on us was removed, except our clothes – we were each in turn led in to meet Garang, the chairman and commander-in-chief. When it was my turn, I found him looking down at a sheet of paper. I stamped my feet and saluted him. He raised his head and looked at me in silence. He then looked at the paper again, and called out my name.

"Yes, Comrade."

"Are you Bol Majok Adiang?" The same old question again!

"Yes."

He asked for my other details, then told me to go. It was a large room, and he was sitting at the far end. When I reached the door, I looked back. Dr John was still looking at me, holding his head in both hands.

The list came out at once. Ninety-two of us were to go to a political school at Isoke. This was the first political course to be offered inside Sudan. Isoke is in present day Eastern Equatoria, south of Torit town. We would be airlifted by helicopter from Gambela to Jebel el Ruad on the Ethiopian border with Sudan, and from there vehicles would take us to Kapoeta. Before we left Gambela, my wife came from Itang to see me.

"I want you to stay in Itang for two more months, no longer." I told her. "Sell all our cows and then travel with the children to Dimo." Dimo was another refugee camp. "From there I hope you will find transport to Kapoeta, and then to Torit. Dr Madut Deng Mayol will put you up in his house."

Our journey from Jebel el Ruad to Kapoeta depended on the availability of military vehicles travelling from Ethiopia to Sudan – which meant that we remained at Jebel el Ruad for a long time. The base commander Captain Makuol selected thirty of us to build a huge store – what it was for, we did not know. The other sixty-two were accommodated on the Sudanese side of the river in a compound known as the house of Dr John Garang.

We cut poles in the morning and grass in the evening, and constructed a fine store. Captain Makuol was happy with our work. But food was again a problem. Within a few days we would run out of rations. Just then two heavily laden military vehicles arrived from Dimo. Captain Makuol asked the Ethiopian drivers to take thirty of us, but they refused, saying that they were not allowed to carry passengers, only military equipment.

"It's an emergency," Captain Makuol told them. "They will face starvation soon."

The drivers remained unmoved.

"Then park your vehicles and join us for supper so that you may share our suffering."

The drivers had brought their own food, but when they saw what we ate, they agreed to take 30 of us, fifteen on each vehicle.

The road was muddy and difficult and we spent a night on the road. The next day around midday we reached Boma. By that time we were very tired and hungry, but Cdr Anthony Bol Madut, who was in charge of Boma, showed no sympathy. Instead, he sent a 1st Lieutenant, an Arab who had been captured and integrated into the SPLA, to inspect us and our luggage.

He did what is called *"farj al matar"* in the army. He made us unload our luggage, untie our bedding, unfold the groundsheets and put our bed sheets and boxes or bags on the groundsheets. Then we were told to move away while the officer and his soldiers searched everything – the sheets, the mosquito nets. They shook everything and opened boxes and bags. They unfolded our clothes and made sure that nothing remained in the boxes and bags. Every scrap of paper they found was read carefully. Then they came to us and searched our pockets, again scrutinizing everything that could be read. They did not find anything they could possibly object to.

Then suddenly we saw an Antonov bomber coming for us from the north, over Jebel Boma.

"Move the vehicles away," Cdr Anthony Bol Madut ordered in a harsh voice. "At once!" We scrambled to put our belongings back into the boxes and get into the vehicles as they moved away from the base towards Kapoeta. When we reached Khor Cuom five miles away, the Antonov was still hovering over Boma base. We asked the drivers to park under some big trees, and we scattered in various directions to take cover. We saw the Antonov dropping several bombs, in a line from north to south, and then from east to west, before it disappeared into the direction it had come from.

When it was gone, we continued our journey and arrived in Kapoeta very late that evening.

CHAPTER 26

More Frustration

The commander at Kapoeta, A/Cdr Bior Ajang, known as "Bior el Aswuod", and all those working with him, including the notorious security officer Deng Aguang Atem, were all from Bor - like the majority of those who came with us. Our group included Aguang Atem, the security officer's father. We spent a month in Kapoeta, and almost every day we were invited to someone's house for a meal. Rams were slaughtered and local beer made in every house, and our health improved rapidly.

The sixty-two men who had remained behind, joined us a month later. The stories they told us were not good. They had run out of food and were forced to hunt monkeys in order to survive. Soon after their arrival we were taken to Isoke.

A/Cdr Kuol Dem was in charge of the political school at Isoke, and we were the first students. A number of trainees had already arrived. There were three classes – one for military intelligence, one for political affairs (for the NCOs) and a third for us, the intellectuals. Our class was kept separate from the other two. The classrooms had already been completed, but we built our own houses.

The classes started well, with paperwork and some military exercises taking up most of the time. It was only when the grinding mill broke down that we had to pound our own maize. And of course, we did our own cooking.

A/Cdr Kuol Dem was a strong administrator, enabling us to complete the training successfully. Unlike A/Cdr Cagai

Atem Biar of Bilpam, he took proper care of us. Besides maize, beans, oil and salt, he also provided some medical services.

We lost only one young man from Twic. He came from the Arab Gulf States and went straight to Itang refugee camp, but he found life very difficult, and developed a mental problem. He spent only three days with us at Isoke before he disappeared into the mountains. Three days later he was brought back by people from a nearby village, but before a car could be found to take him to Torit for treatment, he disappeared again, this time for good.

In October 1990 the chairman and commander-in-chief, Dr John Garang de Mabior, came to Isoke for our graduation. But when the war intensified around Kapoeta, he stopped the graduation and sent the young men in the first two classes to the frontline. They were dispatched to Kapoeta to reinforce the troops. When the enemy had been repulsed, they came back. Some of their comrades had been killed in action.

Dr John Garang Mabior then returned to complete the graduation. He explained the criteria he had used to determine our ranks: University graduates, he said, regardless of when they graduated and their former positions in the Sudan, would receive the rank of 1st lieutenant. Those who were not university graduates, would be given the rank of 2nd lieutenant. He then read out the list of names with their ranks. The graduates who had arrived in Ethiopia after me were given the rank of 1st lieutenant and attached to Shield 2. I was commissioned as 1st lieutenant, but attached to Shield 3. Eli Acol Deng Hot, who was not a university graduate, and who defected and reached Ethiopia after me, and who did the general military training with me, was commissioned as a captain. Dr Garang called it "special consideration". Kau Akol Dhieu, whose qualifications were exactly the same as Eli Acol's, including their previous positions in Sudan, was made 2nd lieutenant, whilst a certain David from Yei, who reached Ethiopia some years after us and who was not a university graduate and who did not do general military training, was commissioned as 1st lieutenant. The rest of the students, primary school teachers mostly from Bor, were commissioned as 2nd lieutenants, and then immediately promoted to 1st lieutenants. Two NCOs who later turned out to be security men attached to us in order to spy on us, were commissioned as 1st lieutenants. In my case, however, and Kau Akol Dhieu's, the criteria were strictly observed.

When Dr. Garang had finished, I raised my hand, but he told me to be quiet. "I know that what I have done is not strictly correct," he told us. "But I know what I am doing, and it must remain like that." He then left for Kapoeta, and we had to wait for him to come back to deploy us.

I had never heard of anybody complaining to Garang de Mabior before, but I made up my mind to do so. I put my complaint in writing, and gave it to A/Cdr Kuol Dem to hand to him on his return to Isoke.

When he returned, we were taken to him one by one to be interviewed. When I stood before him he asked his usual question: "Are you Bol Majok Adiang?"

Then: "Are you married?"

"Yes, I am. I have three wives."

"Any grown-up children?"

I had refused to allow my children to join the army two years back in Gambela, so I merely said, "My son Ajal fought with Kon Anok in the campaign of Rumbek."

He then asked how old my son was and I replied that he

was 18 years old.

Garang then turned to Cdr Kuol Manyang Juk who was sitting next to me, and asked if he had a question for me.

"Yes," Cdr Kuol said, "Given the economic conditions in the Sudan, how do you manage to support three wives?"

I just laughed. "Is there anything wrong with my question?" he wanted to know.

"You should rather have asked how my family is coping alone while I'm in the bush and not receiving a salary."

I knew that he was implying that I must be a member of the Sudanese bourgeoisie. When I was in Torit, I saw how lavishly Cdr Kuol Manyang Juk, was living. There was no woman in his house, but he had a large number of bodyguards. They slaughtered a bull every other day, and all the best food in the town was at his disposal.

"I can tell you that the position you now hold in Torit, is exactly the position I held in the Sudan government, except that I didn't have special privileges," I said.

"Do you have any more questions?" Garang asked Kuol. He did not.

"Then you may go," Garang told me.

After he had completed the interviews, Garang left immediately. There was no opportunity for A/Cdr Kuol Dem to deliver my letter, but he promised to do so at some later stage.

I was next posted to the administration college at Imatong Mountains, so I left for Torit where I was to wait for the others who were going to Imatong, including the students we were going to train. Meanwhile my wife Acol Ayuel Rehan was stranded at Dimo, in the house of Bol Bol Awendit, the husband of her stepsister Arual Ayuel. The military vehicles which came to Dimo, refused to take a woman and children back to the Sudan. When Salva Kiir Mayardit came to Torit, I went to see him about my stranded family, and he sent a message to the base commander of Dimo, ordering him to transport my wife and children to Torit in the first available vehicle, regardless of who was in the front seat. When eventually they arrived, I was still waiting for the others who had been posted to the college, but I decided to go ahead to Imatong with my family.

Our first job was to build classrooms as well as accommodation for the trainees. The officer in charge was A/Cdr Majur Nhial Makol, with A/Cdr Samuel Ater Dak as his deputy. A captain and a 1st Lt (senior to me), both illiterate, were responsible for the administration of the college, while Samuel Ater Dak and I were the teachers.

It was difficult to understand why A/Cdr Majur Nhial was to run the college, whilst Samuel Ater Dak, the most senior administrator in the whole of Southern Sudan, served as his deputy. All the administrators in the Sudan, including me, were trained by Samuel Ater Dak. Majur Nhial graduated a year behind me from the same department, and joined the police. A more suitable posting for him would have been the newly opened SPLM/A police college opened at Loboni. This was just another sign of the mistrust that existed in the movement. As was the appointment of two illiterate officers as my superiors. But, of course, they were the ones trusted by the chairman. I was the most junior officer at the college, and I used to submit to the decisions of those illiterate officers, even when I knew they were not right.

We were ready to start teaching, when John Garang ordered the trainees first to go to Isoke for political orientation before they did the local government administration course. All we could do, was wait for them to return.

CHAPTER 27

Mutiny

As the war at Kapoeta intensified, the officers under training at Isoke were deployed to the battlefield. Then Dr Riek Machar Teny declared a coup against the leadership of Dr John Garang de Mabior – and we waited in vain for those officers - our students - to return to Imatong.

A few days after the mutiny, Dr John Garang went to meet the forces at their various locations to ensure their loyalty. When he arrived at Imatong, the five of us stood waiting for him in a small square in front of the classroom, lined up, in uniform and carrying our guns. Garang de Mabior spoke very briefly, denouncing the mutiny and calling it "a one-man act". He took Majur Nhial's hand (Majur was from Bor) and walked to his house, leaving the rest of us standing. Cdr William Nyuon then left with his fellow Nuer tribesman, Captain David Kong. I went to my house with Cdr Martin Manyiel Ayuel, also from Twic. Cdr Manyiel greeted my family, and returned to where the cars were parked.

The chairman's entourage then left for Torit. We noticed that security measures had been relaxed. Garang travelled with very few bodyguards, and the strong force with heavy guns which used to move with him, had been scaled down.

The coup received very little support. Yet it seemed to have opened the mouths of the people, who began to express their feelings freely. Many of the citizens of SPLA/M-held areas who had kept quiet before, were now talking about the shortcomings of the leadership.

Even before the coup a number of people were not happy with the way the movement was being run and how the war was being fought. Although there was a High Command of five men (later increased with a number of alternate members), they did not sit for a single day as a body to discuss and evaluate their strategy and to plan the way forward or ways to overcome problems. It was John Garang's one-man show instead. Members of the High Command were merely called to receive and carry out orders. Their opinions were not sought. Commanders like Dr Riek Machar and Dr Lam Akol Ajawin were sometimes vocal against the way things were run, but avoided direct confrontation with Dr John Garang de Mabior.

In order to put down the mutiny of Dr Riek, Dr John Garang did exactly what he had done when he disagreed with Cdr Kerubino Kuanyin Bol. Actually, what happened between Kerubino Kuanyin Bol and John Garang, was not a mutiny. It was merely a disagreement. But, in army circles, when a junior officer disagrees with his senior, it could be construed as mutiny. It was true that Kerubino had often in the early days disagreed with Garang and their quarrels had always been resolved in a brotherly manner. But this time the four members of the high command for once met at Itang refugee camp and agreed to imprison Kuanyin Bol. The result of the meeting was an open secret, also that Kerubino ignored it. He fled to Addis Ababa, hoping that the president of Ethiopia, Mengistu Haile Mariam, would intervene on his behalf. The president, however, assisted Dr John by arresting Kerubino and sending him to prison.

Knowing that most of the officers who were in Blue Nile with Kerubino were from Bahr el Ghazal, Dr John sent Cdr

Salva Kiir, who came from the same area of Bahr el Ghazal, to them. These officers, including Faustino Atem 'Gualdit' Koc Ayok, were confident that they had no part in any mutiny or coup, and came to Salva Kiir voluntarily. When Salva Kiir arrived in Ethiopia with them, however, they too were arrested and jailed with Kerubino, indefinitely.

In the case of Dr Riek Machar, Garang sent Cdr William Nyuon, who was Nuer, to Leer, Dr Riek's home village. I do not know what he did there, but I do know what Dr Riek did afterwards in Bor, presumably in revenge for whatever Cdr William did in Leer. His forces carried out a massacre from the extreme north of Bor to the extreme south. They killed soldiers and citizens alike, women, children, babies – many thousands of them. Even the cattle, goats and sheep were killed. Houses and grain stores were burned to ashes. They wreaked total destruction.

CHAPTER 28

Some Order Established

The fighting between the forces of Dr Riek and the SPLA under Dr John Garang could have ended in the Upper Nile, but was purposely transferred to the Bahr el Ghazal region, for several reasons. Most of the SPLA soldiers were from Bahr el Ghazal – men who, before they joined the SPLA, had been fighting against the Arab cattle raiders, especially at Aweil and Gogrial. These soldiers used to go to a place called Majok Yinhthieu where another group of Arab militias would exchange guns for cows. This enabled them to oppose the *Marahliin*.

When the war between the SPLA and the Sudan government broke out, those young men heard that guns were given away in Ethiopia, and they travelled to Ethiopia in large numbers to obtain free guns. They intended to return home and fight the *Marahliin*, but once in Ethiopia they were oriented and persuaded to join the Sudanese liberation army (SPLA).

The news that kept coming from home was not good. The *Marahliin* were reported to have taken all the cattle, killed many men and carried away young women, girls and children. There was no satisfactory response from the SPLM/A leadership. Dr John Garang was quoted as saying that Bahr el Ghazal, especially the devastated areas of Aweil and Gogrial, were like the edge of a field. "Goats and cows can destroy the crops at the edge of a field," he said, "and there can still be a good harvest."

This saying angered many of the soldiers from Bahr el Ghazal, and they tried to escape from where they were fighting for the SPLM/A and go home to fight the *Marahliin*.

Before Dr Riek mutinied he was posted as commander in Northern Upper Nile, while Arok Thon Arok was the commander in Southern Upper Nile. The Bahr el Ghazal soldiers escaping from frontlines in Upper Nile region who used the Northern Axis of Dr Riek Machar Teny were given free passage to Bahr el Ghazal, whereas those who used the Southern Axis of Cdr Arok Thon Arok, were rounded up and executed – a very cruel way of preventing the people of Bahr el Ghazal, who were bearing most of the burden of the war, from escaping.

Among other issues, the quarrel between Cdr Kerubino Kuanyin and Dr John Garang pertained to Cdr Arok Thon Arok. It was assumed that Dr Riek had at least some support in Bahr el Ghazal. Although Bahr el Ghazal at that time was governed by Cdr Daniel Awet Akot, it was Dr Riek Machar Teny who had brought some stability to Northern Bahr el Ghazal when he toured the area long before the arrival of Cdr Daniel Awet. Thus he was still fairly popular with the civil population of Northern Bahr el Ghazal.

The civil population of Bentiu, for reasons best known to themselves, moved in large numbers with their families and cattle to the areas of Yirol, Rumbek, Tonj and Gogrial. They were well received and intermarriage between Dinka and Nuer families was common.

Only God knows what would have become of those innocent citizens of Bentiu and the areas mentioned above if those unlucky people had not been made part of a dispute in which they had no hand in. To bring the war to them was seen as an opportunity to take revenge for what Dr Riek's forces had done in Bor, and to destroy the good relationship that had been built between the Nuer of Bentiu and the people of Bhar el Ghazal – a positive relationship that had never existed before. Nuer high-ranking officers and soldiers in the four areas of Yirol, Rumbek, Tonj and Gogrial were rounded up and killed in cold blood, simply because they were Nuer. Some of them had never even met Dr Riek in their lives. Civilians, old people and babies were murdered alike. The soldiers divided the Nuer cattle among themselves – including the cattle paid as bride price to Dinka families.

Some officers were brought all the way from the Aweil area to be killed at the SPLA base of Mathiangdit in Gogrial. They included a brilliant Nuer officer who brought down a number of Sudanese warplanes over Aweil using SAM – 7 missiles.

Surprisingly, the Nuer members of the SPLM/A in Equatoria including those who were at the headquarters of Dr John Garang, were ot touched.

In my opinion, the present enmity between the citizens of Unity State and those of Warrap and Lakes dates back to that massacre. What prompted Dr Riek to declare a coup was mistrust. Dr John Garang was aware of Dr Riek's movements and he called a General High Command meeting for the first time. It was to be attended by all the permanent and alternate members. Dr Riek regarded this as a trap to get him into Dr John Garang's hands. After the way Dr John had arrested and imprisoned the founder of the SPLM/SPLA, Cdr Kerubino Kuanyin Bol, Dr Riek knew that Dr John would not hesitate to jail anyone else who opposed his system of running the movement. So, somewhat prematurely, he attempted to seize power.

The colleges the SPLM/SPLA had established were abruptly closed. Cdr Awet Akot asked all the local government administrators from Bhar el Ghazal who had been deployed in Eastern Equatoria to return to Bhar el Ghazal to reestablish the local government administration there. Almost all of us who had joined the movement were from Yirol, Rumbek and Gogrial. In December 1991 we assembled in Torit, where we were briefed by Cdr William Nyuon. Then we left for Bor from where a boat would take us to Bahr el Ghazal.

As we traveled from Torit to Bor, the road from Jemeza to Bor was littered with dead bodies - human and animal - killed by Dr Riek forces. In Bor town the human bodies had been removed, but the rotting carcasses of animals were everywhere. We had to move to the riverside for some fresh air.

A week later we took a boat for Shambe and from there we were taken by car to Karic in the Rumbek area. We were warmly received by Cdr Awet Akot, who announced that he would post us to our home counties. "You need to be near home," he said, "so that you can do the work of the movement and at the same time bring together your families that have been scattered by the war." I was posted to Wunrok County in Twic.

At Lietnhom I met Cdr Bona Bang Dhol who told me to proceed to Wunrok directly. He said a letter would follow. When I arrived at Wunrok on 1 February 1992, I found the town almost empty. Everybody had gone to Abindau two miles away to receive the Missieria traders. A peace agreement had been reached with the Missieria tribe whereby they would stop cattle raiding and killing people in exchange for the right to come to Abindau to sell their goods and buy cattle. They were also allowed to bring their cattle for water and grazing. The Missieria carried goods on camels, horses, donkeys and bullocks and in a very short time they brought all types of goods to Abindau. During the dry season when the people of Twic were hungry, they gave priority to the transport of dura. Life had become very good for both the Missieria and the people of Twic, and both were very happy with the agreement.

The peace was sometimes disturbed by the Nuer cattle raiders from Bentiu who tried to rob both the Dinka and the Missieria, but they were halted by the combined force of the two tribes.

When I arrived, Captain Santino Deng Wol was both the army commander and the civil military administrator (CMA) for Twic and Abyei. He handed the office of CMA to me. One of my former rate collectors who had now become a 1st Lieutenant Gaetano Nyuol Atem, senior to me in the movement, attempted with the help of some others to create a problem between me and Santino Deng Wol, but he did not fool Santino. Santino was a student when he joined the movement, but he became a brilliant officer and it did not take him long to understand what some of the officers under him were up to. Most of them were from Twic, whilst he was from Aweil and had been in Twic for a very long time. Some people told him he was lucky to work with me, but these officers claimed that I was junior to them and they would not work under me. He took my side. Santino Deng Wol and I established a strong administration. He was soon promoted to the rank of Alternate Commander (A/Cdr).

CHAPTER 29

Trouble

Three years later, early in 1995, disaster struck again. The news reached us that Kerubino Kuanyin Bol, Faustino Atem 'Gualdit' Koc Ayok and others had escaped from prison in Eastern Equatoria and fled to Kenya. In June 1995 Kerubino was reported to be in the Bentiu area, organizing the Nuer to accompany him to his home area, Twic. In the last week of June he was at Jara, on the border between Bentiu and Gogrial. At Jara he was supposed to be halted by the SPLA forces under A/Cdr Mading Duor Aguar, the deputy commander of Gogrial and Abyei, but the Apuk people petitioned Mading Duor Aguar not to attack Kerubino in their area as he was on his way to Wunrok in Twic, his home area. Mading took the advice of his people and allowed Kerubino's forces free passage to Twic.

A/Cdr Santino Deng Wol, the commander of the forces in Twic and Abyei, sent forces from Wunrok to the southern side of the Lol River to intercept Kerubino. They were supposed to lay an ambush for Kerubino's forces, but failed to do so. In the night of 4 July, Kerubino's forces crossed the river at Abayok, and marched northwards towards Tekajak, the main SPLA military base in Twic. Halfway there, they turned and headed for Wunrok and Abindau on the northern side of the river.

Kerubino's soldiers were mostly Nuer, but as long as they did not talk, no-one could tell the difference between Dinkas and Nuers. They all wore the same SPLA uniform.

So the people who saw them thought they were SPLA forces coming from Tekajak to Wunrok - and Kerubino's soldiers were able to attack the two bases simultaneously from a short distance.

I had spent the night at the house of my wife Acol Ayuel Rehan, and then gone to Veronica's house to repair a bath enclosure that had collapsed. Veronica's aunt was coincidentally joking that I was preparing the enclosure for the Nuer militia that were rumoured to be on their way to Wunrok with Kerubino Kuanyin when we heard the first shot. I wanted to run back to Acol Ayuel's house, but realized that it was not possible, so I turned back halfway.

There were very few soldiers left in Wunrok, mainly bodyguards of A/Cdr Santino Deng Wol. They did not put up any resistance but ran westwards. On my way back to Veronica's house, I saw A/Cdr Santino Deng Wol also running, heading west. I found Veronica standing in front of the house, bewildered, holding her baby son Col in her arms. Col was only six days old. I had no gun – I had left mine in Acol's house. I took the child from Veronica and ran in the direction the others had gone. Veronica followed me, running. When we emerged from the *dura* field onto the airstrip, I saw that the attackers were already ahead of us, chasing and shooting at Santino Deng Wol and his bodyguards. So my wife and I ran towards the river, hoping that the Nuer would be delayed by the SPLA soldiers they were following and that it would give us a chance to escape along the river. But another group turned on us and started shooting at the soldiers ahead of us, including some of Santino Deng Wol's bodyguards who had been left behind. Some of them fell, between my wife Veronica and me. They did not shoot at Veronica and me, though. Perhaps they knew that we would never be able to escape, since the river was deep, and flowing fast.

When we reached the river bank, I stopped and caught Veronica's hand. "Let us rather die on dry ground than drown in the river," I said. We sat down. Kerubino's soldiers were less than one hundred metres behind us. "Get up!" they shouted at us. And at a SPLA soldier swimming in the river: "Swim back, or we'll kill you!"

I addressed the soldiers in Nuer, although I had forgotten much of the language I had learnt in Nasir. "Are you Santino Deng Wol?" they asked.

"No, I'm not, I'm someone else."

Perhaps that was why they had not killed me! They thought I was Santino Deng Wol, and they wanted to question him. They came to my house with me and we sat down in the middle of the compound while Kerubino's soldiers moved from hut to hut. They emptied their bags and filled them with whatever they found I my house, furniture, utensils, anything of value.

Meanwhile my wife Acol Ayuel Rehan had come to Veronica's house, and when she did not find us there, she ran into the dura field and hid there. She found Veronica's aunt also there, with my three-year-old daughter Aker. When they heard our voices in the house, they came out and joined us. By then we had taken most of Veronica and Acol's children and cattle to Acol's parents at village of Gol, north of Wunrok because we were expecting the attack. If the attack had not happened in the morning we would have joined them that day.

The soldiers searched my pockets and took the little money they found, and my watch. I knew that I was their prisoner, but I asked them to allow my wife to go to the nearby village. They refused. Acol quietly took my small daughter and walked away with her. The soldiers saw her and ran after her to stop her. "Please," she told them "I have lost a young child. I think he may be in that house," and she pointed. They took pity on her and allowed her to go and look for the child. Little by little, from house to house, she found her way into the dura field and to Gol village.

When the soldiers had finished their looting, they left Veronica and her aunt in the house, and took me to my wife Acol Ayuel's house, where they locked me up with some others. Among the Nuer soldiers there was a certain man, Majak, from Panaru. He spoke Nuer, but when I heard his name, I knew that he was Dinka. I asked the soldier who was guarding us to call Majak to me, and when he came, I begged him to allow my wife Veronica and her aunt to go to Apukdit north of Wunrok.

The area around my two houses was now occupied by Kerubino's men. At nine o'clock that evening the SPLA attacked, wounding three of Kerubino's soldiers. That same night after the shooting, Veronica was allowed to leave for Gol, where she joined the rest of the family. They were in a safe place now, and worried only about me.

In the morning we left for Tekajak, the SPLA base that had now been captured by Kerubino. Some of the prisoners were made to carry the wounded soldiers, but Madut Angok and I had to carry the guns that had been confiscated from the SPLA soldiers. Each of us carried eleven guns tied together, for twelve miles. At eleven o'clock, when we reached Rumgok, the soldiers decided to take a rest. We prisoners were locked up in a large hut which was guarded. It happened to belong to Santino Malong Deng, one of our officials in Wunrok. Meanwhile Santino had been captured and taken to the other end of his field, while members of his family were taken in another direction, leaving the house empty, ready to be looted – which the soldiers did.

When the soldiers returned with Santino Malong, they pushed him into the hut where we were being kept. He was surprised to find us there.

"Where were you caught?" I asked.

"Here, in my house. I was in this hut taking a rest about ten minutes ago!" The very same hut that had now become a prison to us!

The soldiers had their breakfast but did not give us any. Then we all proceeded to Tekajak where we arrived before sunset and were handed over to the prison unit. The next day Kerubino and his senior officers came to talk to us.

"I have come home to my own people," he said. "I see no reason why my people are running away from me."

When I was asked to speak, I said, "You are hitting a cold iron to mold it into a shape. When you want to make a knife you must hit the iron while it is red hot from the fire. Only then can you achieve the shape you want. Hitting the iron when it is cold will never make a good knife or spear."

"You made mistakes," I continued. "When you refused to obey Garang de Mabior's order, it already amounted to mutiny. As a real soldier, you should not have tried to be reconciled with your commander before the Ethiopian president. Your popularity with your former soldiers has expired. During the long period you spent in custody too many things have changed. Your former soldiers have been reoriented and the commanders commanding them now are no longer the ones you used to know so well. You will find your job very difficult!"

Some officers indicated that they wanted to speak, whether to answer me or about something else I did not know. But Cdr Bipen, a Nuer who was with Kerubino, told them that what I had said did not call for a reply. Kerubino agreed and they left.

I would like to explain that years before, when I first arrived in Itang from the Sudan, I went to see Cdr Kerubino Kuanyin Bol. I wanted to inform him of the conditions those I left behind at home lived in, and I wanted him to enlighten me about the way things were going in the movement. Every time I tried to talk to him, he said there were too many other people vying for his attention, and as soon as he could find some free time, he would sit and talk to me alone. So I remained in my house and waited for him to call me. He never did. He left for Blue Nile and ended up in prison, without even seeing me.

Two days later we moved to Mayen where we were kept in a house near the market. From here Kerubino's forces would go out to Wunrok, Turalei and other places to fight the SPLA forces, and then come back to Mayen. Some soldiers and civilians from our section had joined Kerubino's faction voluntarily, and they cautioned him to separate me from the rest of the prisoners, under close arrest. He was not concerned, and merely said that if I escaped, he would recapture me. Then they suggested to Cdr Simon Madit Ngor that I should be taken to the battle field. So one afternoon Madit Ngor came to the house where we were and pointed at me.

"Why are you not taking part in the fighting?" he asked.
"I don't want to," I said.
"Why not?"
"No reason, I just don't want to go and fight."
"Well, I'm going to take you with me and you will fight."
"I won't fight."
He got very angry. "I'm coming for you in the morning!"
But he did not come. Someone must have reported the conversation to Kerubino and I suppose Kerubino told him to leave me alone.

While I was in Mayen, the SPLA forces were making things difficult for my family, calling them the family of a Nyigat. (The word Nyigat had come to be widely used for Kerubino's forces.) My family decided to come to Mayen with the children and the cattle, but I instructed them to go to Wunrieng instead – a place which was still unoccupied by any force. My idea was that Kerubino would at some stage be forced to withdraw to Bentiu, the area where he came from, and that would give me the opportunity to escape and join my family. Meanwhile Barac Powut Barac, the husband of Ajak Ayuel Rehan, my sister-in-law, had joined my family with his cattle.

As time passed, things were getting more difficult for Kerubino. His forces were running out of ammunition, and the reinforcements he was expecting from Bentiu did not arrive. He secretly sent his security officer Col Mabil Deng, his uncle's son, to Abyei to ask for help with ammunition, but Col did not come back in time. Instead, SPLA reinforcements arrived under Cdr Anthony Bol Madut and Cdr Elias Waya. They engaged with Kerubino's forces at Turalei, but suffered heavy losses. Kerubino's men killed twenty-seven officers and men and wounded many more. Cdr Anthony Bol Madut himself escaped capture narrowly. When Kerubino's forces returned to Mayen in the evening, an urgent meeting was held. Kerubino's officers told him that they had completely run out of ammunition.

Immediately after the meeting ended, we saw people being rounded up in the market and taken to where the sick and wounded soldiers were being kept. Soon we saw them coming back, carrying the sick and wounded. They took the road to Abyei. Clearly Kerubino's foces were leaving Mayen. What we did not understand was why they were going in the direction of Abyei. Perhaps, we thought, they had decided to bypass Turalei and turn towards Aweng or Majok Noon. We were soon to discover that Kerubino actually meant to go to Abyei, to ally himself with the Khartoum forces against the SPLA.

All the units moved together. We, the prisoners, were put in the middle. I walked close to my bodyguard Majok Aguer as well as Bol Majok Angui, my nephew that my wives had sent to me with milk, Mading Piol Majok, my other nephew and Madut Angok whom I was working with at Wunrok. Santino Malong Deng and some others were far ahead, and I could not get to them.

"This is our chance to escape and go back home to the SPLM/SPLA," I told Madut Angok.

"I don't know," he said. "There is no guarantee that the SPLA forces will spare our lives."

So I left him alone, and suggested to the other three, Majok, Bol and Mading, that they escape with me. It was already dark when we arrived at Mabior Ayueldit village. About three hundred metres from us, we saw a forest fire burning. "I want you to escape one by one," I told my three companions. "We'll assemble near the fire."

The fire was in a thick forest where people used to burn trees to make it easier to gather branches for firewood. The four of us met there and started walking back through the forest towards Mayen Abun. My nephew Bol Majok Anguei, led us to Wunrieng where, around ten that evening, we found my family with the cattle. My wives cried when they saw me.

"The SPLA forces are going to kill you!" they said.

"They may, if I fall into the hands of ordinary soldiers," I replied. "But if I meet an officer who knows that I was captured, I will not die. It is normal for a soldier caught in the war to return to his own forces. I have suffered too much in the movement to leave it now and follow people I know are not doing what is right."

I told my brother Piol Majok, Barac Powut and Bol Majok Anguei to remain with the cattle and follow us in the morning, while I immediately left for Wunrok with the whole family and my twin sisters, Alek and Aluel. None of us knew the terrain, and when we realized that we were lost, we spent the rest of the night in a deserted village. I wished that there had been someone I could ask for directions!

CHAPTER 30

Prisoners

Early in the morning we moved again. But that same morning Cdr Elias Waya happened to be moving his forces towards Mayen Abun. We walked right into them near Tekajak, the former SPLA military base. They took my family to a nearby house, and me and my bodyguard Majok Aguer to the end of a field – so that my children would not see what they intended to do to us. They took off our clothes and tied our arms at the elbows behind our backs and began to beat us. One tall young man kept beating me on my head and face even after the others had stopped. He said he would not stop until I cried – like my guard. At last, when he saw my eye bleeding, he stopped, and the soldiers took me to their commander Elias Waya, who was sitting in the shade of a tree some distance away. He ordered them to hand us over to the prison unit.

Meanwhile Bol Majok Anguei, Barac Powut Barac and my brother Piol were on their way to Wunrok with the cattle. Bol and Barac were arrested too and brought to where we were. They at least were not beaten and their hands were not tied. Piol, who was a typical villager and an elderly man, was allowed to continue with the cattle. My family was told to go to Wunrok with him. My wives Veronica and Acol wanted to remain at Tekajak with me, but were told that they would not see me again anyway. And the children needed to follow the cattle or they would not have milk to drink.

The prison was a typical large Dinka hut with a small round door that looked like a hole in the wall. They made certain that we would not be able to escape. Two strong poles were planted in the ground in front of the opening, and thick logs of wood were placed up to the roof between the wall and the poles. It was impossible to force it open from inside the hut.

At three o'clock I was fetched and taken to the security officer, Kondok Mawien, who was sitting under a tree near the hut. It was very difficult to crawl out through the small opening with my arms tied very tightly at the elbows behind my back.

Kondok Mawien kept asking me why I had defected and joined Nyigat, in spite the fact that I repeatedly told him that I did not join Nyigat voluntarily, but was captured during the battle of Wunrok. Before he had me taken back to prison, he asked about Barac Powut Barac and Bol Majok Anguei who were in the hut with me. I told him that Barac was a veterinary officer and Bol was a teacher. This agreed with what these two men and my bodyguard Majok Aguer told him later. Compared to me, they were treated mildly – at least their hands were not tied. Throughout the evening more prisoners, mostly SPLA soldiers, were brought in.

When Kerubino entered Twic, the SPLA members deployed there had to decide whether to join Nyigat or report to their SPLA units. Many of them – including officers such as Macam Atem Barac, Gaetano Nyol Atem Lok, Paul Madut Cyer and others -defected to Kerubino's units. Many others, though, were not ready to join Kerubino, and, instead of reporting to their SPLA units, these undecided soldiers remained at large, moving in small groups, feasting in the deserted villages on the goats and rams the villagers had left behind. It was these men who were rounded up and brought to our prison hut, with their arms firmly tied behind their backs. Cdr Anthony Bol Madut was probably doing the same in Turalei where his forces were based.

That same evening I was taken to Cdr Elias Waya, someone I had never met before. He had Kondok Mawien's notes before him, and he repeated the questions that Kondok had put to me. I told him too that I had been captured at Wunrok. But there was something strange about him. He never looked me in the eye. Every time he asked me a question, he looked away, as if he had something to hide. It was something to do with my fate.

I was taken back to the hut, and my bodyguard Majok Aguer was brought before the commander. A few minutes later he was back. Barac and Bol were not called, but Cdr Elias had asked me about them, and I told him what I had told Kondok Mawien. "Things don't look good for me and Majok," I told Barac and Bol. "I don't think you'll have a problem – but please just tell my family what has happened to me."

More and more prisoners were brought. By nine the hut was so full that there was hardly any space to sit – let alone stretch your legs. Some of the young men had eaten a lot and drunk water before they were arrested, and had no choice but to pass urine and defecate where they were sitting. Soon the mess was running over the floor and out through the door.

Meanwhile Cdr. Elias Waya had sent a report to Cdr Anthony Bol Madut about my capture. On the two-way radio Bol told Waya that there were no prisons in which to keep the Nyigats, so anyone captured – including Bol Majok Adiang – was to be executed directly. But it so happened that the radio operator, Mahguob Lueth Ajak, overheard the conversation. He ran to Cdr Bona Bang Dhel, who rushed to the radio room. Bona Bang called Cdr Elias Waya and told him that when they came to Twic they were provided with lists of officers who had defected and joined Kerubino's forces voluntarily, and those who were captured. "Bol Majok Adiang's name is on the list of captured officers," he told Cdr. Elias Waya. "You will be held responsible if Bol Majok is killed!"

This conversation again was overheard by Cdr Anthony Bol, who came in and said, "Bona, Bona! Where is this Bol Majok you are talking about? Hasn't he already gone with the Nuer? The reason why we are fighting now is because Kerubino's life was spared when he should have been killed. If he had been killed, we wouldn't now be fighting the Nyigat. We can't afford to repeat mistakes. If we spare Bol Majok's life now, we'll soon be fighting his forces."

Cdr Bona Bang ignored all that Cdr Anthony Bol was saying. He told Elias Waya, "We are all soldiers and I am the most senior officer here. As the commander of this area where the fighting is taking place, my orders must be obeyed. If Cdr Bol Madut bears a grudge against Bol Majok, now is not the time to settle an old score."

Meanwhile inside the prison, I didn't know I was being discussed by the commanders. I was sitting in the hut – in agony, like the other prisoners, waiting for our execution. I knew that, being the only officer among the prisoners, I would be taken out first. A soldier in Elias Waya's forces, Adiang Piol Wading, who happened to be my relative was disarmed that night, for fear of his reaction if I was executed.

At eleven that night the executions started. The door was opened, and two soldiers entered the room bearing a light. They selected four of the prisoners, and after the door was securely closed again, they took them about a hundred metres away, to the edge of the *dura* field. We heard their cries as they were hacked to death with pangas. Some of the men in the hut began to wail. When their cries were no longer heard, we knew that they were dead. Then the executioners came back and took another four. And so it continued. Every time the door opened, everyone expected it to be their turn.

By one o'clock only four of us remained in the hut – Barac Powut, Bol Majok Anguei, my guard Majok Aguer and myself. When the door opened again we were in a bad state – with our arms still firmly tied behind our backs, we had collapsed. Then a certain sergeant, Akec Puou, who was in charge of prisoners, entered. He was from Tonj, and he told me that he had known me when I was the assistant commissioner of Tonj Area Council. He untied my arms, and tied my hands instead. He said it was to enable me to lean against the wall, or even lie down. He then left the room. I relaxed a little, although I was still convinced that I was going to die. Maybe, I told myself, because I was an officer, there would be a firing squad instead of a panga. Towards morning Akec Puou came back alone. He untied my hands and tied my arms again behind my back, like before. "The other officers will quarrel with me if they find you with only your hands tied," he said.

By then the rain was coming down in torrents.

For four hours nothing happened. It gave me hope. Perhaps something had come up that could save my life, I thought. When the door opened at eleven o'clock, my guard Majok Aguer was taken out first, but brought back after a few minutes. Then it was my turn. I was taken before a captain who was sitting on a chair in the open. The sun had appeared in the sky. The captain was a security officer – from Bor, I guessed by his accent. In a soft, sympathetic voice he asked me to tell him exactly what had happened. I told him. He said my arrest had been reported by Cdr Bona Bang Dhel and A/Cdr Santino Deng Wol in Twic, who had seen me being captured. He said that their evidence was all they needed to set me free. "You'll remain in custody for a while, as a matter of military procedure," he told me. "But the charge against you is withdrawn." He then questioned me about Barac Powut and Bol Majok Anguei and I gave him the information I had already given to Cdr Elias Waya.

The news of my arrest caused such a stir, that at first no-one was aware that Barac Powut and others had also been captured. No-one was sure what had happened. At times it was reported that I had defected to Kerubino's faction and had then been recaptured by the SPLA forces under Cdr Anthony Bol Madut and Cdr Elias Waya. Others said that I had been captured by Kerubino's forces and had escaped and rejoined the SPLA. The last report by Cdr Bona Bang Dhel who was informed about my capture by A/Cdr Santino Deng Wol was the correct one.

When Barac Powut Barac was captured, A/Cdr Santino Deng Wol did not know about his arrest until he was released by Cdr Elias Waya. If he had known about it, Barac would have perished with the rest of the soldiers that night. A/Cdr Santino Deng Wol believed that Barac and some others had known that Kerubino was coming to Twic and that they used to meet in a church at Mayen Abun to send messages to Kerubino through their special informants. Barac Powut and Bol Majok were released after only one night in prison. I remained in custody with my bodyguard Majok Aguer for another four days. Every evening more soldiers were brought in, and taken out again in the night.

On the fifth day my bodyguard and I were brought out in our underwears, and our arms were untied. We were taken to a nearby pool to take a bath. The pool smelled awful – it was used to wash the entrails of slaughtered goats, sheep and cattle – but it was better than the stench inside the prison. We had no soap, but somehow we managed to get rid of some of the dirt on our bodies and underwear. Then we sat down on a log near the soldiers, happy to be breathing fresh air again, although we were still prisoners. Majok was sent to fetch water and help with the cooking, while I remained sitting alone. The soldiers gave me some meat to eat. For the first time since my arrest, I could use my hands again to put food into my mouth. The first day in prison we ate nothing. When the soldiers started bringing food once a day, they had to put it into our mouths because our arms were tied behind our backs. We had to chew quickly or swallow it unchewed if we wanted more, because the soldiers were impatient and would soon take the food away. Drinking was equally difficult. The soldiers would pour water down our throats from a jerry-can, also pouring some over our bodies and into our noses, until it felt as if we were drowning.

When night came, Majok was taken back to the prison hut, although his hands were not tied. I was given the bedding of one of the soldiers who had been arrested, and spent the night outside near the soldiers. Three days later we were taken to Cdr Anthony Bol Madut in Turalei.

When we arrived in Turalei, we found that Cdr Anthony Bol Madut had gone to the airstrip to see some wounded soldiers off, men who were going to Loki in Kenya for treatment. We were put into a small abandoned hut. We lay down on the bare floor and fell into a deep sleep.

CHAPTER 31

More Bad Blood

At midday, when Anthony Bol Madut came back from the airstrip, he was told about us, but said he needed some rest and that we should be handed over to the prison unit. There they tied our arms again, at the elbows, behind our backs, with very thin but very strong ropes. Then they tied us to the roots of a *lalob* tree. There was some shade at first, but as the sun moved to the west, the shade disappeared and we were left in the burning heat of the afternoon sun. We were very thirsty. Hungry too.

When a soldier came from the stream with a jerrycan of water, I asked him to let us have a drink. He turned to bring us some water, but the soldiers sitting in the shade of another tree shouted at him, "Whose jerrycan are you using to give water to the prisoners?" So he went back to them without helping us.

We could hear the soldiers talking among themselves, but could not hear what they were saying. However, the soldier got up again and brought us some water. As usual, it was very difficult to drink from a jerrycan put to your lips if your hands were tied so tightly behind your back. Some of the water was poured over our dusty and dirty bodies, making us look even more dirty and unkempt.

At last – at five o'clock – an officer arrived with two soldiers. We were untied from the tree, but the ropes tying our arms were held tightly by the two soldiers. Cdr Anthony Bol Madut was sitting on a bed in the shade of a hut.

"Sit down!" he nodded.

He called me "Uncle Bol". "Are you all right, Uncle Bol?" he asked.

"How can I be all right with my arms tied behind my back so tightly, pushing my chest forward, and my arms swollen? Of course it is hurting. It feels as if I'm going to burst."

He ordered the soldiers to untie our arms.

He was very frank. "I ordered Cdr Elias to have you executed, like any other Nyigat," he told me. "I lost several soldiers fighting against the Nyigat at Turalei. I narrowly escaped death myself. But it was God's will that Cdr Bona Bang should overhear my conversation with Elias Waya. There were many charges against you. I wanted you dead before Bona Bang heard about it."

"If there were so many charges leveled against me, why connect me to the Nyigat? The problem with you Southerners is that you don't take the time to find out what the actual facts about each of your prisoners are. And then to try them, so that the ones found guilty can die for their misdeeds."

"Yes," he answered. "I admit that I was acting in haste. Not for the first time, I'm afraid."

He told me the story of a soldier he ordered to be executed on the day they sustained heavy casualties from Nyigat. When Dr Riek Machar Teny rebelled, some Dinka soldiers were stranded in the Nuer area, waiting for an opportunity to escape and go back to the SPLA. One such a person was Captain Adhar Atem who deserted from Kerubino's forces at Jara and reported himself to the SPLA forces. Another soldier took the opportunity to defect to the SPLA on the day the SPLA and Nyigat were fighting at Turalei.

"We arrested him," Anthony Bol Madut told me. "He told me that he had not fired a single shot since he entered

Twic, and asked me to check his gun. I told him he should have defected along with Captain Adhar, but he kept repeating that joint defection was very difficult. In spite of his pleas I ordered his execution. I admit that I regretted it afterwards."

"Yes. You kill your friends and keep your enemies alive. Like that Arab 1st lieutenant who was with you in Boma – the one that inspected us when we arrived there. And Abu Lela Adam!"

Cdr Anthony Bol Madut handed me over to Captain Aguek Atem Angap, telling him that I should not be allowed to go home. I was to remain near the captain until I was handed over to Cdr Bona Bang Dhel.

I was still wearing underwear only. When my family received the news that I had been taken to Turalei, they sent my son Bol Bol Majok (Bol Junior) to see me. He gave me his own jalabiya to wear. It was much too small for me, but better than nothing. The boy walked home in his underpants and returned the next day with a pair of trousers and a shirt that my wife Veronica had bought for me.

In my absence something unbelievably good had happened to my wives Veronica Nyanut Elario and Acol Ayuel Rehan. I had bought them some very nice clothes from the market at Abindau before the Nyigat came and an expert tailor sewed two jalabiyas for them. On the day the Nyigat attacked Wunrok and captured me, both of them were wearing their new jalabiyas and a type of beads known as *"majok"* round their necks. Veronica had sixty Sudanese dinars in her possession - at that time a very large amount of money indeed, equivalent to six cows. She put it in a piece of cloth that looked like a belt, open on the inside, and tied it round her waist, inside the jalabiya. When we all fell into the hands of Nyigat at Wunrok they did not search my wives. They confiscated the little money I had in my pocket and my watch, but left my clothes. They did not take anything from the women, not even their beads, which was not like them at all. They liked beads! When a man called Majok Majok once refused to hand over his beads to them, they killed him. A song has been composed about him – Majok, the man who allowed himself to be killed for a string of beads.

Later, when we fell into the hands of Elias Waya's forces, they stripped me of my clothes. They did not strip the women, but they took some of the clothes they had brought, like the sheets with which they covered themselves. The sheets were very dirty as the women slept on them on the bare floor. But fortunately they did not touch their jalabiyas, otherwise they would have found the money.

When Cdr Bona Bang Dhel later met my wives, he asked them how they had managed to hold on to their beautiful jalabiyas and beads when the Nyigat and especially the forces of Cdr Anthony Bol Madut and Cdr Elias Waya were known to take everything they could lay their hands on. Actually, the Nyigat were in a great hurry when they looted Twic and missed the hidden things. It was the SPLA forces later who found whatever was hidden in the grass, in the trees, bushes and rivers, even what was buried. They took whatever they could carry, and destroyed what they could not. They took the aluminum pots and dishes, but broke the clay pots and calabashes after using them. So my wives were indeed lucky!

Two days later, we left for Mayen Abun, where Bona Bang's forces were now based after Kerubino's forces left for Abyei. Here Cdr Anthony Bol Madut handed me over to Cdr Bona Bang. I was sitting under a tree with Cdr Bona Bang, when my sister-in-law, Ajak Ayuel Rehan came to us, weeping. I got up and met her at the edge of the field. She told me that her husband Barac Powut Barac (who had been arrested with me at Tekajak and released) had been rearrested by SPLA security personnel and taken to the headquarters of A/Cdr Santino Deng Wol on the other side of Mayen Abun. This had happened at Gol village, where he had joined my brother Piol Majok with the cattle.

"Go back to the children. Leave the problem to me. I'll settle it with Cdr Bona Bang," I told her.

When Bona Bang heard that it was Cdr Daniel Awet Akot's brother-in-law, Barac Powut Barac, who had been arrested again and taken to A/Cdr Santino Deng Wo; and how Barac had been arrested at Tekajak and what Santino Deng Wol had in mind for him then, Bona Bang called his adjutant and told him to write to A/Cdr Santino Deng Wol ordering him to release Barac Powut right away.

At that time a rally was organized for the citizens of Twic around Mayen Abun. At this rally, Cdr Bona Bang told the people to be calm, and that once Kerubino had left the area, no further arrests of those who remained in the area would be made.

Then Cdr Anthony Bol Madut told them how surprised he was to see them well dressed again when he knew that the SPLA soldiers had looted the villages. He was frank. He said that he was taking his forces back to Tonj area. He had intended them to rescue the people from Nyigat, he admitted, but instead they were finishing off everything Nyigat had left, making life even harder for the citizens of Twic.

Barac Powut Barac was back. He and I returned to Wunrok with Cdr Bona Bang, but after Bona left for Akon, Barac was arrested for the third time and taken to Tekajak. A/Cdr Santino Deng Wol called me to Tekajak too, and told me he had received information that I was the one who had told Cdr Bona Bang Dhel about Barac's arrest at Mayen Abun.

"Barac's wife came to me when I was sitting with Cdr Bona," I explained. "I have already told you that she is my sister-in-law, and it was my duty to make every effort to rescue her husband. If Bona Bang hadn't been in Mayen at that time, I would have come to you to plead for his life."

Santino Deng Wol would not listen to my reasoning. "I have advised you repeatedly to stay away from people who are connected with the Nyigat," he said.

"I usually take your advice," I told him, "but I can tell you that Barac is not one of them. He has no connection with Nyigat. He has never been interested in politics, he focuses on his own private affairs and has become rich working hard."

It was true that Barac was one of the best hands-on farmers in the area. Although he was a university graduate, he took care of his cattle himself. He cultivated his own lands, something most intellectuals cannot do.

"Barac is being wrongly accused by those who envy him," I said.

"Barac will remain here, in custody," A/Cdr Santino Deng Wol told me. "You can go."

But A/Cdr Santino knew that while Cdr Bona Bang was in the picture, he could take no further action against Barac. So he kept him in custody for some time and then released him.

We briefly stayed in Wunrok. Then Kerubino decided to return to Twic from Abyei. The Nuer were deserting him, going back to the Beniu area through Abiemnhom.

CHAPTER 32

Surviving

When Kerubino Kuanyin Bol's forces were crossing the Kiir River back to Twic, my family and I crossed the Lol River and fled southward. We went to a village called Acebut, south-west of Panliet, about sixteen miles from Wunrok. My elder wife, Acai Ayuel Dual was also with us. When the Nyigat first attacked Wunrok, she had fled with her children and cattle from her house on the southern side of the Lol River.

Kerubino remained for some time in the Kiir River area, his movement stopped by the forces of A/Cdr Santino Deng Wol. From the beginning to the end, it was Santino Deng Wol, more than anyone else, who fought the war against the Nyigat. About three-quarters of his forces consisted of young men who used to sleep on the southern side of the river Lol and then go back to Wunrok in the morning to harvest the *dura*. The harvest was almost over when Kerubino's forces reached Wunrok. They crossed to the southern side of the river and then moved up to Thur Adiang.

My family and I remained at Acebut, expecting Kerubino forces to go back to the Bentiu area via Mangol Apuk. If he decided to go to Gogrial, instead, we thought, he would follow the road through Panliet. We at Acebut were about six miles away from that road.

Meanwhile a huge SPLA force was waiting for Kerubino to move away from Thur Adiang. We were all still waiting, when I was called to Akon. I left my family at Acebut, telling them not to move until the Nyigat had passed to Gogrial. "Leave Acebut when you hear the two forces fighting," I instructed them. "If the road to Gogrial is blocked by the SPLA, Kerubino's forces may take the alternative route through Acebut."

In Akon, I reported to Cdr Paul Malong Awan. "In Nairobi some elders from Twic have complained to the SPLM/SPLA leadership that the citizens of Twic are being randomly killed," he told me. "I want you to go and tell them what is actually happening. You are an example of someone whose life has been spared."

"I know very little about the fighting between the SPLA and Nyigat," I said. "On the first day of the fighting, I was captured by Nyigat and locked up in their prison. When I escaped from them, I spent only one night outside before I reported to the SPLA and they arrested me and locked me up. I can only tell the leadership what happened to those who were in prison with me."

"What did happen to them?" he asked.

I explained to him that I was not a good source of information when it came to the battle against Nyigat. Especially not a sole source! There are many others he could consult. I told him I shouldn't be the source of information regarding the attrocities being committed by the SPLA in Twic because afterwards the commanders in the area who would be questioned would blame me for passing information to the leadership about the way they treated the people of Twic.

"Well, I want you to wait here in Akon. You'll be picked up by a plane and taken to a place where you will meet someone."

He did not disclose the destination of the plane or the name of the person I was to meet. I waited and waited, watching a plane carrying ammunitions coming and going. It landed four times, but I was not picked up.

It delivered only a few boxes of ammunition. John Garang was rationing ammunition, because he did not fully trust those who were fighting the war against the Nyigat. Most of the SPLA soldiers were issued with only four or five rounds of ammunition when they were sent to attack the Nyigat. The only good thing was that the Nyigat did not know that their opponents had run out of ammunition. When the SPLA soldiers attacked them and then ran away, the Nyigat called them cowards. "They're afraid of us!"

One morning while I was still waiting at Akon, the Nyigat were ambushed by the SPLA at Liet Manangui. I became worried about my family when I heard shots, so I decided to leave for Acebut immediately without asking anyone's permission. In the evening I arrived at a place called Kueel. Meanwhile the SPLA forces had run short of ammunition and they allowed the Nyigat to pass. The Nuer soldiers in Kerubino's Nyigat's force turned eastwards at Liet Manangui and took the way to Mangol Apuk, taking along with them all the cattle and valuable items they found on their route. Kerubino's remaining forces spent the night at the Awudou Paniet airstrip.

My family fled Acebut and spent the night at Amoth-moth, about five miles from Acebut. It was late evening when I managed to cross the Kuom River, and the SPLA soldiers advised me to sleep over at Kueel. The next morning I came to a place called Wacjang, and here I found many families who had arrived with their cattle. I asked them about my own family's whereabouts, but received different information from different people. They all knew about where our cattle were, though, so I decided to make my way to Maluil cattle camp.

That same day the Nyigat passed through Acebut on their way to Gogrial. The house in which I had left my family, was near the main road, and they passed through my compound, collecting all they could use from the house and outside. They did not see the boxes my wives had hidden in a nearby bush. A blind old woman they found nearby, told them that the house belonged to me, so some of them wanted to burn it, but, as I was told later, Cdr Faustino Atem "Gualdit" refused, saying "It is not Bol's house. Don't burn it!"

I spent the night at Maluil cattle camp and left very early the next morning in search of my family. Meanwhile my brother Piol had joined me, and I told him to follow with the cattle back to Acebut. That evening, at last, I found my family at Aganythii. We all spent the night there, then returned to Acebut where we rested for two days before I sent my family back to Wunrok, with the cattle. Cdr Paul Malong never called me back to Akon, so I went to Panliet to have the airstrip maintained so that relief organisations could deliver food items to the devasted civil population by air.

There wasn't much to eat at Wunrok. What the Nyigat had not consumed of the newly-harvested dura, was being stolen by those who had returned home earlier. From Panliet airstrip I sent a full report to Akon's office of Sudan Relief Rehabilitation Association (SRRA) - a movement relief body that was working in SPLA controlled areas. I reported the damage caused by the opposing forces to the civil population of Panliet and the surrounding villages. In twenty-four hours a small plane landed to check maintenance work done on the airstrip, and in less than a week non-food items were brought in, followed by the dropping of food. I did not attend the food distribution as I was called to Wunrok to open the peace market. The old market had been closed as a result of the fighting, and a new one was opening at a place called Warapec. The Misseriya traders who had left the area were now coming back with all kinds of goods, and life in Twic was returning to normal.

In 1996 the whole of Gogrial was made a county, and the small counties such as Wunrok for Twic were abolished. Acuil "Manoli" Tito was appointed commissioner of Gogrial County. Abyei (which used to fall under Wunrok) became a county, governed by James Ajing Path.

When I defected to the SPLM/SPLA Acuil "Manoli" was a police captain in Wau. Later he was promoted to major and when he joined the movement, he was appointed as alternate commander (A/Cdr), a rank much senior to mine. Now I became his executive director, the same position I had held twenty years earlier, before I joined the movement.

Kerubino settled in Gogrial side by side with the Sudan army. He quickly built a strong army and soon his Nyigat forces started coming to the villages to collect food and recruit young men from the villages and cattle camps. They did not tolerate resistance. The commissioner, "Acuil Manoli" Tito was in Twic when the Nyigat came to Panliet Airstrip. It was at this time that they captured my nephew Agok Bol Mayom, whose story I related at the beginning of the book. The county had no headquarters, but we worked while on the move, avoiding being captured by Nyigat. Acuil "Manoli" mostly stayed near Kuajok, his home town, while I stayed in the Twic, Pan-nyok and Akoc areas.

In 1997 Dr Justin Yac Arop announced the separation of Twic County with its headquarters at Turalei. James Yol Kuol Bol, a former army brigadier, who had spent less than a year in the movement since coming from Khartoum, was appointed commissioner. Because I was from Twic, I was posted to Twic as executive director and judge. In a small meeting of elders, intellectuals and army officers, James Yol Kuol was informed of his appointment by Dr Justin Yac Arop and Bona Malual Madut. James Yol Kuol pulled his chair out of the circle to talk privately to Dr Justin and Bona. They were close to where I was sitting, and I heard him saying that he did not want to work with me as the executive director. Both men knew me well though, and told him that he was lucky to have me. I was in the dark – I could not recall any problem between us, or our parents, in the past. But everything I did in my capacity as executive director – or as the only judge for the whole of Gogrial and Abyei – was questioned by James Yol. He even ignored the independence of the court and reversed some of the cases I settled.

Ever since that beating I was given years before by the SPLA soldiers my eyes had caused me problems. Now suddenly my eyesight became very poor. I sent a message to John Mangok Kuot to book a seat for me on a relief flight to Loki in Kenya, and asked James Yol Kuol for permission to go so that I might see a doctor. But he refused, informing me instead that an auditing team had been formed to audit all my work, including what I did before he became the commissioner. The team was composed of five persons – Stephen Dut Ring (chairman), the security officer 1st Lt Deng "Kuei" Malual Chan, 1st Lt Tor Kondok, Nyuol Ring Col and Atem Dumar Atem. The first three persons were from James Yol Kuol's section, and the other two from Amiol and Adiang respectively. Nyuol Ring Col refused to be a member of such a committee. Atem Dumar came to me once, with the others, but then returned to Mayen Abun and never showed up again. I cooperated with the other three, and finally asked them to declare the result of the audit before I went to Nairobi for eye treatment. Stephen Dut Ring, an innocent man who was unaware of James Yol's motives, was sympathetic. The other two turned their backs and walked away whenever they saw me coming. Stephen told me he could not announce the result alone, and I gave up trying to persuade the other two. So I started preparing for my journey instead.

Those two, Deng "Kuei" and Tor Kondok, knew when the plane was coming, and on that day they sent a soldier to me with instructions that I should go to Pan-nyok market, a considerable distance from the airstrip. I refused and went to the airstrip. Tor Kondok, who did not want to arrest me himself, asked another security officer, Malual Tong to do so instead. When Malual Tong arrived, I told him what was going on between the auditing team and myself. He simply said that he did not want to get involved in such a complicated affair, and left.

The plane landed and I prepared to board with Dr Lawrence Majok Yak. Then suddenly Deng Angok Arop, a bodyguard sent by the two men, appeared and grabbed my shirt, trying to pull me down. Dr Lawrence and Macar Malok (the SRRA representative) freed me from his grip and pulled me into the plane. The bodyguard then grabbed my bag, and I let him have it. Luckily some citizens of Pan-nyok who did not like what was going on, took my bag from him and came running to the plane with it. The pilot was confused. He had already closed the door, but opened it again, and took my bag. And so we took off for Loki.

It was while I was in Kenya that Kerubino's forces returned to Wunrok and occupied it. Kerubino had recruited a large army, composed of deserters from the SPLA and young men drawn from the villages and cattle camps. My family moved to the Aweil area. From Wunrok, the Nyigat devastated the whole area of Twic, from the east to the west. I received the news of the death of my son-in-law, Ajak Kol Ajak, the husband of my eldest daughter, Aker. He had been killed by Kerubino's forces in a battle at Turalei. The year before, in 1996, his elder brother, Nyuol Kol Ajak, a brilliant officer, had been killed by the same Nyigat forces at Nyok Thiang near Gogrial town.

When I arrived in Kenya, my son Wal Bol, who was in the USA, sent me some money to pay for my eye treatment, but not enough to allow me to go to a private hospital. Dr Justin Yac Arop, in whose house I was staying, advised me to contact Arthur Akuien Col, the then SRRA secretary-general in Nairobi for assistance. I went to see him with Dr Lawrence Majok Yak, who also needed an eye operation, and we each explained our problem to him. Arthur told me that there was no money to help pay for my treatment, but he told Dr Lawrence that, since he was working for Norwegian Church Aid (NCA) in Southern Sudan, he might continue with his treatment with the little money he had and present him his bills for settlement later. There was nothing he could do for me.

"What if I borrowed the money to pay for my treatment and bring the bills to you later?" I asked.

"I'm afraid not," he said.

"May I ask you why I'm being treated differently? Dr Lawrence and I are from the same county, and members of the same movement," I asked.

"Sorry – I can't help you," he responded.

I was in trouble. Dr Lawrence at least had a job with NCA and a regular salary. I was unemployed. But the money I did have was enough to take me to Kikuyu Eye Hospital that belonged to the Presbyterian Church and charged less than the private clinics. I was examined by a young Kenyan lady whom I thought to be a doctor. She took me to the white doctor in charge of the hospital.

"His right eye is slightly better, the left eye is badly damaged," she told him. "Will you perform the operation on the right eye?"

He refused, telling her to do it herself. I had no choice. So the next day my right eye was operated on by the lady. When the pressure in the eye would not come down after a month, another white doctor examined it. "Your problem is glaucoma", he told me. "Your operation doesn't seem to have been very successful." So he performed more surgery. I also convinced him to do surgery on the left eye which they said couldn't be rescued. They gave me some eyedrops and asked me to visit the hospital once every month for review. My eyesight did not improve, so after about a year I decided to go back home.

CHAPTER 33

From Pillar to Post

When I got back after a year, my family was still in the Aweil area. Kerubino's forces were no longer in Wunrok. After a heavy attack by the SPLA they had moved to Abyei. So I returned to Akak in Twic with my family. At this time Kerubino reached a secret agreement with the SPLM/SPLA to join their forces to capture Wau from the Sudan government. On the other hand, he tricked the government of the Sudan, into providing arms for the population of Wau and the southern traders, ostensibly to enable them to fight the SPLA in Bahr el Ghazal. The Sudanese army provided the arms and Kerubino distributed them to all the Southern officials and traders in Wau and told them they were for their own protection.

The combined forces of the SPLA and Kerubino duly attacked Wau and almost captured the city. The SPLA forces, however, did not trust Kerubino, and failed to attack some of the military garrisons assigned to them in their secret operation plan. This enabled the Khartoum forces which had been dislodged from Girinti, the main government base, to regroup and make a comeback. Kerubino's forces sustained heavy losses and were compelled to pull out of Wau, taking with them the officials and traders that Kerubino had armed.

I returned to Wunrok and continued my work as the executive director of Twic County. In September 1998, however, the commissioner James Yol Kuol sent me to Loki to attend a women's conference. In my absence he announced that I had been granted forty days' leave, and when I returned, Manyang Bol, my deputy refused to hand over the office to me.

"Why?" I asked. "What is wrong?"

"You are on leave. The commissioner will give you details," he said.

The commissioner told me that it was compulsory leave and I was to come back after forty days. I had no option but to go home. When I returned to work, I was told that I had been pensioned off by Alfred Deng Aluk, the deputy governor of the Bahr el Ghazal region. Strange! There was nothing like pension in the Movement and they would not be able to afford giving me the benefits of a pension. The deputy governor had the power to remove me from my assignment, but not to grant me a pension. They called mine an "exceptional case". It was obviously a tactic designed by James Yol Kuol to get rid of me. So once again, I returned home.

In April 1999 I went to Yinh-Kuel in Tonj to see Cdr Nhial Deng Nhial, the governor of the Bahr el Ghazal region, to lodge a formal complaint. My complaint was in writing, but instead of replying in writing, Nhial sent me his deputy Alfred Deng Aluk, the same man who put me on pension with a verbal reply.

When I arrived in Yinh-Kuel, Nhial never showed me hospitality. Neither did Alfred Deng Aluk who in 1980 before the war, was a commander of Sudanese forces while I was an assistant commissioner in Nasir. And again in 1981, when I was the assistant commissioner of Gogrial Area Council, Alfred Deng Aluk was appointed the commissioner of Bhar el Ghazal Province. At Yinh-Kuel, the two gentlemen regarded me as a 1st lieutenant and asked a bodyguard to take me to their mess when I arrived – the mess they shared with the commander of the SPLA and overall commander of SPLA forces in Bahr el Ghazal. The mess was at the residence of Cdr Salva Kiir.

I was not happy at all with the way they were treating me.

I spent one night with their bodyguards and in the morning went to the house of 2nd Lt Kuanyin Wek Kuanyin. It was here that Cdr Alfred Deng Aluk came to see me that afternoon. I was asleep, but got up when I heard the clapping of his hands, and invited him in, leaving the guard outside. I offered him some water, but he declined.

"I have come to tell you that Governor Nhial Deng Nhial has confirmed my decision," he said. "You will remain on pension. You will be given six soldiers as bodyguards. Two of them will remain with you, two will look after your cattle, and two will serve as runners." He also told me that I would retain some privileges which I had when I was the county executive director.

"That is a good arrangement," I replied. "But what shall I do with the verbal arrangement I have received from the governor? To whom shall I take it? I realize that I have become a very unimportant person in the movement, but I do think that for courtesy's sake Nhial Deng Nhial should meet me face to face before I go back to Wunrok," I told Alfred Deng Aluk.

I waited for three days for Nhial Deng to reply, but in vain. Then I wrote another letter of complaint against the governor's decision, this time addressing it to Cdr Salva Kiir Maryardit. I took the letter to Cdr Nhial, and he passed it directly to Cdr Salva Kiir. I followed the letter to Kiir's office. His adjutant told me to wait – I would be called.

By that time Majok Mayar Majok, my nephew who had accompanied me, and I were starving. We had spent sixteen days in Yinh-kuel. There was no woman to cook in Kuanyin Wek Kuanyin's house where we were staying. Kuanyin himself would leave the house very early while we were still sleeping, and return late when we had gone to bed. The little money I had brought had all been spent - on groundnuts, the only food we could buy.

After another three days a soldier took me to Cdr Salva Kiir Mayardit's office. "The reason the county commissioner gave for pensioning you off is that you are practically blind," Salva Kiir told me. "He said that a blind man cannot keep government secrets. Of course there is nothing like pension in the movement. You can't be discharged from the movement and your blindness cannot be used to compel you to retire. I know of a number of blind people who have held high positions in other countries. There is the home minister in Britain, for example, who was led to his office by a dog. And the former minister of education of Egypt, Taha Hussein. James Yol Kuol just doesn't want you, and to impose you on him wouldn't be good for our work."

He told me that he wanted me to go back to Twic as a judge, and that I would receive a letter of recommendation to that effect from the governor.

Two days later the governor, Nhial Deng Nhial, did call me to his office and he gave me a letter addressed to the judge of the high court of Northern Bhar el Ghazal. It granted me judicial powers for the Gogrial and Abyei areas. Since I could not read, I asked Nhial to read the letter to me and he complied. The letter stated that because I had become blind, I was moved from local government administration to the judiciary.

I laughed. "You are a lawyer yourself, Nhial," I said. "You know perfectly well that my assignment as a judge will require more writing than I would do as executive director."

All cases settled by a judge must be in his own handwriting, and signed by him. In local administration I could just draft a statement and give it to a clerk to type before I would sign it.

"If he didn't respect your authority so highly, the judge of the high court would just let you know that the judiciary is no place for a blind person like Bol Majok Adiang," I told Nhial.

Nevertheless, I took the letter to the judge of the high court, honourable Agoth Wek Agoth, and he appointed me 1st class judge for Gogrial and Abyei. I left the administration to James Yol Kuol, but even so, he was not happy with my presence in Twic as a judge, and from time to time, interfered with the cases I settled. He would reverse my decisions, not because they were wrong, but just to frustrate me. There could be no doubt that I was an experienced judge. I had been a first class judge ever since 1979 when I was the assistant commissioner of Nasir, and continued to be one in the area councils I was transferred to. As a matter of fact, I was a 1st class judge in Gogrial when honourable Agoth Wek Agoth, who had now appointed me, was a second class magistrate. Unlike Yol Kuol, I knew exactly how to do my job. When Yol Kuol interfered with the independence of the judiciary, I simply directed those affected to raise their complaints with Agoth Wek Agoth.

When the Movement appointed Justice Ambrose Riiny Thiik as the chief justice in the SPLA controlled areas, he visited Twic County, and met in Turalei with Dr Justin Yak Arop and James Yol Kuol to discuss my case. The result was that he relieved me of my position as first class judge. I was not a professional lawyer, he said.

Later, in 2001 I met Justice Riiny Thiik in Rumbek and talked to him about my unfair sacking. "During

British rule, as you know," I told him, "local government administrators used to be given judicial powers in the areas under them. The same practice continued after independence and after Southernization. I was the only judge in the Gogrial area until I defected and joined the movement. Moreover, the Sudan government had a law faculty at the University of Khartoum, and they offered special courses in law for the administrators they trained, and maintained them as judges. The SPLA has no law college. How can they reject the administrators working as judges? I was the only judge in the SPLA controlled areas of Gogrial and Abyei long before the arrival of Agoth Wek Agoth and before other judges could come out from the Sudanese army controlled Wau town after Kerubino Kuanyin attacked it. And if you removed me because I was not a professional lawyer, why don't you remove the local government administrators who are working as judges in Equatoria and Upper Nile?"

I also mentioned to Justice Riiny Thiik that he had appointed his own uncle, Ngot Riiny Thiik, and Jok Dau Kacuol of Cueibet as second class magistrates. They were both illiterate. When he appointed the two, he stated that appeals to their decisions should be lodged at the court of appeal, not the first class magistrate court as used to be the case.

"You got rid of me to satisfy the whims of James Yol Kuol," I said.

But I was tired of complaining, and stayed at home, unemployed, in Wunrok. In 2004 Cdr Pieng Deng Kuol asked me to accompany him to Rumbek to attend a senior officers' conference. I was reluctant to go. I did not want a repetition of the embarrassment I experienced at Yinh-Kuel. But the commander persuaded me to go, telling me that junior officers who were overdue for promotion were also wanted.

Upon our arrival at Rumbek, we were met by A/Cdr Marial Chanuong, who was responsible for accommodation. I knew him well – I met him in Yirol when I went to Ethiopia, and he stayed with me briefly as the commander for Gogrial and Abyei when A/Cdr Santino Deng Wol was transferred from Twic. A/Cdr Marial Chanuong had come to the airstrip with two Toyota pick-up trucks. He put Cdr Akuei Adal in the front seat of one of the vehicles, and me in the front seat of the other. The other officers were told to find seats in the back. We were taken to the Panda Guest House where I was to share a double room with Cdr Akuei Adal. The other senior officers were put up at Rumbek Secondary School.

Later a captain who was in charge of accommodation at the guest house, came round. He noted down the name of Cdr Akuei Adal, then asked me, "You are Commander who?"

"I am 1st Lieutenant Bol Majok Adiang," I said.

"I'm afraid you are in the wrong place," he said. "Only the most senior commanders are accommodated here."

"That is not my problem," I replied. "I was brought here by the responsible officer. You were present!"

"All right," he reluctantly agreed. "I'll put your name down without a military rank."

"I have no problem with that," I said.

The senior officers knew me well, and I found it easy to rub shoulders and have meals with them.

Before the conference started, the chairman and commander-in-chief, Dr John Garang de Mabior, announced some promotions. Some alternate commanders were promoted to the rank of commander or colonel. I was promoted to the ranks of captain, major and lieutenant colonel. We stayed longer than planned in Rumbek as the chairman would go to Kenya from time to time for peace talks, then come back to the conference.

After the conference I returned home to Wunrok, where I remained until the Comprehensive Peace Agreement (CPA) was signed in Kenya, and the SPLM took over the administration of the ten southern states.

CHAPTER 34

After the Comprehensive Peace Agreement (CPA)

When the peace agreement was signed, ten top SPLA officers were assigned to the ten states of Southern Sudan as supervisors, pending the institution of the government and the appointment of governors. They worked with the officials they found in the towns. When the governors were appointed, they rushed to the towns and took over the offices and went ahead with the staff they found there, disregarding the fact that there was an equivalent state administration set up by the SPLA in the liberated areas, outside the towns that were held by the Sudan government. These staff members now waited in vain for postings. The governors were quite comfortable with the former Sudan government employees they found in the offices. In the CPA it was stipulated that the Civil Authority of New Sudan (CANS) would absorb the existing Sudan government staff. The governors appointed were content with the Sudan government staff they found in offices and disregarded those working in the administration of the liberated areas. They forgot about CANS's role in bringing about the CPA they were now enjoying.

In Warrap, the staff of CANS started coming to town one by one. They met the directors-general of the ministries. These directors-general had been juniors to most of us before we defected to the movement. Now we had to be satisfied with the junior positions they offered us – the very positions we had left several years before. I refused. The governor Anei Madut Kueidit wanted to appoint me director general of local government in Grade 2.

"In 1985 I was at the top of the list of officers recommended for grade 1," I told him. "I would definitely have got it if I had not left for the movement early in 1986. After 22 years of serving the movement, I deserve better!"

"I'm sorry, all the constitutional positions are already filled," he replied.

"Then forget it. I'm going home."

When I was in Khartoum for treatment, Anei Kueidit appointed me local advisor – a position above director-general and below a constitutional advisor. This is the position in which a governor keeps people he cannot accommodate in constitutional positions. Some important, but uneducated, retired men in the town were appointed with me.

Then Anei Kueidit was removed as governer, and Cdr Anthony Bol Madut was appointed in his place. He discharged me, but reinstated me after three months. Next Anthony Bol was removed and Tor Deng Mawien became the governor. He removed me and throughout his tenure I remained out of the system.

When the 2010 elections arrived, I decided to run for the office of governor, but was dropped at the screening level. When Madam Nyandeng Malek Dielic was elected, I thought I might be appointed to her cabinet, but it did not happen. In 2011, after she had been in office for nine months, she appointed me as local advisor in the local government. I remained in this position until she was removed in 2015.

CHAPTER 35

The States

There are ten states in the Republic of South Sudan. The largest part of the population of the country lives in the rural areas, and the state authorities are responsible for the security of the people and the property.

The rural population is highly organized. In every village there is a headman who knows everybody in his village, particularly the elderly people. He knows when a woman gets married and moves away. He is like the squad commander in an army. Then comes the *Gol* leader (clan leader), who may be compared to a platoon commander. He knows every village headman under him. A group of *Gol* leaders fall under a sub-chief, who is like a company commander. He is acquainted with all the *Gol* leaders, and runs his sub-section through them.

Above the sub-chiefs is the executive chief, who may be likened to a battalion commander. He rules his section through his sub-chiefs. All the executive chiefs in a county fall under a county commissioner, who is like a brigade commander. He knows every executive chief personally and runs his county through them. He is assisted by a number of local government officers who are like the support units in an army. The governor is in charge of the state, like a division commander in the army. The governor appoints the county commissioners and runs the state through them. Through the governor one has access to the president of the country.

Given the above channel of authority, one would expect it to be simple to manage a state. The problems that crop up in a village are settled by the village headman, and only cases that exceed his capacity such as those involving residents of other villages are referred to the *Gol* leader. The *Gol* leader would take difficult cases, or problems involving other *Gol* leaders, to the sub-chief, who will settle the cases within his jurisdiction and refer the difficult ones to the executive chief – who in turn, could hand the really tough ones over to the county commissioner.

With all his administrative apparatus in place, the county commissioner should be able to solve almost any problem that is brought to his attention. Very few cases may reach the governor. The governor judges his commissioners by the number and nature of problems that reach him/her via them every year. The governor has the power and the facilities and the supporting bodies such as the law enforcement agencies and the legislative assembly to solve almost any case. Only in very extreme circumstances would a case reach the president of the republic.

But the truth is that from day one most of the states have not performed well at all. Most of the governors appointed by the SPLM had been great commanders - who might have been successful on the battle field, but were not the best peace-time administrators. Some were politicians – who uttered very nice words on political platforms but made poor administrators. This was coupled with the appointment of young military officers as commissioners. They were still students when they joined the movement and had no experience in civil service. Thus the ethnic unrest erupting in states like Warrap, Unity Lakes and Jonglei was the result of maladministration.

A crisis starts like a wildfire. A child drops a burning

stick on a rubbish heap and it catches fire. If there is no adult present to put it out immediately, it spreads to the tall dry grass and soon bursts into huge flames which are very difficult or impossible to extinguish. What happened in the triangle of Bentu, Rumbek, and Kuajok and in Jonglei, the other triangle of Dinka Bor, Lou Nuer and Murle - started as very small problems, cattle theft by individual thieves or small groups. If proper administration had been in place, these problems would have been nipped in the bud. The thieves would have been apprehended and brought to book and the stolen cattle would have been returned. Unfortunately that did not happen, and when theft developed into small-scale cattle raiding, it still received scant attention. So the people took the law into their own hands. The robbed ones joined the thieves and took part in the cattle raiding in the hope that they would recover their own looted cattle or at least make up for their losses.

Raiding led to resistance and besides cattle, human lives were lost. Even women and children were killed, and in Jonglei children were abducted and carried away with the cattle. The people of each state expected their government to put an end to the atrocities, but instead, the governors took sides and stood with their own factions. What followed, was total anarchy.

During the war, the SPLA forces attacked Sudan government garrisons, killed the soldiers and took whatever they could carry, destroying the rest. They were received back as warriors and heroes. The same happened when the Sudan government forces attacked and destroyed SPLA bases. What they did was certainly not regarded as crime. What used to happen between the warring forces, was now taking place among the states of one new country, the Republic of South Sudan.

When the people of Warrap carried out a raid in the Unity or Lakes areas, they were received back as warriors and heroes for killing their brothers on the other side of the border, and looting their property. They simply shared among themselves whatever they had stolen. Likewise, when the citizens of Lakes caused havoc in Unity State or Warrap, the authorities turned a blind eye.

I once overheard a commissioner talking to people who had come to him to complain about what the cattle raiders from across the border were doing to them. "There's nothing I can do about it," he said. "But those raiders coming to your area are men like you. What is preventing you from crossing the border and doing the same to them?"

"Anyway," he added, "Those raiders are *Mujirimiin* (criminals)." This was as if the criminals had their own territory which the state authority couldn't reach!

When governors meet in the presence of President Salva Kiir Mayardit, they embrace and pretend to be brothers and sisters – while the citizens they rule cannot come face to face without attacking one another! Yet some of these men have remained in their positions for a long time, and are hailed as "good governors".

I fail to understand why they are called "good". Are they being praised for allowing the people they are responsible for to die in great numbers? More people have died in the last six years of the so-called peace period, than in the twenty-one years of the war between the SPLA and the Sudan Armed Forces (SAF).

CHAPTER 36

Excluded

In 2008/2009 I went to Juba to meet President Salva Kiir Mayardit. I had two issues to discuss with him.

The first was my personal problems. Governor Tor Deng Mawien had removed me from the position of local advisor, which paid just enough to keep me living from hand-to-mouth. The person he appointed in my place was already receiving a pension from the Sudan government, whilst I had no pension. I wanted to remind the president that, whereas he had accommodated some of my colleagues in key positions, I had been thrown away like a broken tool. While they had built themselves concrete houses, I was still living in a thatched hut with mud walls, without any hope of ever building myself a proper house. The very people who had hidden in safe places during the war, or, even worse, had fought against the SPLA on the side of the enemy, were now walking away with big slices of the cake they had collaborated with the enemy to prevent the South from getting. I, who had served in the midst of the struggle, was still waiting for my fair share.

The second matter I wanted to discuss with the president was the way the states were being run, especially our state of Warrap. I wanted to share with him my thoughts on the best way to manage the states and put an end to the ongoing cattle raids and local fighting among the citizens of one country.

I found President Salva Kiir Mayardit surrounded by people I had never seen with him in the bush, and who were not keen to let me speak to him. His manager, Yel Luol, said, "The list of people waiting to see the president is just too long. I'll add your name to the list. I suggest you return to Kuajok for two or three months, and return when the list is shorter."

By then I had already spent five months in Juba, so I told him I would just wait there until the president was ready to see me.

"Where will you stay? What will you eat?" he asked me.

"I have accommodation with a relative," I told him, "but I'll need some food from the president's office."

"I'm sorry," he said. "We no longer have a budget for those waiting to see the president."

I left his office, but kept returning, until the gatekeepers were saying "That blind old man again!" Some were fed up with my visits, but others were sympathetic and reported my arrival. I was always disappointed when I was turned away like a beggar.

After eleven months in Juba I was about to book a seat on a plane to Wau, when I met a young man called Atem Powut Barac from Wunrok, my village. I told him that I was going home as it seemed impossible that I would ever see the president. "Why don't you stay for one more month?' he asked. "That will make a full year. If you refer to this time again later, a year would be easier to understand than eleven months." I took his advice, stayed for another month, and then left for Kuajok.

The elections, as I have mentioned before, came and went, and so did the referendum. I was not allowed to run for office, and Nyandeng Malek Dielic excluded me from her government. So I decided to go back to Juba.

CHAPTER 37

Dr Riek Machar Teny

In January 2011 I once again left for Juba. This time I decided to change my strategy. Instead of going to the office of the president, I contacted some people I knew who had free access to his house over weekends. I asked them to take me with them, as I was sure that when Salva Kiir Mayardit saw me, he would warmly welcome me and make time to talk to me. They agreed, but kept saying "tomorrow" and "tomorrow" and "tomorrow". The visit never materialized.

So I gave up the idea of seeing the president, and after two and a half months in Juba, I tried to meet the vice-president, Dr Riek Machar Teny instead. His office manager, Deng Deng Akoon promised to arrange the meeting for me. On the day I was allowed in, Deng Deng was not in the office, but a lady took me to the waiting room. It was nine o'clock in the morning. Dr Riek arrived at ten o'clock and saw many other people, some of whom had arrived after me. Among them were some tribal chiefs from Bentiu who spent a long lunch time in discussion with him. After lunch, Dr Riek left for a while, then came back and saw some more people. I thought I might as well give up, but kept waiting. At four o'clock I was ushered in.

By then I was exhausted, hungry and thirsty. I had never met Dr Riek before, so I gave him a detailed introduction. I told him who I was, where I came from, my education and my occupation in the old Sudan. I told him about my defection to the movement and everything I had done and what had happened to me up to the time I came to his office.

"I graduated from the University of Khartoum," I told him. "The year you entered."

"Oh? What did you study?"

"I did accounting."

"*You*? You studied accounting?" He sounded surprised.

"Yes. We were the first batch of accounting students graduating from the university – thirteen northerners and two southerners."

When I told him, that I had wanted to contest the election for governor in Warrap in 2010, He told me that I should not have tried.

"Why not?" I asked. "Is the position too high for me or is it because of my poor eyesight?"

He said, "No", but failed to tell me why I was not a suitable candidate.

"Well," I said, "then I need your help. My car has overturned, and since I have no assignment, I need assistance to put it back on the road."

"You have cows, don't you? If you have cows surely you can maintain your own car!"

"Dr Riek, have you spared my cows?"

He knew what I meant. "You are from Adiang, aren't you? You would have reason to complain if you were from Akuar, Amiol or Apuk," he said.

"During the dry season all the sections of Twic including Adiang take their cattle to the same *toch* between us and Nuer. I, Bol Majok Adiang, personally blame you and President Salva Kiir Mayardit for what is taking place in the triangle between Bentiu, Rumbek and Kuajok," I told him.

He did not bother to reply – he just told me that he had no money in his office. He did give me a small note though, in which he approved the amount of five thousand Sudanese pounds to be given to me.

Five thousand pounds! I did not want to take the scrap of paper. If I had been an ordinary old man from Wunrok and I had travelled all that way to see him, he would rather have told me that he had no money than giving me such a pittance!

The young man who I came with to Dr Riek's office took the note when I refused it, and gave it to the financial officer in Dr Riek's office. He made several efforts to collect the money for me, but failed. I gave up and left for Kuajok without the money.

CHAPTER 38

The Future

The future does not hold much for me. I consider myself lucky to have been born South Sudanese. On the other hand, it was very unfortunate that I had lost my eyesight - I am ninety-eight percent blind. And I happen to be in South Sudan where disability is equated with inability. I do miss my eyesight a lot, but I have not lost my way of thinking, and my way of doing things.

I sincerely believe that I am still capable of doing important jobs, perhaps better than some of those with perfect eyesight who have been placed in key positions. In many other countries, disability is not considered inability. Educated and experienced people remain useful even after they have been disabled, provided their injury does not affect their mental faculties. Taha Hussein of Egypt is one good example of this. He was blind from birth, yet became minister of education and one of the most influential writers of Egypt. His autobiography *Al-Ayam* has added to his fame. John Milton, a blind English poet, wrote *Paradise Lost* and *Paradise Regained*, two great epic poems. Sheikh Ahmed Yasin was in a wheelchair and had difficulty talking except through an interpreter, yet he became the most important man of his time in the Hamas movement. (He was also the most wanted man, later killed by the Israelis.)

In the old Sudan it took me only fourteen years to progress from Scale Q to Grade One Super Scale. I caught up with and passed some of the university graduates who had joined the local government several years before me. Since I was efficient and honest, I was always selected to serve in the most difficult areas. My prestige declined only when I joined the movement.

Back home, the local commander, Major Deng Ajuong, kept telling me that I was very much wanted "up". The people in the movement used to refer to the headquarters of John Garang de Mabior or Ethiopia as "up". I knew that Deng Ajuong, who was a police corporal when he joined the movement, was uncomfortable with my presence at home – the people remembered me as their assistant commissioner, and still respected me highly. But I left for Ethiopia anyway. There I found no sign that I was wanted by anyone. The chairman did not even for courtesy's sake give me a word of welcome.

To my dismay I discovered that no-one in my category was required by the leadership of the movement. The most wanted groups were (1) soldiers who defected from the Sudan army, police officers, prison wardens, wildlife officers and members of the fire brigade; (2) students and (3) young men from the villages and cattle camps. Elites and politicians were not welcome, except some who had joined earlier, mostly from Upper Nile, like Dr Riek Machar Teny, Dr Lam Akol Ajawin, Elijah Malok Aleng, Kuol Manyang Juk and Dr Amon Wantok. They were given special military ranks, and deployed. But I, and others like me, who had joined later, did both the military and the political training, were then commissioned and given low military ranks to serve under the members of the three groups mentioned above. Our superiors were led to believe that we had worked against the movement when we served the Sudan government, and had only joined the movement to destroy it from within. We were regarded as dangerous and untrustworthy.

Some said that it was in the interests of the movement to shun the intellectuals, mainly the former high-ranking officials of the old Sudan. But what danger could we possibly pose to the movement, if we were given proper consideration? I was convinced that the movement needed our skills in many fields. We could manage the refugee centres in Ethiopia, or the SPLA training bases very efficiently. Among us we had the rare skills that the movement needed for diplomatic missions. We were fit to lead the army in warfare, which also called for people with brains! A wise commander knows when and how to use his forces against the enemy and when to avoid contact with them. He knows how to catch the enemy at a disadvantage and inflict heavy losses on them with minimal cost to his own soldiers. A brave but stupid commander destroys his own forces for hardly any gain.

It took me over twenty years to reach the position of Lt Colonel in the SPLA – a rank junior to the position I reached in fourteen years in the old Sudan. It was a position I shared with officers who could not read or write – men who were still at cattle camps when I returned home in 1992. They only happened to have joined Kerubino Kuanyin Bol in 1995. Those young men from the villages and cattle camps were given high military ranks when peace was made with Kerubino in 1998.

There were intellectuals and politicians who could not bear the humiliating way in which we were being treated in the movement, and defected back to the Sudan government. When the Comprehensive Peace Agreement (CPA) was signed and the SPLM/SPLA took over, mainly top SPLA officers were appointed as supervisors to run the ten states of Southern Sudan. As I have mentioned before, they soon became very comfortable with the civil staff they found in the states – people who had learned how to handle their bosses during the long years of war, when rampant corruption was the norm. As they embraced the former Sudan government officials, the newly appointed supervisors disregarded the parallel systems of government that the movement had established in the liberated areas.

The governors who were appointed to succeed the supervisors, followed their example. They took over the offices in the towns, formed a government and appointed new commissioners for the counties. The commissioners, especially those in Warrap State, worked with the staff of the Civil Authority of New Sudan (CANS) that they found in the counties. The exception was Gogrial West, which was not among the liberated areas. In Warrap State the civil staff in the headquarters and the state ministries of the old Sudan would not budge for the personnel of the CANS, and the governor and his ministers found it convenient to disregard the officials from the CANS.

During the war and long before the Comprehensive Peace Agreement (CPA), Dr John Garang de Mabior once said that there would be no such thing as the absorption of CANS by those who were already in the towns. CANS, he said, would take over as a ready government. It was CANS who would absorb the staff of the old Sudan, not the other way round. We in the once liberated areas waited and waited in vain for this to happen.

Dr Garang's words were: "Nobody is going to be thrown away like a broken tool." When it became apparent that the governor and his cabinet were "throwing us away", we – one by one - began to walk to Kuajok, the headquarters of Warrap State. There we found men who had been our juniors in the old Sudan government, installed as directors-general and directors of the various departments. They received the new governor and his ministers warmly, but were not comfortable at all with our return from the bush. But they had been instructed to try to accommodate the CANS staff under them. So they – who used to be our juniors - offered us work, but in positions similar to or lower than those we had left several years before. Coming from the bush, we were desperate. The resources we had depended on during the war had dried up. So most of us swallowed our pride and accepted whatever they handed us.

As for me, I found it very difficult to be absorbed under the director-general of the ministry of local government. He was in Grade Two, while I was due for Grade One when I left for the bush. The governor of Warrap State, Anei Kueidit, offered me a position as director-general of the ministry of local government in Grade Two, but I told him that I was not prepared to move back while others who had been in the movement with me, progressed to higher positions.

"Just leave me alone," I told him. I'll go back home. It is enough that South Sudan has achieved peace."

I went to Khartoum for medical treatment. In my absence Anei appointed me local advisor.

When I returned to Kuajok, I sat down to reflect on all that had happened when I visited Dr Riek Machar Teny in Juba. I was grossly underrated by him, I realized. It was clear from his response when I told him I was an accounting graduate from the University of Khartoum. "You? You studied accounting?' he said. And when I told him I had wanted to run for the position of governor in the 2010 elections, he just said I shouldn't have done so – refusing to tell me why. And when I tried to provoke him into justifying his own actions by telling him I blamed him and Salva Kiir Mayardit for all that was happening in the states, he simply ignored what I said, and changed the topic. Didn't he see me as a worthy participant in such a discussion? Or did he think that what I said was just the careless talk of someone who had come to his office to ask him for a favour?

Perhaps Dr. Riek Machar Teny just did not know how to handle criticism, because the important South Sudanese leaders surround themselves with advisors who tell them that whatever they do is always correct. I wish I had met President Salva Kiir Mayadit when I was in Juba. I would have told him exactly what I told Dr. Riek Machar Teny. I am sure the president would have asked me to explain my words. I meant what I said, and was ready to give my reasons.

I am not saying that the leadership did not attempt to solve some of the conflicts in those states. I am aware of the many conferences held in Bentiu and Tonj and attended by President Kiir. I acknowledge that conferences can contribute to a solution – but they cannot solely bring an end to the massive conflict in the four states. Further action is required. The criminals have to be brought to book, and the looted cattle and abducted children returned and handed to the rightful owners and parents. And the most competent persons have to be appointed to run a well established government system.

Good governance requires putting the right person in the right place. The counties and states need county commissioners and governors who would not point fingers at their counterparts on the other side of a border, but would settle down and control their own people. True, controlling a civil population in a country like South Sudan, where the majority of the citizens are not educated, is not a simple job. It requires tough decisions. Tough decisions are not popular initially, but they are understood, admired and accepted in the long run when they yield good results.

The Future

When citizens gather in a village preparing to cross a border to commit atrocities there, it surely cannot escape the attention of the village headman, the *Gol* leader, the sub-chief and up to the commissioner and the governor. When the citizens ignore the authorities and go ahead with their campaign, then the authorities must use force to stop them. Of course for a government to fight its own citizens in an attempt to stop them from crossing borders and committing crimes requires tough decisions – but it has to be done.

If, by any chance, citizens escape the attention of the authorities and reach the other side of a border to kill people and loot cattle, they must, on their return, be considered criminals. They should be rounded up – by force, if they resist – tried in a court of law and jailed. And the looted cattle should be returned to their rightful owners.

Actually, if these problems are nipped in the bud – and it is possible to do so – those tough decisions may well be avoided. Instead, some governors gang up with the lawless citizens. I know of a case where a governor followed these raiders to the border with an organized force, and when they returned, pursued by the owners of the cattle, he provided cover for then, enabling them to escape. Is he not also guilty of looting? He calmly left his people to divide the cattle among themselves as if they had not committed a crime. And he is not the only one. Some county commissioners are known to have done the same.

If this is not stopped, the government of the Republic of South Sudan will continue to spend huge amounts of money and human resources dealing with internal disputes, resources that are sorely needed for development or defending the country from external attacks.

Since I am not in a position to put into action what I believe should be done to bring about stability in the four states, I can only sit back and watch the South Sudanese run their affairs the way they deem best. A blind man can, after all, watch a situation! But it is not like watching a game of football. The mistakes made on the football field are discussed for a while, and then forgotten as the spectators walk back home. Administrative mistakes can have long-term undesirable consequences.

The fact is that the great death toll and the loss of property in the mentioned states are the result of maladministration - of officials who are entrusted with the running of these states, not doing a proper job.

If I just sit back and watch my people die, my conscience will not allow me any rest.

Aker ku Majok riang kou Wunrok!

Appreciation

My deep appreciation and sincere thanks go to the following persons whose assistance enabled me to write this book:

Ustaz Lino Angok Kuek, who copied my draft. He patiently helped me to sort out the paragraphs which I wrote in longhand and which were, due to my blindness, often in a mess.

Sannie Meiring, for editing the book and putting it in proper shape.

Aher Arop Bol (Aher Dot Ajok Majok Adiang), who edited, typed and printed Usta Lino Angok's handwritten draft and made hard and soft copies. Together with Sannie Meiring in South Africa, he once again edited the printed copy before sending it back to me for final corrections.

My son, **Mariak Bol Majok**. He assisted me in revising the printed and soft copies of the book and adjusting some edited parts to reflect the exact meaning I wanted to convey. He added some chapters and pages that were omitted during the typing done by Aher Arop Bol.

www.ingramcontent.com/pod-product-compliance
Lightning Source LLC
Chambersburg PA
CBHW071857290426
44110CB00013B/1182